Testimonials

"I have had the privilege of knowing Badiul Alam Majumdar for many years, and I deeply admire his unwavering commitment to social justice and community empowerment. His story is one of courage and resilience, showing us that real change begins with a vision and a willingness to act. Badiul's leadership is marked by his ability to inspire others, to bring out the best in people, and to unite them around a shared purpose. His journey is a powerful example of how one individual's dedication can light a spark that ignites change on a much larger scale."

Prof Muhammad Yunus, Nobel Peace Laureate, Chairman of Yunus Centre

"This story of Dr. Badiul Alam Majumdar will inspire millions of young people who are trying to find meaning and purpose in their lives. I have been fortunate to personally meet many resource-poor women and men who told me that they discovered their own strength to address the myriad challenges they faced after attending Badiul's programs. This is a must-read book for all—young and old—who aspire to make a difference in this world."

Professor Rounaq Jahan, Distinguished Fellow, Senior Research Scholar, and Adjunct Professor of International Affairs, Columbia University

"Badiul Alam Majumdar is one of the boldest and most articulate activists within Bangladesh's civil society. His mobilizing, writings, and dialogues have kept him on the frontline of Bangladesh's ongoing struggle for a credible and sustainable democracy. This biography should serve as both a historic account of one person's contribution toward democracy and ending human deprivation, as well as providing an object lesson to activists in civil society on the importance of perseverance in the face of adversity. It highlights the necessity of sustaining the struggle to serve the people of Bangladesh."

Professor Rehman Sobhan, Chairman,
Centre for Policy Dialogue (CPD)

"When I first met Badiul, The Hunger Project was pioneering a new expression of development, which was all about empowering people to end their own hunger. This was revolutionary at the time. Badiul incorporated this approach as consistent with his own understanding of effective leadership. His work transformed people and communities and made clear what is possible when individuals become authors of their own development. People living in the condition of hunger were no longer seen as the problem; they were seen to be the solution. The contribution Badiul has made to Bangladesh is immeasurable."

Joan Holmes, Founding President and
CEO, The Hunger Project

"Professor Badiul Alam Majumdar has been an activist of exceptional stature on many fronts, including political and civic rights, transparency and accountability, the rule of law, and the environment. He and I were instrumental in banning the highly polluting two-stroke engines that were widely used in three-wheelers in Bangladesh. In my view, his most important contributions are in awakening and mobilizing the present generation of youth in Bangladesh, and imbuing them with vision, hope, and a sense of direction."

Abdullah Abu Sayeed, Chairman, Bishwo Shahitto Kendro

"Badiul Alam Majumdar's biography deserves reading because it tells the story of a person who has remained steadfast for decades in working for the downtrodden who face adverse conditions—many of which were engineered by state apparatuses and vested interests. His tenacity and hard work continue to inspire many, as does his ability to bring people together to achieve something larger than any one of us. His commitment to establishing democracy, good governance, accountability, and transparency has made him an iconic figure in Bangladesh, but his contribution transcends national boundaries. I feel honored to have known him for the past decade and proud to have had the opportunity to work alongside him."

Ali Riaz, Distinguished Professor, Illinois State University, United States

"To change systems requires an indomitable spirit, clear vision, resilience, and cutting-edge tools. But, most of all, it means working with people to help them see — often for the first time — the bottomless well of their own capacity. This wonderful alchemy of relentless passion and 'can-do' spirit is Badiul Majumdar's gift to the world and to those whom the world has forgotten. *Today, I Saw a Revolution* is a story of social, political, and personal transformation in Bangladesh. It is a powerful story of the making of a true Defiant Optimist."

Durreen Shahnaz, Founder & CEO, IIX, 2017 Business for Peace Award Honoree, Author of *The Defiant Optimist*

"Nobody has unleashed the vision and leadership of women, men, and youth like Badiul. And nobody has so successfully advanced the principles of democracy and good governance in Bangladesh. If you yearn to live in a more just and sustainable world, learn from Badiul how to make it happen."

John Coonrod, PhD, Founder and US Chair, Movement for Community-led Development

"I greatly admire Dr. Badiul Alam Majumdar for his persistent and intense advocacy for civic rights and democratic principles even in the face of physical threats. His amicus curiae brief prepared for the Bangladesh High Court in an election case was an important contribution to the jurisprudence on elections and helped pave the way for Bangladesh's recent 'Monsoon Revolution'. He is a brilliant man, widely loved by Bangladeshi's for speaking truth to power and for his work to empower the young and disadvantaged by building democratic institutions."

Dr. Kamal Hossain, Senior Advocate, Supreme Court of Bangladesh, Principal author of the Constitution of Bangladesh.

"It has been a great pleasure knowing Dr. Badiul Alam Majumdar over the last two decades. I have known him as a dreamer and visionary with extraordinary leadership, commitment, and service to others. His two remarkable initiatives—The Hunger Project and SHUJAN (Citizens for Good Governance)—bear ample testimony to his unwavering commitment to the ideals of democracy, good governance, social justice, and the empowerment of people. May Dr. Majumdar succeed in his mission of 'chairaibeti' (moving ahead)—his relentless pursuit of an inclusive, democratic, and prosperous Bangladesh.

Mohammad Abu Hena, Former Chief Election Commissioner of Bangladesh

"Badiul Alam Majumdar showed courage when most others stepped back, fearing the consequences; he relentlessly advocated for accountability when others had given up all hope for it; and he repeatedly defied the supreme authority when nobody else dared. His constant fight for transparency has earned him widespread public respect. During our darkest days of repression, Badiul stood like a beacon of light for democracy and human rights.

Mahfuz Anam, Editor, The Daily Star

"*Today I Saw a Revolution* tells the remarkable story of Badiul Majumdar and The Hunger Project transforming villages and ending hunger in Bangladesh. Meeting Badiul in 2005 and seeing his work changed the trajectory of my own life, including causing me to step up as a leader in my commitment to end hunger. To all of us who share the desire to make this planet a better place, this book is a powerful account of what is possible."

Sheree Stomberg, Chair of the Global Board of Directors, The Hunger Project

“A few brave voices have stood out in the crowd, relentlessly fighting for Bangladesh’s democracy and the people’s right to self-determination and civic rights. Badiul Alam Majumdar’s courageous activism, articulate voice, and precise writing have unveiled the misdeeds of the autocratic Hasina regime and paved the way for our second liberation. *Today, I Saw a Revolution* is the story of a fearless fighter who never lost hope and never stopped speaking for the people.”

Matiur Rahman, Editor, Prothom Alo

“Badiul Majumdar is one of the greatest moral and professional authorities in Bangladesh, holding firm to his convictions and commitment to those in need, even under very challenging circumstances. The story of his amazing life journey is an inspiration and a true testament to what the will to persevere and a deep affection for the people can achieve.”

H.E. Achim Tröster, Ambassador of the Federal Republic of Germany to Bangladesh

Best wishes —
Badiul A. Majumdar
23 Oct 2024

TODAY I SAW A REVOLUTION

From Grassroots to Global Change: The Badiul Majumdar Story

CATHY BURKE

Published by Cathy Burke

First published in 2024 in Australia

www.cathyburke.com

Typeset by BookPOD

Front cover photo by Ahsanul Kabir

ISBN: 978-0-6453879-2-6 (paperback)
ISBN: 978-0-6453879-3-3(ebook)

A catalogue record for this book is available from the National Library of Australia

To that revolutionary spark in all of us that knows a better future is possible.

CONTENTS

Introduction

I first met Badiul Majumdar nearly three decades ago during a Hunger Project global meeting in New York City. It was 1997, and I was new to the team, still finding my way in an organization filled with strong voices. Badiul was the Country Director for The Hunger Project Bangladesh, and from the start, his cheeky humor and irreverence made him immediately likeable—but it was his unwavering sense of purpose and humility that really drew people to him. Badiul was outspoken and direct, always willing to provoke deeper thinking. He had a way of shaking people from their complacency, pushing them to confront uncomfortable truths.

I went to Bangladesh in 1998 as the newly minted CEO of The Hunger Project Australia, and that is when I saw Badiul in action on his home turf. While erudite outside his country, when speaking with a group of villagers, he shone with a kind of intensity and freedom that is hard to describe. His immense love for his people was (and remains) an essential expression of his leadership style—one that is fully in service to a greater purpose. In village after village, I watched as Badiul brought people together, offering them a way of thinking that broke the chains of dependency and despair, and his utter confidence in the power of ordinary people to do extraordinary things was irresistible. This confidence was then taken up by the people themselves, sparking a movement of millions who changed their lives and ended their hunger. But as this book will show, this journey was far from easy. Badiul faced immense resistance—from political powers, entrenched cultural norms, and even his own doubts. But he continuously adapted, learned, and grew, pushing the boundaries of what was possible.

It was in September 2019, during a catch-up with Badiul in Australia, that the idea for this book first came to life. I had left The Hunger Project staff two years earlier and was busy running my leadership coaching practice. As Badiul shared updates on his latest efforts in Bangladesh, I felt a growing sense of urgency. At that time, Badiul was in his mid-70s, and I couldn't bear the thought that his life's work might fade away without a proper record—I dreaded his legacy being reduced to a few old training manuals gathering dust in a Dhaka office, with no cohesive narrative on how this huge movement to awaken the people to end hunger happened. How did thousands of women break out of their deep subjugation and into their leadership? How were the mindsets of resignation and despair, honed through centuries of colonization and a brutal war of liberation, transformed? I wanted that story told so we, and the generations following, have it in our toolkit as we work collectively to bring about a better world. Badiul didn't have the time to write a book, and truth be told, neither did I, but the need to share his story was too strong. Less than two months later, I found myself on a plane back to Bangladesh.

Understanding the significance of Badiul Majumdar's work requires understanding Bangladesh—a country born out of the brutal struggle for independence from Pakistan. Bangladesh has endured poverty, political instability, and natural disasters, and was saddled with an unenviable reputation as a "basket case," as Henry Kissinger infamously called it. Countless aid initiatives were launched, and it is against this backdrop of charity and hopelessness that Badiul's success in mobilizing people for self-reliance was all the more remarkable.

Badiul's approach to ending hunger is grounded in the unshakeable belief that the poor and hungry of Bangladesh were not the problem—they were the solution. This paradigm was an outlier as traditional responses saw the poor as pitiable, a mass of need that needed to be fixed or saved. Badiul and his team rejected this and instead developed and implemented programs that placed the poor at the center of their own development. Because of this, people stepped into their agency and power, ending hunger in their own lives and villages. His approach has been replicated in countries across Africa and Latin America, proving that people, when given the tools, can reshape their destiny.

Badiul's life's work is one of the most remarkable untold stories in the global fight against hunger and inequality. His achievements are extraordinary not just in the context of his country, but as a case study on the power of grassroots movements and people-led leadership. His work has global relevance; humans face overwhelming issues, including rampant inequality, climate change, and the despair and alienation that accompanies late-stage capitalism. Badiul's journey from a poverty-stricken village to leading his country's largest grassroots movement is a powerful example of what is possible when someone sees what could be, rather than gets stuck on what is.

Today, Bangladesh stands at a crossroads. Political upheavals and a renewed push for democracy have brought Badiul's work to the forefront, reminding us how relevant his story is. His advocacy for governance reforms and his commitment to people-powered leadership laid the foundation for the student-led uprisings we're seeing unfold now. His work reminds us that real, lasting change starts at the grassroots level, with ordinary people working together, daring to believe in their own power.

Now is the time for his story to be told; we are at a critical point in human history, and the model Badiul developed offers a roadmap for how change can happen. The title "Today I Saw a Revolution" is both a quote, and it grounds the biography in the idea that revolutions don't only occur in grand, historical moments; they also occur in the everyday acts of courage and determination that shape our world. Badiul's revolution is not about fear or chaos—it's about a new future that breaks from the past. It points to what we can build—and—what must also be dismantled for people to flourish. This biography isn't just a tribute to a man who changed his country—it's a guide for how others can change the world.

"Today I Saw a Revolution" captures many of the pivotal moments that have defined Badiul's work—some of which I have been fortunate enough to witness firsthand. For the writing process, there were numerous intense conversations with Badiul in Dhaka, Australia, and over WhatsApp that lasted years. Through these, I attempted to delve beneath the achievements to try to understand the thinking that led to them. I felt this was important for the reader—to see the figuring-out-part and not just the end result. I wanted to reveal the actual process of creating something new—the uncertainty, mistakes, and vulnerabilities—that often gets overlooked when writing about someone as accomplished as

Badiul. Many hours were spent writing up interviews with youth activists and village Hunger Project leaders called *animators* whom I interviewed when I was in Bangladesh in 2019 to do the research. I read government reports and sifted through research papers documenting his impact. Newspaper articles, Hunger Project archives, and data collation and sense making from the surveys I did of more than 600 village women leaders added to the richness of the picture of Badiul's work and impact. Many discussions with his wife Tazima, both when I was staying in their home in Dhaka and on long distance chats gave additional insight, as did talking to Badiul's Hunger Project colleagues including Founding President Joan Holmes and Nasima (Jolly) Akhter who sadly and unexpectedly passed away while this book was being finished. My own experiences as Badiul's friend and colleague also informed the narrative—I have spent countless weeks and months over the years, traveling through the villages Badiul mobilized, speaking to the women, men, and young people whose stories—raw, real, and filled with challenges and hope—provided unique insight into the intimately personal difference Badiul's leadership has made. All of this brought me closer to understanding the man behind the mission, and any mistakes, failings, or omissions in the book are my own.

The book follows Badiul's journey in three parts. First, we explore his life chronologically, from his birth in the shadow of the Bengal famine and partition, to his academic career in the United States, and then his return home to Bangladesh, where he was determined to make a difference. The second part delves into key pillars of his work, revealing how he pioneered these concepts, the highs and lows of building a movement, and his ongoing struggle for democratic justice. The final section looks at his legacy, beginning with his philosophy of change and empowerment, and then looking toward what is next for him.

As you read, I hope you see beyond the life of a single individual, as this book is also a call to action. It shows what is possible when a group of courageous people come together to achieve something that was once deemed impossible. Badiul and his team didn't just work to end hunger in a world that said it couldn't be done—they created a new paradigm of leadership and development that lit a global path. His approach upends the narrative that systems of oppression are too strong to be dismantled, and we, as individuals, are too small to make an impact.

"Today I Saw a Revolution" is an invitation for each of us to contribute to shaping a more just and equitable world. At the heart of this book is a simple but powerful message: we don't need to wait for permission or for ideal conditions. We are enough, just as we are, to begin.

A team from the United Nations Democracy Fund (UNDEF) was in Bangladesh to evaluate the programs of The Hunger Project, and they met with village volunteer leaders from across the country. On returning to Dhaka to report their findings, the head evaluator, a seasoned professional who had worked at the U.N. for years, turned to Badiul and declared, "*Today I saw a revolution.*"

PART ONE

FROM POVERTY TO PROFESSOR

CHAPTER ONE

Birth and Becoming a Young Man

In Bangladeshi society, even today, it's expected that when people marry, they will become parents quickly. But this didn't happen for Badiul's parents. Badiul's mother, Anjumennessa, was thirteen when she married his father Rangu Meah Majumdar, who was twenty years her senior, and both the young age of the bride and the age discrepancy were quite common. For many years, Anjumennessa couldn't conceive, and people thought it was her fault—that was the prevailing view at the time. Neighbors and family members strongly advised Badiul's father to remarry because they believed it was the wife's shortcoming if she could not bear a child. But his father somehow resisted this pressure and decided not to marry again. Finally, Badiul Alam Majumdar, who would be the only child born to his parents, arrived, and it was welcome news.

Badiul was born in Bengal of British India in 1945, during a very calamitous and uncertain period. Poverty stalked the land.

The country had suffered under the brutal legacy of two centuries of British colonial power, which had reduced India from one of the richest to one of the poorest countries in the world. When Badiul was born, the catastrophic Bengal famine, in which three million people died of hunger and millions more were crushed into generational poverty, had happened only two years earlier. World War Two had just ended, and the departure of the British, which caused the chaotic and bloody partition of Bengal and the creation of Pakistan, would happen two years later.

Badiul was born between October 23 and November 21, 1945,[1] in the Bangla month of *Kartik*, the month before Agrahayan—the harvesting time, which is the lean period before the harvest, often accompanied by widespread starvation. In his family and his village there was dire poverty.

When Badiul was a baby, there was a serious communal riot close to his home, around the time of the creation of Pakistan in 1947. Many people, mostly Hindus, were killed by aggrieved Muslims in retaliation for a riot in Kolkata. The riot was primarily in Noakhali district which is next door to Laksam where he was born. His mother's parents were from the Noakhali district and there were widespread massacres there, so much so that Mahatma Gandhi visited Noakhali to try and stop the killings and he stayed there for some time.

1 Confusingly, Badiul's official birthday is February 21, 1946, which is different from his actual birthday. When children were enrolled in school, teachers arbitrarily recorded a birthday for them. They decided on February 21, 1946—not 1945—as his birthday. But his father didn't mind. February 21st is the International Mother's Language Day, commemorated for the Dhaka University students killed by the Pakistani police on February 21, 1952, for demanding Bangla be recognized as the state language for the people of East Pakistan. Considering his future activism around restoring sovereignty to his people, this became a perfect birthdate for him.

Badiul's father, Rangu Meah, was the only educated person in his village, having completed a little high school before needing to withdraw due to poverty. When Badiul was born, his father worked as a revenue collector for the family of a well-known landlord (or *Zamindar)* named Nawab Faizunness. *Zamindars* were the new class of aristocrats, created by the British as part of more than 1,000 Indian Civil Service officers, who were known as the "steel-frame" of British colonial enforcement, to rule India. When the *Zamindari* system was abolished in 1950, his father lost his job and it was a while before he could secure a seasonal position at the Land Settlement Department, where he was assigned to a sub-district of Chattogram. This provided some badly needed income stability which was unfortunately short-lived.

In a ruinous turn of events when Badiul was six, Rangu Meah became permanently incapacitated when he suffered a stroke that paralyzed his entire right side. Due to a lack of professional medical attention, his symptoms were not recognized as a stroke and were misdiagnosed as gout. The village quack treated Rangu Meah with medicines made from herbs mixed with gold, but to no avail. His father could hardly move, and became bedridden for the rest of his life, unable to work. Besides being personally devastated to have the proud, strong husband and father laid so low, it made the family's situation even more worrisome as there was no source of income to provide for basic needs or to cover the debt from his father's treatment. The poverty became so chronic they sometimes did not have enough to eat and at times starved. Badiul's mother Anjumennessa held the family together. She was responsible for her husband's care, as well as managing the affairs of the family. When Badiul became old enough, he started doing mundane chores and eventually was able to till the soil. The family plot was also leased which helped them survive.

While this was very hard, Badiul didn't know any different. Life was tough for everyone he knew. He was very fortunate in one respect; the marriage between his parents had grown to be one of deep love, and he in turn was cherished by them. There was a lot of mutual care and happiness in his home, and he developed a closer relationship with his father than he otherwise would have, spending time every day sitting with Rangu Meah on his bed, sharing what he'd seen and learned.

The most common meal served in his village was rice and lentils, cooked with mustard oil bought in small amounts. Fish from the pond provided occasional protein, and the deltas, rivers, and waterways provided a natural habitat for fish which people could also access. Chickens were not raised commercially, though most families kept a few, and small amounts of vegetables were eaten as well. Cows for milking were not common, though some fortunate people had cows for tilling the land (though not Badiul's family). Families were mainly self-sufficient—they produced what they ate, and this made for a very low standard of living.

During the lean season when people did not even have rice, boats from other areas would bring sweet potatoes and jack fruits so that people could survive. The long rainy seasons also disrupted food supplies. The whole area would flood, and the houses were like isolated islands. People used to move around in boats created by hollowing out palm trees.

Badiul's home was like all the others in the village. It had a thatched straw roof which leaked in the rainy season, and sometimes during a cyclone the whole roof would be blown away.

Earthen floors would need regular maintenance by adding a fresh layer of dirt and smoothing it down. The structure of the walls was made from bamboo and filled in with sticks from the jute plant. It had two rooms, one for eating and storing the utensils, and the other for sleeping. The family slept together on a wooden bed made of planks. The mattress was hard and lumpy, stitched together and stuffed with old clothes.

The village had no electricity, corner shops, or tea stalls. No one even had a radio. There was no source of entertainment other than what they created. Lighting was by kerosene lanterns, which were used as little as possible. Not long after dark the village would be as quiet as midnight, with no signs of activity. When his family ran out of kerosene and there was no money to buy more, they would sit in the darkness from sunset onwards.

Families did not have sanitary latrines and people practiced open defecation. There was no potable water, not even hand pumps for fresh water. Instead, there were two ponds that women would collect water from with a pitcher. Water used for drinking and cooking was drawn from the same place where people washed clothing, bathed, and fished, which caused frequent diarrhea outbreaks. In those days unsafe drinking water and lack of sanitation would kill many children. When Badiul was a baby and nursed by his mother, he had cholera, which killed a lot of people in those days, including some of his relatives. He was so sick that his parents thought he would die. He became the miracle child who survived cholera!

There was no health care system as such. Penicillin had just become available, and the untrained village healers would push antibiotics when people had any health problem. It was a miracle drug—the cure for all—and it worked a lot of the time.

People used to have a lot of infections then including typhoid, and penicillin would cure them. In addition to the village quacks, there were homeopaths who were able to do small surgeries. Once, his mother had a tumor under her ear and Badiul came home to see the homeopath operating on her. She could have gotten an infection and died, but the homeopath gave her an injection of penicillin and there was no infection. His mother soon recovered.

Hunger and illness weren't the only threats to a child's survival. One night Badiul woke to his parents frantically pulling him out of bed and taking him outside. They had heard the hissing sound of a cobra, so they went to their neighbor's house and stayed the night there. In the morning his mother returned to their house and saw baby cobras crawling out of a hole in the ground. Rats had made the hole, and the mother cobra had come in to lay her eggs. It was that cobra, hissing and slithering around in the middle of the night, that his mother heard.

Neighbors gathered in the morning and started digging, soon finding the nest. They killed about a dozen or so baby cobras but could not find the mother. They kept digging and finally found her at the end of the tunnel. She was at least a meter and a half long, and though they killed the huge cobra, for many weeks afterward his parents were afraid that her mate would come to bite them in retaliation. It was a nightmarish experience for Badiul.

Another time, his mother boiled the milk Badiul brought home from milking a neighbor's goat, and they all sat down to drink it mixed with rice. Suddenly a small snake fell from the thatched roof of the house and landed in his bowl, splashing milk everywhere and causing the family to leap back in fright. Although he managed to escape being bitten then, Badiul's luck would run out. Coming home from school after a football match on a dark evening during the rainy season, he was bitten by a snake. After he was carried home by his fellow students, all kinds of remedies were administered by the village quack. His mother wailed at the top of her lungs, as many people died of snake bites every year. Fortunately, the snake that bit him was not poisonous.

There were plenty of other challenges to contend with in the village, not least the widespread oppression of women, though Badiul was not aware of this at the time. For him and everyone else, that was the way things were. Females were often married around age thirteen and had no control over the number of children they had, or decisions that involved them economically. The man's word was law.

Illiteracy was also widespread. Young Badiul witnessed an incident when his father left a diary behind at home that he needed to maintain as part of his job. He sent a telegram from his place of work which read: "Send diary immediately." No one in the village was literate enough to understand the telegram, so they found someone from the next village who was. Unfortunately, they poorly translated the message to say that Badiul's father was sick with diarrhea, and he needed help to be sent. Upon hearing the news, Badiul's mother started wailing. She fainted and fell, breaking her wrist.

When Badiul was old enough to go to school, there was a disagreement between his parents as to where to send him. His father wanted him to attend religious school and become a *Hafiz* by memorizing the holy Quran. The belief was that once the child memorized the Quran, the parents would go to heaven, and the child would join them when it was their time. Rangu

Meah was adamant that Badiul tread that path, but his mother, Anjumennessa, said no. She wanted him to go to a regular school, and in the face of her determination, Rangu Meah acquiesced.

His mother was a very strong and capable woman. She had no education as such—she could barely sign her name in Bangla, nor read and write, yet she was the best manager Badiul could imagine. She managed the whole family with the very few material things available to them, and she took care of her invalid husband and young son in a calm manner. She also looked after the neighbors, who were very poor.

At Anjumennessa's insistence, Badiul went to Uttarda Junior Madrasha, a few kilometers away from his home. In 1953, he was enrolled in class II—having skipped class I because he had already learned some of the basics. A boy in the senior class had been lodging in Badiul's family's outbuilding because he lived too far from school to walk there and back each day. He supported himself by tutoring the younger children in the village in exchange for food, or in Badiul's family's case, in exchange for a place to sleep. Badiul had joined the tutoring sessions for something to do and picked up some literacy essentials along the way. Hence it was decided he would start in the year above other students his age.

Badiul loved school and took to formal learning like a duck to water. Bangla was the language of instruction, though he started to learn the English alphabet the following year. He made friends easily with the other boys and enjoyed playing games with them. As an only child he relished the interactions and playing with the other kids. There were a few girls a year or two older than him in the class, which was unusual because girls' education was not valued—their families preferred them to take care of the younger children or work in the field. Badiul was the smallest, so the teachers made him sit next to them. The girls were nice and affectionate, and he was a good student. Both boys and girls from his village would walk to school together every morning and return as a group in the afternoon. In the morning the students learned to read the Quran, and were taught the basics of Islam, including how to pray. Up to age eight or nine the girls received the same instruction too, but after that they left school—there was no more education for them.

Meals were not served at school, so in the early morning Badiul would eat puffed rice or crushed rice with coconut, or homemade *pithas* which were a type of cake made with rice powder. He would not eat again until he came home from school in the afternoon to share a simple meal that his mother prepared. Like most growing boys, he was always hungry and there never seemed to be enough food. He learned to keep his appetite in check because in truth there wasn't enough food to satisfy everyone, and he knew his parents would give him their own food if they thought he was hungry.

Transport and moving around had not changed much in centuries. People walked, some lucky few cycled, and goods were transported by bullock carts. Even on the main District Board Road, which connected the district of Cumilla with Noakhali, there were no motorized vehicles, not even rickshaws.

Badiul and his friends walked the four kilometers round trip to and from school every day, but in the rainy season, walking was not possible. The downpours were so frequent and intense that roads turned into rivers. The only way village students could leave their flooded village was to be taken to the main road in handmade boats paddled by a family member. In the afternoon, children would shout at the top of their voices, and someone would come to fetch them from the road and float them back home.

During the rainy months, men would congregate and read aloud from *puthis*—the fictional stories of historical heroes, especially Muslim heroes. They were not only means of entertaining the village; they also commemorated the stories of the historical heroes. In winter, which was much more severe in those days, men would come together and build a fire to keep everyone warm. People huddled under homemade quilts called *kathas* made by sewing old clothes together, and children would tie hay together to make balls to play soccer. They also played *hadudu*, which was a local game often played in the rain.

Though he had the care of his parents, village elders were the guardians of all the children, and though Badiul's life was harsh and difficult, with many challenges and loss, as a young boy he felt carefree, safe, and protected.

Badiul was admitted into class VII at Laksam High School in 1958. He walked about seven kilometers to and from school each day. In addition to studying, throughout all his years of schooling, he worked his family's patch of land to ensure that he and his parents had enough to eat. When Badiul turned fifteen his father wanted him to leave school, get married, and give him grandchildren. However, Badiul's mother had a different vision for him. Despite her own limited education, she had a strong sense that education was essential for her son. She convinced her husband that Badiul should not be constrained in this traditional way, and as a result they both became strong supporters for his continued education.

During Badiul's adolescence, there was a national conversation about the growing discontent East Pakistan (where Badiul lived) felt in being yoked to West Pakistan. The two wings of Pakistan could not have been any more different. They each spoke different languages, the food was different, and the growing economic disparity between them was becoming untenable for East Pakistan. As an adolescent, Badiul was oblivious to this, not just because he was caught up in the normal life of a teenager, but also because national affairs were not spoken about in his village or at school. Radios were not common and as most people could not read, news sources were limited. People were concerned with trying to get by, so national affairs were not considered relevant.

Badiul began to gain awareness about the country's political situation during his half hour for tiffin (refreshment) at high school. Students normally bought peanuts or roasted beans to eat, and since he could not afford those, Badiul instead would go to the dispensaries (pharmacies) in the nearby market and stand in line to read the newspaper. There was only one newspaper in the country in those days, *Ittefaq,* which would normally be available a day later. Sometimes he had the opportunity to read the newspaper, and even though there was no guarantee that he would see the paper, this became his daily routine. This was how Badiul became more aware of what was happening within and outside the country, and it helped him become informed and socially conscious.

He learned that West Pakistan exploited East Pakistan even though the main export item for the country was jute which was grown in East Pakistan. During the Korean War, the price of jute had skyrocketed, earning a windfall for the country. All this money was invested into West Pakistan. Pakistan's economy was dominated by a few families and all of them were from West

Pakistan. Economic disparity grew, and tension and protests were increasing. Badiul's people were deprived of government jobs. They had very little representation in the army. East Pakistan was like a colony.

This political education sparked the beginning of his motivation to inspire and lead others to champion a greater cause, and in 1962, when he was sixteen and in class X, Badiul got involved in student politics for the first time. He became a member of Student League and immediately began mobilizing other students, informing them of the terrible policies Pakistan's President Ayub Khan was inflicting on East Pakistan. The students held rallies, chanted slogans, and demonstrated at school. Even at this young age, Badiul could galvanize others into action.

After passing the matriculation exam in 1962 (which required traveling about fifty kilometers from his home to the district town Cumilla to take the exam), Badiul was enrolled at Nawab Faizunnessa College—the institution founded by his father's first employer. It was a two-year college for XI and XII classes. He became further involved in student activism, primarily to agitate against the exploitation of East Pakistan by the West Pakistani rulers and he was eventually elected vice president of the student union for the 1963-64 school year.

He got an early taste of the partisanship of politics that was to come when one of his closest friends ran against him, carrying out a negative campaign with made-up allegations against Badiul. Despite the smear campaign, Badiul won the election handily by strategically distributing posters with the Bengali Nobel Laureate Rabindranath Tagore quote, "Good people say good things about people, but bad people say bad things." He and his opponent later reconciled and remained friends.

For Badiul, life at this time was an exciting mix of activism, friendships, and study, all contained within the reliable foundation his family gave him. This was soon to change forever, when in 1964, just before taking the Higher Secondary Certificate (HSC) examination, Badiul suffered a devastating loss. His beloved father, Rangu Meah Majumdar, died. Even though he had been bedridden for many years, his father's passing was unexpected to the youthful Badiul and came as a huge shock. Badiul had felt very loved by his father and loved him greatly in return. Losing him increased his sense of responsibility to look after his mother. He took on the patriarchal belief that as the closest male relative he was now responsible for her, and this only spurred his ambition to do well even further.

Despite this great tragedy, Badiul passed his exams. He shared his deep desire to go to university with his mother, even though that meant moving to Dhaka and leaving her without a son or a husband. He was conflicted, but Anjumennessa was not. While others in the village looked down on the decision, she was steadfast in her belief that her son must continue his education. And so, after passing his HSC exam with good marks, and with the blessing of his mother, Badiul left for Dhaka and enrolled at Dhaka University.

With only a small government scholarship to support himself, he arrived in Dhaka with just a quarter of a taka in his pocket. He had briefly been to the capital once before to attend a meeting of the student organization he belonged to. For that previous visit, he traveled with others and the organizers took care of everything. Arriving in Dhaka on his own was daunting—the city was huge, and at the same time chaotic and modern. There were cars, buses, rickshaws, and people everywhere, it was hard for him to get his bearings. He also didn't have a place to stay yet but fortunately, one of the student leaders heard about his situation and gave him temporary shelter. Badiul eventually found more permanent lodging at Iqbal Hall (now Zahurul Hoque Hall), which was a student hostel. He needed to earn his keep and find a way to feed himself, so in exchange for free meals he taught night school for young people who worked in the dining room, and in addition to his studies he tutored students to support his mother.

On campus Badiul was instantly identifiable as a village boy coming from extreme poverty. He did not speak as smoothly or dress as smartly as those from the urban centers with middle class privileges that made up the overwhelming majority of the student body. He was an anomaly—so few kids with his background finished school let alone ended up at the best university in the country. It took some adjustment for him to ignore the comments and to feel as if he belonged. But he was determined and resilient enough to overcome these challenges and make his mark.

1965 was a turbulent time at Dhaka University, and Badiul dived straight into student politics. Chhartra Union was a left leaning student organization and the dominant student organization on campus. Chhatra League with its middle of the road orientation, was the second largest student organization. The third largest group was the National Student Federation (NSF), which was right leaning and created by the Pakistan government to keep any challenge to government authority at bay. Islami Chhatra Sangha, the organization of the Islamists, had no formal structure at the University, although it had supporters.

Badiul's residence at Iqbal Hall was the hotbed of all movements against the government and it was often a violent place to live. Regularly, three NSF goons named Khoka, Paspathu, and Zamir Ali would attack, using hockey sticks and knives as weapons. Khoka would also attack with a snake in his hand to terrorize students. (Some years later Khoka's body was found in the racecourse track, and Paspathu was killed when Badiul was still a student, his body dumped in a manhole.)

Badiul was in the thick of it all. On one occasion during an NSF attack, he jumped from the second-floor roof of the mosque and broke his ankle. He had been holding on to a light fixture before jumping and could have been electrocuted and killed. He escaped death a second time when a group of body builders from the old part of Dhaka, who were all supporters of Chhatra League, came to the Arts Faculty Building to retaliate against the NSF. When they arrived on the campus, the NSF goons started chasing them, so they ran into Badiul's hall. He was caught up in this dangerous melee and an NSF attacker was moments away from throwing acid at him. From the other side of the hallway, a quick-thinking friend shouted, "Our boy," meaning he was an NSF supporter, and thus, Badiul was spared.

Faculty members were not immune to the chaos. Professor Abu Ahmed, a left-oriented faculty member in the Economics Department, filed a case against the University Vice Chancellor Osman Ghani, who was enabling the NSF on behalf of the government. When Ahmed won the case, NSF goons attacked him. In retaliation, the student leaders of other organizations attacked the Vice Chancellor's residence.

It was a volatile and dangerous time to be at the university, but Badiul was passionate about political activism as he believed wholeheartedly in the liberation of his country. Fortunately, he was not left to solely fend for himself. Professor M. Habibullah, a popular teacher in the Commerce Department, had also come from humble beginnings, and he took Badiul under his wing. Badiul became close with him and his family, and their home became Badiul's home away from home. Whenever there was violence at the university, Badiul could take refuge there.

In 1966, Sheikh Mujibur Rahman, the charismatic nationalist leader of East Pakistan, unveiled his famous six-point formula designed to foment a movement to promote autonomy for East Pakistan as a way to address the growing economic disparity between East and West Pakistan. Like millions of others, Badiul was captivated by this vision and he actively participated in the movement by arranging demonstrations and picketing to help garner attention and support. The six-point plan galvanized the country and gave people something specific to get behind. In time it would be recognized as a critical point towards East and West Pakistan becoming separate nations.

With all the violent incursions and risks to his life, Badiul never considered leaving student politics. Instead, the volatile situation had the opposite effect, making him more convinced that he was meant to keep fighting injustice. These terror campaigns waged by the NSF and funded by the government only deepened his commitment to put his energy toward ushering in change.

Despite all this turmoil, Badiul's education progressed. He studied commerce and business, with economics as a minor. He enjoyed economics as he found it more analytical than his other courses. Badiul found his school work easy, and even though activism was his passion and took up most of his time, he attended nearly all of his classes, and passed his examinations without studying. He completed his undergraduate degree with distinction. In recognition of this, in 1967, Badiul was picked to join an official Dhaka University delegation to visit West Pakistan, sponsored by the central government, to promote national integration, which was proving nearly impossible to achieve. The delegation included the best students at the university and was led by the legendary Mrs. Akhter Imam, the Provost of Rokeya Hall.

They visited many areas in West Pakistan, including Landikotal near the border of Afghanistan, which was famous for its black market. Badiul found it wild that anything could be acquired there—drugs, guns, tanks—anything at all. They were expected to stay in the Lahore Government College Hostel, and when they arrived at the campus and entered a room, a light bulb exploded. Mrs. Imam raised hell, and they were all transferred to East Pakistan House which was built for MPs and dignitaries. Badiul left a shirt there which he had borrowed from his friend in Dhaka. Amazingly, it was returned to him.

Badiul was studying for his master's in commerce, and in 1968, one of his Senior Faculty, Sadequr Rahman, got him a job at Quaid-E-Azam College. With this promise of regular income, Badiul bought his first pair of new shoes. Unfortunately, the cobbler put pieces of crushed brick in between pieces of leather to make the sole, so when Badiul went out in the rain wearing the shoes, the soles collapsed—he realized he had been cheated.

In the late 1960s, all the student organizations came together and formulated an eleven-point formula, which included Awami League's six-point demand, to wage a larger movement. It was called 1969's People's Movement, and Iqbal Hall was the center of the student movement against the Pakistani regime. Badiul, as an elected secretary of the Iqbal Hall Student Union, had a leadership role in this movement, occasionally meeting with Sheikh Mujibur Rahman, the Father of the Nation, and other student leaders. They discussed the political movement with him and what the students were doing. These briefings helped coordinate activities with student activists and prominent figures across the country.

In 1969, Badiul passed his master's exam and joined the university as a lecturer. He was in awe of his good fortune and shared the news excitedly with his mother. During his university years, Badiul visited her at least twice a year and kept her informed between visits through correspondence, as there was still no phone in the village. It was at this time that he focused his leadership goals on achieving something not related to national politics.

Professor Habibullah had been a senior faculty of the department when Badiul was a student, and now that he had been hired as a lecturer, the hierarchy between the two men lessened, to the extent they would meet to catch up about what was happening at the university and exchange ideas. One of these ideas involved turning the Commerce Department into a Commerce Faculty, similar to a business school. This would give more students the opportunity to study business and commerce, for which there was a big demand.

They brought this proposal to the new Head of the Department, Professor Farouk, who refused. Badiul thought this was shortsighted, so he staged a protest in favor of it. He mobilized students and faculty members to write a memorandum to the department chair, and newspaper stories were written to support it. It was a very stressful situation for Badiul and even more so for Professor Habibullah, who suffered a heart attack from which he recovered. There was a lot of pushback by Professor Farouk and some other teachers, who applied pressure to stall the proposal, but eventually the push for faculty status was accepted by the university. This was a big win for the quality and accessibility of business education in Bangladesh, and though the journey was not a pleasant experience, both Badiul, and Habibullah felt deeply satisfied by the outcome.

One of the department chairs was a member of the Rotary Club, which offered a scholarship called Rotary Foundation Graduate Fellowships for International Understanding. This gave the selected student the opportunity to study at a university in the United States for nine months. The professor and the department chair—well-known and respected figures in the university—had a discussion, and the professor recommended Badiul as the perfect candidate for the fellowship.

Badiul was thrilled to learn he had been selected for this highly competitive global scholarship, especially when he learned he was the only one chosen from all of Pakistan, both East, and West. This was a very exciting opportunity for him—this village boy being picked to live and study in the great United States. Although he was already a lecturer, he was keen to pursue higher education and make the most of this opportunity.

The fellowship was assigned to the Rotary Club of Claremont, located in Southern California. To start the process, Badiul had to enroll at Claremont Graduate School, however, he faced several challenges during the application process. The application forms sent to him by the university kept getting stolen, so in the end they were mailed to the Governor of the Rotary District in Dhaka and then hand delivered to Badiul to complete his enrollment.

Once the admission problem was sorted out, another issue arose—that of getting his passport. He applied for one, but the police had filed a report against him due to his political activities, which made it difficult for him to obtain a passport. The Vice Chancellor of Dhaka University, Justice Abu Sayeed Chowdhury, who was a Rotarian, intervened on his behalf, and he was finally granted the passport. If not for the vice chancellor's help, Badiul would not have been able to travel to the United States.

He was very focused on his studies and politics in those days, but love also found him. While teaching at Quid-E-Azam College he met his future bride, Mahbubon Nessa (or "Lucky," her nickname, by which he knew her). She was teaching social work and was one of only two women teachers. When he met her for the first time, he really liked her, but she was very formal and reserved. She later explained that living in a patriarchal society and being surrounded by male colleagues, women who worked outside the home had to be like that. Friendliness was often misunderstood, and men would try to exploit it.

Gradually they became friends, and as time went on the relationship became deeper and they fell in love. Badiul took her to meet his mother, who approved of her and immediately gave Badiul her blessing. They were married in 1970 without any ceremony, in the company of a few friends in Dhaka. Even though he was newly married, his education continued to be a priority for him, and he spent many hours in the library gathering data to write a thesis, which was required for a Master of Business Economics (MBE) degree.

Lucky and Badiul initially lived in a one-room apartment next to the Awami League office in Purana Paltan. Later, his wife was allocated a house which was once inhabited by Hindus, many of whom had left for India after the 1965 war between India and Pakistan. They lived there until he left for America in late August 1970.

With his passport, U.S. visa, and, due to serious exchange control, only $10 from the State Bank of Pakistan in hand, it was time for Badiul to take flight. Before leaving for the airport, he had a moment of questioning his decision to leave behind the woman he loved, who had also recently become pregnant with their first child. He was also leaving his mother in his cousin Shamsul Alam's care. But he only hesitated a moment. Lucky was supportive of his scholarship and didn't ask him to stay, as was his mother. But that said, Badiul was also a man of his era, determined to do what he thought was best. He adored his wife and was excited to become a father—of this there was no doubt. He also loved his mother and was grateful for all her sacrifices. Yet the future beckoned brightly and the opportunity to study in America was something that would only come once. Besides, he would be reunited with Lucky and his new child in under a year, and he was satisfied that both she and his mother would be well looked after by their families. With that settled in his mind, he boarded the PIA flight to Karachi, and from there Swiss Air to London.

Little did he know it would be six years and a civil war later before he next stepped foot in his homeland again.

CHAPTER TWO

Life in the United States

Since he only had $10 in his pocket, the Rotary Governor in Dhaka arranged for someone to come to Badiul's hotel in London to give him 10 GBP. With very little cash, along with some Pakistani Rupees, Badiul was determined to eat at a Pakistani restaurant in London, which were mostly run by Bengalis. At noon the next day, he went out to find a Pakistani restaurant, and came across a man coming from the opposite direction who looked South Asian. They stopped to chat, with Badiul sharing he was from East Pakistan, and the man said he was from South Africa. Badiul asked him for directions to a Pakistani restaurant when, without any hesitation, the man demanded Badiul hand over his wallet. Badiul was young and naïve and thought he could easily physically handle the other man, so he refused to give him the wallet, and quickly crossed the road, leaving the man behind. Badiul found he was not afraid. Nothing could bring him down from the excitement he was feeling to be on his way to a new life.

The next day he flew from London to Zurich, en route to New York City, the circuitous route a consequence of the Rotary Club booking his flights for the cheapest possible price. Badiul did not have a visa for Switzerland and when he arrived in Zurich that evening, the immigration official let him into the country, on the proviso that his passport would be held in customs, and he was taken to the hotel to stay overnight. The next morning on returning to the airport, he got caught up in chaos. During that time, the PLO had hijacked some airplanes, diverted them to the Sinai desert and blown them up. In those days there was no security equipment to scan the passengers, and he was strip-searched before boarding the plane, perhaps because he was dark-skinned and looked like an Arab. Despite this humiliating experience, his excitement for reaching the coveted dreamland was not dampened.

Badiul eventually arrived at JFK Airport and was driven to Manhattan. He was amazed by the car ride through tunnels, which he had never seen before in his life. At the hotel, he did not feel comfortable going to their restaurant because of his experience in London, and instead went to the deli downstairs for a loaf of bread, which became his dinner. The next morning, he flew to San Francisco and then on to San Clemente by Southwest Airlines. He was met in San Clemente by Mr. William Bergman, the President of the Rotary Club of Claremont, and his wife, who took him to a restaurant for fried chicken. It felt like he was now truly in America.

Badiul's new home was a graduate student dorm apartment with three bedrooms, one common bathroom, and a kitchen. As he entered the apartment, he met his roommate, Yoshi Amakawa, a

Japanese man who had come to the U.S. as a high school student. Yoshi then introduced Badiul to his girlfriend and said she was living with him during the summer. It was the first culture shock—an unmarried man and woman living together in a student dormitory!

That night Badiul's feelings were complex. After the excitement of coming to the dream world of the United States which offered him this incredible new future, for the first time he realized he was alone. He had left his family back home, including his mother and his pregnant wife. But he did not have time to wallow in his loneliness as he was there for a mission—getting an education while promoting brotherhood among people of different cultures and backgrounds. He eventually fell asleep and woke up in the morning with a stuffy nose, almost certainly due to the air conditioner—the first time Badiul had slept in a climate-controlled environment.

Badiul joined the graduate program at Claremont Graduate School (now Claremont Graduate University). Claremont was a small college town with the university comprised of five colleges. To Badiul, it seemed quiet and sleepy, with few other buildings besides the campuses. Downtown there was a bank and several shops where Badiul and Yoshi would go to buy groceries and other things. They could buy boned and skinned chicken pieces, fish, fruits, and vegetables. Back in Bangladesh, they used to slaughter live chickens, but here you could buy parts of a chicken, skinned and wrapped in plastic. He was fascinated that the shops had only a few clerks to ring the cash register, but nobody else to prevent shoplifting. The streets had orange trees, and no one would pick the oranges, which also seemed strange to Badiul. There were many small things that were so different from home, but he was determined to get used to life in the United States as soon as possible.

The fall semester was about to start, so the morning after Badiul arrived, he went to the university's Business Office to enroll. The office had a few small cubicles in the middle occupied by men, which were surrounded by many desks occupied by women. He was not used to seeing women in offices like that. Back home only men worked in business offices, except in teaching and medical professions. It was one of many culture shocks for Badiul.

Badiul had a designated Rotary Club advisor who was an administrator at Scripps College. But soon he became close with Dr. Ronald Bell, an optometrist, and his wife, who lived close to his dorm on Dartmouth Street. Ronald examined Badiul's eyes and also arranged for him to see a dentist for the first time in his life. He was still taking pills for tuberculosis, which had been detected in Dhaka before he left for the U.S. (it was a mild dose, so luckily it did not affect him too badly).

The Rotary Club of Claremont met once a week for fellowship and lunch in a restaurant, and Badiul would attend those meetings, occasionally addressing the group to share about life in East Pakistan. The members were curious about him and would invite him to their homes and to different events. While people seemed nice, it was in this forum Badiul experienced overt racism for the first time. While it was understandable that most of the members didn't know much about people from other cultures, especially the cultures of South Asia, many of them were plain ill-informed. At one meeting, someone asked Badiul whether people still lived in trees in his country and the room broke out in guffaws. Badiul was shocked at how ignorant some Americans were, and he didn't like it.

At that time, there were no other South Asians on the whole campus except for a lone Indian from Punjab, and as a result, there was no one to speak Bangla with. During the Christmas break, Badiul met an American clergyman who had lived in Kolkata. Knowing that Badiul was from East Pakistan, he spoke to him in Bangla, but initially Badiul could not respond in his native language. He was disconcerted that he had forgotten his own mother tongue after only a few months away. It took Badiul a moment to get his native language flowing again in conversation.

On the campus, there were parties, some of which he attended. People would drink and dance, but Badiul would watch and talk with people. There were also weekend get-togethers in the dorms. This was during the "Summer of Love" and the behaviors he saw were the opposite of the conservative values with which he had been raised. It took quite some time to adjust and be less uptight and judgmental about what was accepted in America. Later Badiul received fewer invitations since he would not drink or stay long as he had studying to do. Everyone knew he was married since he prominently displayed a picture of his wife. He also lived a clean and disciplined life, which perhaps made them uncomfortable.

Getting his Master of Business Economics (MBE) degree at a U.S. college would require nine courses and a thesis. Normally students would take three semesters to finish the course work and then write the thesis, but Badiul was in a hurry. He didn't have eighteen months. His scholarship was only for nine months, and primarily focused on fostering international understanding—

there was no Rotary Club expectation that he should finish a degree while he was in the United States. However, Badiul was committed to completing his master's in those nine months, after which he hoped to apply for his PhD at an American university once he returned home to Dhaka. The plan was that he, Lucky, and their soon to be born child would then live as a family in the United States while he worked toward his PhD. With these goals in mind, he enrolled in four subjects that first semester.

Badiul found the American educational system flexible, but demanding, and the teachers much friendlier than what he was used to back home. The American informality took some getting used to. In some classes teachers would sit and put their feet on the desk. In another class the teacher brought in soft drinks during the exam. Students in general worked very hard and libraries were open all night.

Making do with little money required some quick workarounds. For example, the first term paper he wrote had to be typed by a professional, the cost of which was $30. This was a lot of money in those days. Badiul subsequently borrowed a mechanical typewriter from his Rotary Advisor and learned how to type. He needed to write his master's thesis to complete the requirements of a Master of Business Economics (MBE), which he finished and typed up himself during the Christmas break.

Even after taking four courses each semester, Badiul was one course short to get his MBE. Professor Paul Albrecht, who was the head of the Business Economics Program, transferred a class from Badiul's studies at Dhaka University. Thus, he was able to fulfil the requirements for his degree.

After handing in the final coursework, the foreign student advisor took Badiul to a steakhouse for lunch, and it was quite an experience for him. The barbecued steak was not only big but also over an inch thick. More interestingly, he saw pieces of neckties hanging on the walls of the restaurant. Apparently, anyone who came to the restaurant with a necktie would have it cut up by the restaurant employees and hung on the wall.

It was at this time that Badiul was taught by management guru Peter Drucker. Little did he know the impact Drucker's ideas would have on his future activism when he returned home to his country. Drucker was hired by Claremont Graduate School from New York University and started teaching in the Fall Semester of 1970—the same time Badiul became a student there.

Drucker was a world renowned intellectual and a management guru. When he died in 2005, *Business Week* called him a renaissance man, and "the man who made management." Drucker was a visionary. He conceptualized many ideas about the future, society, management, and business, and he brought these new concepts to life. Drucker could see things that others could not.[2]

Drucker was an immigrant from Austria who had worked with Robert Sloan and other automobile entrepreneurs. He wrote the influential "The Practice of Management" which conceptualized what he had learned from this experience, as well as developing the Management by Objective (MBO) concept. One of his favorite sayings that stuck with Badiul was "Management is doing things right; leadership is doing the right things."

Drucker's reputation brought in many students—particularly business executives from the Los Angeles area who enrolled in classes which were offered in the evening, and Badiul was lucky

2 Claremont Graduate School—now called Claremont Graduate University—later built a business school, which was named after Peter Drucker.

to be in his class. Unfortunately, Drucker was a poor teacher and the students who came with high expectations were often disappointed, with some even dropping out. The reason he was a poor teacher was that he would not remain focused on the topic. Rather, he would philosophize and frequently wander away from the subject being taught. However, Badiul could see his brilliance. Drucker's requirements were also easy—there were no exams! Students were required to submit some case analysis and a book review. He told them in class that the best book report he ever got was once sentence long. Badiul wrote a short paragraph long report and got the highest grade—H, meaning Honors.

Badiul was the only South Asian student and the only minority in his class. Upon learning that he was from East Pakistan—which was at that time receiving wide coverage in the international press, and that he had a pregnant wife back in his country, Drucker took a special interest in Badiul, and became a father figure to him. In later years Drucker wrote a letter of reference for him and said he was Badiul's "godfather" during a difficult period in his life.

Badiul's time in America coincided with the ramping up of hostilities between East and West Pakistan, and as the conflict increased in intensity, so too did his desire to return home. Personal news from his family was sparse, and Badiul worried for his wife, unborn child, and his mother. He also desperately wanted to be involved in the liberation work. It was anguishing to be so far away and watching from the sidelines. He went to Drucker for advice as he had developed ideas that made American businesses the world's leaders; Badiul wanted his insight on what it would take for a new nation to move forward. This relationship was seminal for Badiul. Drucker recognized him as a future leader and helped him think longer term. He told Badiul that leadership is not a short-term thing—leaders must think for the long haul. He also told him that his leadership would be needed in the future, and if he develops himself and prepares for it, he will be useful. The liberation of the Bangladeshi people wasn't only about ending Pakistan's occupation and atrocities. A lot more needed to happen than that—it required the building of the nation. He convinced Badiul to stay back and prepare to build the Bangladesh of the future. Drucker told Badiul, "You will be needed."

1970 and 1971 were very difficult years for all people of East Pakistan. The country was still under the control of West Pakistan, and people were struggling for independence. The only way Badiul could get any news about his family was through letters, so when a postal strike stopped all letters from the region in October 1970, Badiul was cut off from news about his family. One month later the devastating Bhola cyclone hit Bangladesh, washing away at least half a million people from the coastal areas of Noakhali and other coastal areas, causing total dislocation for millions more. It drove Badiul's anxiety sky high as he had no way of knowing if his mother was ok as she lived in nearby Laksam.

Badiul tried to do what he could to help his people in the cyclone's aftermath. He had come to know the foreign student advisor well, and with the advisor's help he embarked on an initiative to raise money for the victims of the cyclone. He sent letters to the faculty and administrators of all the colleges and used the student newspaper for a fundraising campaign which raised several thousand dollars that was sent to the cyclone affected areas of East Pakistan.

Things only got worse for his country when the ruling West Pakistani junta responded far too slowly to the magnitude of suffering and death the cyclone caused. People of East Pakistan were already agitating against the economic disparity and exploitation, so the inept and heartless response to the cyclone victims made people really angry. Against that backdrop, Pakistan's national election took place in December, which for the first time was based on adult franchise. This meant East Pakistan had more seats than West Pakistan in the national assembly, with the Awami League, led by Sheikh Mujibur (Mujib) Rahman, winning almost all the East Pakistan seats. Zulfikar Ali Bhutto's People's Party won the majority of West Pakistan's seats. The time was coming when East Pakistan would not be subjugated for much longer.

Badiul followed these events with acute interest and concern. His heart ached for his country, and he was greatly relieved by Mujib's victory. However, he was worried the military might of Pakistan would not be shaken off so easily—and he was right. Pakistani Army strongman Yahya Khan, on the prodding of Bhutto, would not allow Mujib to form a government and become the Prime Minister of Pakistan. Bhutto wanted to share the power, so while pretending to carry out negotiations, he and Yahya instead planned and prepared for a military crackdown. The early months of 1971 were a very chaotic period; the central government's authority over affairs in East Pakistan virtually disappeared, from government offices to private banks. Many people were killed in clashes with the security forces, and students—some of Badiul's former associates—declared the independence of Bangladesh and formally unveiled a flag for the new nation.

This all came to a head on the evening of March 25, 1971, when the Pakistani Army launched a horrific crackdown against those agitating against Pakistani rule. The army arrested Sheikh Mujib from his home and unleashed its brutal killing operation across Dhaka, causing massacres which created headlines around the world. The first place the army attacked was Iqbal Hall, where Badiul had resided as a student, and which was the center of the movement against the Pakistanis. Many people fled to India and ultimately nearly ten million Bengalis took refuge in West Bengal. A provisional Bangladesh government was formed, which made a formal Declaration of Independence on April 17th, 1971. Thus, the war of liberation started.

Badiul felt angry and frustrated following this news from afar. He was cut off from home with no way of returning. Despite Drucker's counsel, in his heart he knew that if he had known what was going to happen, he would never have left Bangladesh, He would have stayed and joined the country's Freedom Fighters. As the sickening news continued to come, all he could do was ramp up his own stateside activism and pray for his family.

Even though the postal strike had ended, during this chaotic time, still no letter from home arrived. Badiul had no idea what had happened to Lucky and their unborn child, and he feared the worst as she was living on Bonogram Road, Dhaka with only one other woman to help her around the house. Lucky was also surrounded by Biharis who had sided with the Pakistanis—some had even participated in the killing of their non-Muslim Bengali neighbors. Rotarians and some of his professors wanted to help and they tried to contact his wife—but she did not have a telephone. They did everything possible to help Badiul reach his family during those months, including giving him a ham radio to stay in touch, but it did not work. A former Claremont Graduate School student was able to get out of Bangladesh and contact him, telling him about the killings, but he knew nothing about Badiul's family.

Every day the mailman would come and give Badiul the disappointing news that no mail had arrived for him. That became a routine until finally, one morning in May, Badiul received a call from the mailroom with news; there was a letter for him which would be brought to the dorm. Badiul waited with feelings of extreme anxiety, desperate to receive it yet terrified it contained bad news. When he was handed an envelope, he recognized his wife's handwriting, and he swiftly opened it. Reading the letter Badiul broke down—his wife was safe, and he had become a father! Both mother and son were doing well.

Unbeknownst to Badiul, his son Mahbub was born less than two weeks after the Declaration of Liberation, on the 30th of April. When Lucky went into labor, her maid took her to the hospital as Badiul's uncle, who used to visit, was no longer able to because of the turmoil. The area was dangerous because of the beheadings, especially of Hindus and those who supported the liberation movement. Traveling to the hospital, Lucky passed many dismembered bodies on the street. It was truly horrifying. She survived because she was a respected professor who taught at a school in old Dhaka, where the principal was Bihari and most of the students were also Biharis.

During this time, there was occasional fighting on the streets. The guerrilla war was one-sided, controlled by the Pakistan Army and its collaborators, who would behead Hindus and Muslims who were not supporting Pakistan. The Muslims who were uprooted were migrants who had come from India in

1947, themselves victims of the atrocities committed during the partition nightmare. They didn't want Pakistan to disintegrate, and many of them became butchers who killed a lot of people. It was a miracle that Lucky survived.

While Badiul was deeply relieved his wife was ok, and ecstatic he had become a father, he had no news about his mother who was living in his village home in Laksam about one hundred kilometers away. Badiul was deeply worried about her unknown fate and had no way of assuaging his fears.

Not long after receiving Lucky's letter, Badiul's nine-month scholarship came to an end, and he graduated with his MBE from Claremont Graduate School. While proud of what he had achieved, celebrating this milestone was a muted affair for him given what was happening at his home. It also left him pondering his future. Due to the war, there were no avenues for safe travel back to East Pakistan, so he decided to heed Peter Drucker's advice by continuing his studies in the U.S. and get a PhD. He could not discuss this with Lucky, but he knew she would agree considering the plan had been for him to apply for his PhD back in Dhaka. And given his mother's vision for her son's education, Badiul felt she would also approve, and in lieu of knowing if she was safe, he could at least make this decision that he knew would make her proud. With this settled in his own heart and mind, he applied to various universities. It was Case Western Reserve University in Cleveland, Ohio that gave him the best scholarship offer, so in June 1971 he took the three-day Greyhound bus trip from California to Ohio. It was not easy to leave Claremont, where he had made a lot of friends. It was also hard to leave his mentor, Professor Drucker.

It was early summer when he arrived in Cleveland, and his first priority was to find a place to live. He found two other people in the same predicament, both South Indians, and like Badiul, were married and expecting their wives to join them soon. They all decided to rent an apartment together for the summer.

They found a place on Murray Hill Road located in what was called Little Italy, adjacent to the Case Western Reserve University (CWRU) campus. The Italian American Brotherhood Club was downstairs from their upstairs apartment. They were only inside the club once to meet the landlord Mr. Milano, and they saw people playing cards and other games. They later learned that Mr. Milano was the local mafia boss and known throughout the area as a man not to be trifled with.

CWRU was a well-known university with a prestigious medical school and a Nobel Laureate on the faculty. Badiul attended the Weatherhead School of Business (which was also known for developing the unique training methodology called "Appreciative Inquiry," which Badiul would later use in Bangladesh). In the business school was an operations research department created after World War II that was based on the quantitative tools developed to help the war efforts. The whole curriculum of the department was highly quantitative and most of the students were from India, with a few from Israel; there were very few American citizens. (The Chinese inflow was not there in those days.) Badiul was happy to discover another student from East Pakistan, and while there were also some West Pakistanis, Badiul had no interaction with them as fighting was still raging back home.

The Chairman of the Economics Department was Bela Gold, a Jewish immigrant from Hungary. Gold was a man with an interesting background, and his maverick nature appealed to

Badiul. A few decades earlier, he and his wife Sonia were accused of being communist spies and had to testify before the House Un-American Activities Committee to prove their innocence. Gold had worked a lot with the Japanese steel industry, which challenged the principle of economies of scale by building larger and larger steelmaking plants. He was a very good teacher and more importantly, an outstanding human being.

Gold knew about the atrocities unleashed by the Pakistani Army, and that Badiul's family was stuck there. He was very sympathetic and wanted to help Badiul, so even though his graduate assistantship would not start until the fall, he gave Badiul a cubicle in the Sears Library Building where the department was located. Badiul was initially a research assistant and soon became a teaching assistant. His time in the U.S. had sharpened his English proficiency, and he confidently taught small sections of undergraduate students. Badiul found teaching a fun experience, and it solidified his interest in economics, which he found analytical and interesting. This was instrumental in his decision to switch from commerce to economics.

Badiul's studies did not take his focus away from doing what he could to help his country. He was instrumental in forming the Bengal Relief Group at the university and served as its secretary, with Professor Ranan Banerjee as the President. The group raised relief money to send back home for the war effort. They also lobbied important senators including Senators Mike Mansfield, Frank Church, and Edward Kennedy. Badiul traveled to Washington, DC by bus a number of times to speak directly to those important politicians. It was daunting for him show up in DC and meet these figures in their fancy offices, but Badiul knew it had to happen. Mostly, those he met were on the same side of the issue, against Nixon's support of the Pakistani military regime, so the conversations were amicable and productive. Badiul was surprised at how much American policy was shaped by public opinion, and he was glad to take the time away from his studies to do this. Anything he could do to sway decision makers to support the freedom of Bangladesh was worth it.

Once settled in Cleveland, Badiul started the process to bring his wife and son to the United States. He contacted the Pakistan Embassy, but they refused to cooperate. He was not surprised, as the war of liberation was still going on in East Pakistan. They told him that as a student he would not be able to bring his wife as he must be a Green Card holder.

After hearing about the position of the Pakistan Embassy, Professor Gold gave Badiul a faculty appointment—rather than a graduate assistant position—which would be helpful in getting his Green Card. Getting the Green Card required certification from the U.S. Department of Labor. The foreign student advisor of CWRU discouraged him from applying, as she was almost sure he would not get Labor Department certification. Nevertheless, Badiul decided to give it a try since he was desperate to bring his wife and son out of East Pakistan, so he filed the application. Professor Banerjee from the Computer Science Department and Professor Chatterjee from the Social Work Department took him to see Charles Vanek, a Congressman from Cleveland, and the Chairman of the powerful House Appropriation Committee, who wrote a letter supporting his application for labor certification. This was successful and Badiul finally got the Green Card and applied for visas for his wife Lucky and their son Mahbub.

Back in Dhaka, Lucky was preparing to come to the U.S. The

war of liberation was still going on and it was a very difficult and unsafe period to move around. It was dangerous and risky for women to leave their home as the Pakistan Army was kidnapping them. Lucky had to get passports and visas for herself and the baby, and she navigated this process with great courage and resilience. She also made it her mission to find out the status of Anjumennessa, which was not easy. Badiul broke down when he received her letter advising him that his mother was indeed alive and well, still living in their small village home! This was such indescribably welcome news to him, and there would be even better times to come.

In October 1971, the long awaited day arrived—Badiul's little family would be reunited. He borrowed a friend's car to drive to the airport and pick up his wife and son. Waiting in the arrivals hall, Badiul was agitated and emotional. He and his wife had been apart for far too long, and so much had happened. Lucky had lived through a war and had faced those uncertain and treacherous times without her husband by her side. In the months apart, they had become parents, and he would soon share the responsibility for the care of their little baby. When the doors swung open, Badiul peered over the heads of the travelers coming through, not seeing them at first, when all of a sudden Lucky was there, carrying Mahbub, who was six months old. Badiul rushed to them, and he couldn't decide where to look, his eyes darting from Lucky's cherished face to that of his new son, and back to Lucky. He couldn't believe what he was seeing, people so beloved who had been so desperately missed. Hugging them closely, all anxiety melted away. With them in his arms, he said in English, "Welcome to America!"

It was a great relief for Badiul to have his family with him, but it was a difficult adjustment for Lucky. In Bangladesh, even with the chaos and danger, she had a meaningful and respected life. She had lots of friends and was a professor of social welfare at a college. People knew her and looked up to her. In Cleveland, she felt isolated, and socially found people friendly but not friends. The weather was cold, and it snowed often. Mahbub struggled with ongoing croup and chest infections, and because they were poor and didn't have a car, there were many long treks through freezing rain, sleet, and snow, with Badiul carrying Mahbub over his shoulder, to take him to the doctor or hospital.

During all of this, Badiul's political activism did not stop. In December 1971, the Nixon Administration's support for West Pakistan increased with the United States dispatching a ten-ship carrier task force, known as the Seventh Fleet, from South Vietnam into the Bay of Bengal as a way of flexing its muscles. While Badiul was at Case Western Reserve University with only one other student from Bangladesh, there were a number of students and some faculty from West Bengal in India, and as they spoke the same language and shared many customs, they were brothers in action. The Nixon administration was out of step with the U.S. people, who were shocked at what they were witnessing on their television screens. Badiul organized meetings with local political representatives, and sent petitions to the federal government to urge the U.S. to help stop the atrocities. Regular marches and rallies were organized and for the first time, Badiul appeared on television to bring awareness to the American people of just what was going on. Even though he was away from his country, he was very much part of the liberation struggle, doing what he could.

On the December 16, 1971, the war between Pakistan and Bangladesh ended, with Bangladesh the mighty—and unlikely—victor. Badiul and Lucky held each other tightly when the news was confirmed. They had been glued to the radio in the preceding weeks as the United Nations Security Council reconvened to push for a ceasefire. After four days of negotiations, it was taken out of the Council's hands when Pakistani forces in the East surrendered to the Indian Army. The war was over.

This brought up a lot of emotions for them both. There was immense pride in the David vs. Goliath victory, and excitement about what this might mean for the fledgling country, as this would be the first time the people would be their own nation, not colonized or governed by outside powers. There was also much sadness and grieving; so much had been lost and so many lives sacrificed.

They discussed their options at length: should they return to Bangladesh to help where they could? Or should they stay in the U.S.? Even though his little family was now in the United States building a new life, Badiul was pulled to go back and assist with the immediate reconstruction. However, Lucky, having just left Bangladesh, wanted to stay to continue her studies and make use of the opportunities to further her education. Drucker's advice to play the long game and wait until he was skilled enough to make a meaningful contribution, also rang in Badiul's ears. In the end, they decided to stay in the U.S. so they both could complete their educations.

In 1972, Badiul, Lucky, and Mahbub moved out of the Murray Hill apartment into a one-room apartment on the opposite side of the campus. It was considered a violent area and was called the "combat zone"—they were told not to cross Road 107, where the worst of it happened—but the apartment was cheap, $100 a month, everything included. The family's income came from a few different sources and totaled $375 per month. The stipend for the assistantship was $250, the family alliance was $40, and Lucky's work contributed $60. Professor Bela Gold gave Badiul an extra $25 per month because he was pleased with his work.

Lucky was admitted to the Master of Social Work program at CWRU, so they were both students and very busy. She also started working in the library to supplement the family income. They organized a co-op day-care center with several families, so parents took turns caring for all the children. Since Lucky was very busy with both work and her studies, Badiul had to help with the day-care center duties, which included changing diapers, something he was not used to doing. Lucky and Badiul's domestic life mirrored that of the times; while a loving parent, Badiul was not a hands-on father, leaving the practical care of his child largely to his wife.

Badiul was one of only eighteen students admitted to the incoming class of graduate students. At the end of the first year, they were given the core theory exam, and then entered into candidacy as doctoral students. After the exam, only two of the students passed, and the rest were given master's degrees and booted out. Badiul was one of the two who remained—he was on his way to receiving his PhD. His professors were so impressed with his performance they allowed him to recommend two students from Bangladesh for the incoming class. Badiul recommended his old friend Shamsul Huq, a brilliant student with a master's degree in physics, and Nasiruddin, who was teaching at Dhaka University. Both were given full scholarships.

Around this time, their stay in the United States took on a more permanent flavor. On a local noticeboard, Badiul read that a three-story house in Cleveland Heights was to be auctioned, with a minimum bid of $30,000. He and Lucky talked it over and submitted a bid for $30,001, not expecting they would win. However, a few days later, Badiul got a call that they won the bid. This presented a challenge as they did not have the entire $6,000 needed for the down payment. They negotiated with the university to be paid in advance for some of their work, and as a result, they were able to buy the house. This was an exciting time for them, though it increased their monthly housing costs from $100 to several hundred dollars. Thus, they fulfilled the American dream of buying a house.

The 1972 class of graduate students included Chi Schive, who was a teacher at National Taiwan University. Badiul and Chi became friends and wrote several papers together, including one where they tried to explain the unexplained part of Nobel Laureate Robert Solow's famous production function. One of the papers was sent to him, and Solow, a towering figure in economics, found the paper "ingenious." Chi went back to Taiwan and some years later became the Chairman of the Taiwan Stock Exchange, and later a government minister.

Badiul's research collaboration with Chi proved prescient. He received some important insights on how Taiwan became an Asian Tiger by using industrial policy to develop a technological base in the country. A case study Chi wrote about Singer sewing machines in Taiwan left its mark on Badiul. For example, it outlined how they stopped importing sewing machine parts from abroad and instead developed a supply chain within the country which had made critical contributions to the development of Taiwan's industrial base. This showed Badiul how appropriate policy interventions were crucial to fostering the economic development of poor countries. Policies were needed to promote certain industrial activities, including developing indigenous technology, to create an industrial base. A country needed this, along with large-scale manufacturing, to create labor opportunities for its citizens, and this should not be left to market forces alone. Without helpful policy interventions and investment in the physical and industrial infrastructure of a nation, people's efforts toward self-reliance could only go so far.

After completing his coursework and passing the qualifying examination, Badiul wrote his dissertation titled *International Economics: Dynamic Comparative Advantage*, focusing on the effects of technological change on trade in the calculator industry. It explored how a country with poor resource endowment could prosper through innovation by using newer technology. He showed how the comparative advantage in the calculator industry shifted with the adoption of newer and newer technology. Historically, the U.S. was the dominant producer and exporter of mechanical calculators, but other countries subsequently gained dominance by producing cheaper and more reliable electronic calculators. Badiul's study showed that constant innovations in the technology of the electronic calculator also impacted the trade pattern of the calculator industry. This area of comparative advantage, which is the economy's ability to produce a particular good or service cheaper than its trading partners, was also interesting to Badiul, in the context of what would be needed to lift Bangladesh from poverty.

In 1976, after much hard work, Badiul completed his dissertation under the supervision of Professor Asim Erdilek, who had been a student of legendary economist Wassily Leonief, the originator of the famous input-output table. Badiul was Asim's first PhD student and made him work extremely hard. He was so demanding that questions occasionally arose in Badiul's mind whether it was worth it. However, the hard work finally paid off, and Badiul earned his PhD. This was a huge milestone. His thesis was published and his findings were reported in several academic textbooks.

Badiul's thesis contributed toward understanding the changes in the pattern of trade caused by technological advances. It provided an explanation of the export-led growth of the East Asian Tigers, who had little to no resource endowment. They did it by producing cheap consumer electronic products using Western inventions in the semiconductor industry, such as the development of transistors and diodes, integrated circuits (ICs), and very large integrated circuits (VLIC), and then exporting them to the U.S. and other developed countries. Professor Harry Johnson, the towering international economist from the University of Chicago, encouraged Badiul to pursue this topic for his research, and Badiul felt incredibly proud of his achievement.

On the day of the convocation, Badiul reflected on his unlikely life journey that brought him, a poor village boy from a war-torn country, to this place. It meant a lot to him. Old doubts left him. He had a huge sense of accomplishment—he realized he can compete with others and not only survive but achieve with pride and confidence. In preparation for the convocation, he dressed carefully. He felt this PhD wasn't just for him. It was for his wife and family who had sacrificed a lot for this day, and his mother, who always believed in him and supported his growth and education at every turn. He also remembered Professor Habibullah, his mentor, who was instrumental in him getting the Rotary Foundation Fellowship that had started this journey. More than anything, he felt a sense of possibility: if he could do it, then others from his country could too. Anything was achievable for regular, village raised Bangladeshi people. The word "impossible" was removed from his vocabulary.

In 1976, Badiul, with Lucky and Mahbub, visited Bangladesh for the first time since he had left home to study in the USA. He had not seen his mother Anjumennessa in all that time, and even though he wanted to bring her to the U.S. to live with them, she was reluctant to leave her village and the life she knew. Seeing her and being together as a family was a top priority. While excited to be traveling back to Bangladesh, there were some mixed feelings. While Bangladesh would always be his home, he also had a home in America. The country that raised him had been through so much—would he feel like he still belonged? Whatever apprehensions he had evaporated when he stepped off the plane at Tejgaon International Airport in Dhaka. The sights, sounds, and smells assaulted him in the best possible way. He was home.

The visit to the newly born country, created with the enormous sacrifice of millions of people, was a rude awakening for Badiul. The country he had left, and the optimism for change that was bubbling up then, seemed largely gone. The catastrophic flood and famine that had raged in parts of the country two years earlier were still being felt with terrible aftereffects. The vast majority of people were in serious distress. Visiting his mother in his home village, he noticed that when the trash was swept from the floor and thrown outside, people went through it hoping to find grains of rice. People were surviving on water drained from cooked rice—life was that precarious and it was shocking to Badiul. He had grown up with many deprivations, but he had never seen anything quite like this. He was relieved Anjumennessa had not suffered from a lack of material needs, since the money he regularly sent to her was able to buffer the worst of the calamities that befell the majority of the people in the nation.

Although he had remained reliably informed while away, Badiul was still shocked to see how the enormous goodwill following liberation had been squandered away. Sheikh Mujibur Rahman, under whose name the war of liberation was fought and for whom people gave their lives, had become very unpopular following the war. He failed to form an all-party government to solidify the country's unity achieved during the war of liberation, and this disavowal of democracy by instituting one-party rule alienated the people and thwarted the reconstruction of the nation. Young people under the banner of JSD—Jatiyo Samajtantrik Dal—united against Mujib, the corruption of the party members, and the excesses of Rakhi Bahini, a paramilitary force created by Mujib.

Mujib had nationalized the main industries, and without a cadre of trusted officials to help govern, the results were chaos, looting, and plundering. The Bangladesh economy was in shambles, heavily relying on foreign aid to supply the most meager of services. When Mujib was assassinated the year before Badiul's first visit home, some people danced in the streets. Despite having the official authority, he had clearly lost the moral authority. Badiul was deeply saddened by the killing of Mujib and most of his family, because Mujib had been his leader when he was a young activist, and he still remembered his courage and fierce determination. Badiul found it hard to reconcile how far Mujib had moved away from his own philosophy. Prior to the Pakistani crackdown, he had asked people to resist the enemy with whatever they had and turn their homes into fortresses. Mujib's clarion call turned Bangladesh's war of liberation into a people's war, which achieved nationhood against the odds. But he failed to galvanize the collective energies and creativity of the people toward creating a prosperous and democratic nation, and for that, Bangladesh paid the price.

The visible devastations from the war were a daily reminder of the losses the country had endured. The World Bank estimated that six million homes had been destroyed, and that some cities looked like "the morning after a nuclear attack." Bridges had been blown out by explosives, and there were buildings everywhere that had been bombed. Repairs were slow, if not non-existent. The inadequate leadership following the war had not progressed the nation. The country was in chaos.

This unworkability was on display during Badiul, Lucky, and Mahbub's flight to Dhaka. Flying Bangladesh Biman, the new airline of independent Bangladesh, they were stuck for three days in London, because the airplane suffered mechanical problems due to not being properly maintained. When they finally reached Bangladesh, horror stories of the atrocities the Pakistani Army had committed were shared by everyone, with people suffering from a collective trauma, and this was compounded by those newly committed by the Bangladesh government. Infighting and resistance against the new government was not tolerated, and the crackdown was brutal, with many people killed by their own security forces. Distrust was rampant and people were divided into bitter, partisan political lines. It was clear that the people's democratic aspirations were dashed.

Yet with all of that, it was exhilarating for him to be back amongst his own people. Seeing his mother for the first time in six years was intensely moving for them both. Badiul had left as a boy and now returned as a man. Anjumennessa was sick and needed surgery, so Badiul decided to stay back to care for her. Lucky needed to leave on the scheduled departure date because of her job in Cleveland.

Anjumennessa was physically fragile, but her bright spirit and pride in her son were undimmed. After her operation, they spent treasured weeks together sharing what had occurred over the previous years. Badiul regaled her with the quirks of America, which amused her greatly. She was immensely proud of her son and the life he had made for himself. The visit reconnected him emotionally to his homeland and rekindled the fire he'd always had to make a significant contribution to his country one day. Leaving was bittersweet, especially saying goodbye to Anjumennessa. Yet he was resolved to make the best of his time in the U.S. while committing to return to Bangladesh more regularly.

In 1978, Badiul was hired by Seattle University as a tenure-track Assistant Professor of Economics and Finance in the Albers School of Business. As part of his contract, he had to go to Seattle to teach summer school, leaving behind his son and Lucky, who was working and also pregnant again. While they did not want to be separated, they made the financial decision for her to stay behind—their health insurance with Kaiser Permanente could not be transferred to cover the family in Seattle. It was tough for Badiul to leave, so before he left Cleveland, they bought a van, with the intention of them driving together for the move to Seattle after the summer.

After finishing summer school, Badiul went back to Cleveland to drive the family to Seattle. By that time, his son Mahfuz had been born and was two months old. This addition to his family pleased him immensely. Like many only children, Badiul had wanted a sibling for Mahbub and a family with many children. But this happiness was nearly extinguished when near Madison, Wisconsin, a big semitruck abruptly changed lanes in front of their van. Lucky, who was driving, lost control, and the van overturned and landed on its side. As they were trying to get out of the vehicle, they realized with horror that Mahfuz had been thrown from the van and was lost in the rubble. After sifting through the debris, they finally found him. By some miracle, he—like the rest of the family—was uninjured, though they were all shaken, and their vehicle was totaled. Watching the news of the accident, a very kind local Indian family contacted the police and offered Badiul's family the chance to stay with them, which they did for a couple of days, while they made arrangements to fly to Seattle.

Badiul and his family settled happily on the West Coast, buying a house in Kirkland, where Microsoft is now located, and Lucky became a PhD student in Social Welfare at the University of Washington.

In 1979, Badiul went to Bangladesh alone to see his mother, who was in her late fifties. It was a curious time to be home. The political situation appeared to be stabilizing, and a sense of hope was burgeoning. The military had ushered the country toward democratic elections earlier that year, so he returned to a new government. It seemed to him that the frustrations and disappointments of a few years earlier had largely lifted. There was a sense of possibility and the promise that things were getting better. During this visit, Badiul took his mother to perform Hajj at Mecca, fulfilling his duty as her son. It was quite an experience. It was incredibly hot, and his mother passed out when they went to pray in the main Mosque. Badiul literally carried her; she was so frail. Although a spiritually uplifting and exhilarating experience, it was a very physically challenging journey for them both.

A year later, in July 1980, Badiul and Lucky welcomed the birth of Shahirah, which brought great joy. After two boys, they had really hoped for a girl. Shahirah was thus a much-coveted addition to the family.

Shortly afterwards, a unique opportunity presented itself to Badiul. NASA was searching for someone to help design a unique initiative called the "Space Industrialization Project" and Badiul, once approved to take leave from his university job, was hired for it. His appointment was based on a nationwide competition among business school faculty, arranged by AACSB (American Academy Collegiate School of Business), and his PhD dissertation on the effect of technological change on trade made NASA interested in him. Peter Drucker's letter of reference must have also helped. For Badiul to pursue this very prestigious appointment, another move for the family was required. This was not a small thing, especially for Lucky, who was immersed in her own PhD study at the University of Washington. For Badiul to take up his dream opportunity meant she had to put hers on hold—which she did —they both agreed that working for NASA was the opportunity of a lifetime. As the role was not permanent, the family made plans to move to the East Coast and then would return to Seattle for Lucky to continue her PhD once the role was over.

NASA was a highly respected agency of the United States Government, whose mission was to explore space and expand the frontier of human knowledge. Badiul was proud to have received the offer from NASA, which was putting a lot of resources into developing the Space Shuttle program. There were serious technological challenges involved in developing the space shuttle, causing big delays and cost overruns. To many Americans, the agency that put men on the moon had lost its magic touch, and some doubts were being expressed about the future of the agency. NASA wanted not only to develop the space shuttle, but also to unveil a new economic possibility, that of processing materials in space—since whatever was produced on the Earth's surface was compromised due to the presence of gravity and impurities. NASA hoped that by helping to produce low volume and high-value products like drugs and electronics in space stations, they would utilize America's technological superiority and open a new economic frontier for the future. One of the obstacles was that the government was not geared toward manufacturing—they needed to collaborate with private industry. However, in creating a potential partnership with private industries, under the procurement rules, if the government invested even a penny in their activities, the patents and data rights that would come out of that activity would belong to the government.

Badiul was asked to work with a group of senior NASA officials to solve that particular problem. They came up with what was called a "Joint Endeavor Agreement Program," under which NASA would provide space in the shuttle and the private industry would design their own experiments. Since there would be no fund transfer, the results of the experiment would belong to the relevant company. This arrangement worked and there were countless experiments conducted in space, although the two space shuttle explosions created a huge setback in later years.

While at NASA, Badiul was given another assignment. The aerospace industry, which had been booming, faced hard times during the late 1970s. In the past, all satellites that were launched by NASA were made in the U.S.. Gradually other countries began to make satellites, and they used NASA's services to launch them. The aerospace industry lobbied to prevent that from happening and legislation was introduced in Congress barring NASA from launching satellites made in other countries. NASA was required to monitor whether the satellite was made in America. Badiul analyzed the proposed piece of legislation and ascertained that this was a regulatory role and NASA's mandate was different—the agency had no business getting into regulation—which killed the idea.

After he finished his assignment at NASA in 1981, the family moved back to Seattle, and before Lucky resumed her PhD, the family of five visited Bangladesh for a few weeks. Badiul found the country had changed again. The chaotic years of Mujib's rule were over, and order had been somewhat restored under the presidency of Rahman, who reinstated multi-party politics, and helped stabilize the food supply through digging canals for irrigation and food production programs. However, a few months before Badiul's visit, a new blow was dealt when President Rahman was assassinated. Hundreds of thousands of people attended his funeral, and in his place the vice-president, a frail Abdus Sattar, became the acting president of Bangladesh, who was then subsequently deposed by the military strongman, General Hussain Muhammad Ershad.

From Badiul's vantage point, Bangladesh was a nation cycling between hope and despair, without ever being able to pull itself out of those two gears to actually achieve the potential people had given their lives for. He was dismayed at how the political dramas, coups, and killings kept people constantly reactive, hampering their ability to move forward. These observations would only deepen in the years ahead and informed his belief that stable, transparent governance was critical for the people to succeed.

While at NASA, Badiul was up for tenure, and although he was very productive in his research and had good evaluations from students, the university postponed the decision. Badiul felt aggrieved, and although Dean Eshelman tried to persuade him not to, he resigned, believing strongly that an injustice was done to him.

This led him into an unusual career detour. One of his former students at Seattle University, Waleed Al-Mahdi, introduced him to Prince Bandar bin Muhammad Al Saud, and his father, Bandar, with a view of Badiul working for them. They were part of the Saudi Royal family, and Muhammad's mother, Bandar was a daughter of late King Abdulaziz Al Saud, the founder of the Saudi Kingdom. Muhammad was the second oldest son in the family, and the family was very rich, with a lot of real estate holdings in the UK and other businesses.

Even though Muhammad had a very decadent lifestyle, throwing parties frequently—he was a playboy, devoted to young women and drinking, and his time was spent on fun and games—something about working for this family intrigued Badiul. Saudi Arabia was beginning to come into its own. Oil prices were up, and money was flowing. Enormous riches were being amassed by a few, in a country that was not economically or psychologically prepared for such a transformation. Saudi Arabia did not have the comparative advantage in other products they would need to thrive beyond the oil boom, and they were wasting resources and missing out on the opportunity to take advantage of the country's full potential. As this was the area of Badiul's expertise based on his PhD research, he felt he could make a small contribution.

Badiul helped the family set up a company in Seattle, a shop for electronics products, and a travel agency. He negotiated and signed a contract with a British company to build the largest poultry farm in Saudi Arabia, with seventy-two broiler houses, each the size of a football field, and twenty-four houses for breeding parent stock. He frequently traveled to Saudi Arabia, London, and other countries to look after the affairs for the family.

While working with the family and other members of the royal family, as well as meeting and getting to know other global movers and shakers, the whole experience was not as satisfying as he hoped. His romantic view of being able to help fell apart. He found the culture of Saudi Arabia antithetical to modernity, and not adaptive. Resources were squandered without people understanding what they were doing, why money was spent, and what outcomes were expected. A culture of patronage eliminated any commitment to accountability. Even more disheartening, he found that while the rulers would "kiss the feet of Westerners," they would exploit their own people, and people of color who came from other parts of the world.

The failure of the elite to achieve a transformation of the country, and their unwillingness to include people outside their circles in the decisions they made, hit home. The failure of a centralized system, where people were only pawns to serve the rulers, meant there was no possibility for sustainable change to happen. It was Badiul's first exposure to the people's best interests not being taken into consideration in any way, and he found it disheartening to witness the cost to society and people's agency when they remained at the mercy of the largesse of rulers. But despite the disappointment, the experience would be worth it, as it was here that he learned many ideas he would later put into practice at The Hunger Project.

While working for the Saudi royal family, a devastating tragedy befell Badiul and his family, which significantly influenced his decision to return to Bangladesh more permanently.

One Sunday, Muhammad and his entourage were going to Mount Rainier for a picnic, and he invited Badiul and his family to join them. Badiul and Lucky agreed to go, leaving the children behind with Lucky's brother's family, who had moved to Seattle a few years earlier. As Badiul was driving the prince's BMW toward the mountain, a large SUV with some young people in it crossed over the line and plowed straight into them. The car was totaled in the catastrophic head on collision; both Lucky and Badiul were knocked unconscious and were taken to Harborview Medical Center by Army helicopter.

Lucky hit her head on the dashboard, and Badiul broke his ribs and partially collapsed his lungs through the impact of his body on the steering wheel. He regained consciousness while being transported in the helicopter and was told his wife was alive and stable, though unconscious. After a few days, Badiul recovered sufficiently, but Lucky was still in a coma. The decision was made to transfer her to another hospital for the long-term institutional care which she would need. However, while being prepared for the transfer, she suffered a respiratory arrest and was declared brain dead, with only a machine keeping her alive while they administered experimental medicine. Doctors advised Badiul that Lucky would never recover, and the toxicity of the experimental medicine would eventually end her life. It was only a matter of time. Badiul consulted religious leaders and Lucky's brother for guidance. In the end, three days after the collision, Badiul had to do the hardest thing he'd done in his life and decided to stop medical life support for his wife, his partner, his best friend, and mother to their three young children. Mahbubon Nessa died on April 23, 1983, a week before Mahbub's twelfth birthday.

This devastating loss sent Badiul into deep grief and introspection. Why had he survived, and Lucky was taken? Badiul's chest was crushed from impact with the steering wheel —logically, he was the one who should be dead. What possible reason was there for his survival? He wondered why he was alive with relatively minor injuries when his wife had been killed. He questioned whether there was a purpose for what happened. All this heightened the compulsion he felt to make his life matter.

After losing his wife, life was extremely traumatic and became very difficult. Not only was Badiul dealing with his own grief, but he also had three small children who had lost their mother. There were too many heartbreaking moments. While work was both a financial necessity and a refuge for Badiul, it was an added loss for his children not to have their father around more. They had a live-in housekeeper, but it was not enough. His children needed continuity and care. They needed a mother. Badiul decided that marrying again would be best for the family. Though still grieving, he was resolved, and so he spoke to his mother and friends back home in Bangladesh to seek their help and advice. This decision, and taking the initial steps, was a nerve-racking experience for him, but one he knew was the right thing to do for his family.

He was introduced to his future wife Tazima by one of her cousins, whom a friend in Washington knew, and the possibility of marriage was broached. Tazima lived in Dhaka and worked in the U.S. Consulate there. She came from a well-known family; her father was the director of the railway, and her youngest uncle, H.T. Imam, was a cabinet secretary, later becoming the most influential political adviser to Sheikh Hasina, when she was elected Prime Minister in 2008.

When the marriage was first suggested as a possibility, Tazima and Badiul spoke a number of times to get to know each other. In February 1984, Badiul went to Dhaka to meet with her, and they both agreed to the arrangement. While Tazima had spent time in the UK, she had not been to the USA, but she was prepared to move there, and so Badiul and Tazima were married on February 24, 1984. Tazima would become Badiul's most important and stalwart partner for the trailblazing work ahead.

Coming back to Seattle with his new wife, Badiul knew things couldn't remain the same. He needed to limit his overseas absences that were required for his job with Muhammad's family and spend more time both with his children, so they could adjust to Tazima, and his new wife. It was time, in any case, to leave the job with the royal family. It wasn't fulfilling, and the global travel was too destabilizing. In 1985, Badiul returned to teaching, securing a professorship in business and economics at Washington State University's Tri-Cities campus.

In 1986, Tazima and Badiul welcomed their first child, Rozana, in Richland, Washington, which brought them great joy.

At that time Badiul was in Bangladesh, making arrangements to bring his mother to the U.S., with plans for her to settle there. Anjumennessa was in her mid-sixties and had lived in her home in the village her entire adult life. She didn't want to leave that familiar place, but after much prodding, she relented. She arrived at Tazima and Badiul's home in the evening, and in the morning asked Badiul where the people were, as there was no one on the street. No matter what answer he gave, she was not satisfied—she could not fathom a street and a town where people were invisible. His mother was also initially suspicious of some basic things. Never having seen a television before, she was convinced people on the TV could see her, and she became agitated whenever the television was on. Anjumennessa also hated the cold weather and never adjusted to it. Even though Badiul and his family lived in a nice house in a beautiful part of Richland, his mother was miserable and felt very unmoored by American life. In the end, after eight months, Badiul resettled her back in her village, where she immediately felt content.

Over the next few years, Samirah, another daughter, was added to the family in 1989. Rozana and Samirah were greatly adored by their older siblings, and they were a happy family, with all the children doing well. In 1989, Mahbub won the Westinghouse Talent Search competition to become one of the forty young scientists of America. In the same year, he wrote an essay on the U.S. Constitution, which was sponsored by the Bicentennial Commission, headed by Chief Justice Warren Burger. It was published in the Congressional Record, and President Reagan declared him the national winner in a White House Ceremony. Mahbub won $11,000, and after graduating from high school, he further made his parents proud by becoming a student at MIT.

Even though Badiul was living abroad, he stayed informed about what was happening in Bangladesh and visited often. From America, Badiul had watched the ongoing disasters befalling his home country—flooding, famine, and poverty. He noticed the global celebrities getting involved, using images from his nation of starving children and people begging to raise money and awareness. It felt very patronizing and disempowering. It created an inferiority complex in him; he felt bad that Bangladeshis were seen as so hopeless and calamitous.

He thought that maybe he could do something about it. He had been a participant of the War of Liberation, which started long before the Pakistani crackdown of March 25, 1971, and saw how, at the beginning, overcoming the subjugation by the Pakistanis seemed insurmountable. When the Pakistani crackdown took place, many people believed going against Pakistan's huge, disciplined army was impossible. Suicidal. It meant only death. But millions of people defied that mindset and took the courageous step of resisting Pakistan. It was a People's War. This was also the mindset of being young—based on defiance and taking risks. Young people don't have obligations to families and can be daring. Because of that, even though three million Bangladeshis lost their lives, they won against Pakistan.

Following the war was a heady period, where people believed and hoped something new would happen for the nation based on ideas of democracy and secularism. Over time, these ideals evaporated and disappeared for many people. They gave up. They became cynical and resigned.

But Badiul did not. As a professor, he arranged a session at the American Economic Association annual meeting in 1988 called "Economics of Growth and Stagnation." It was inspired by a comment he read in *The Wall Street Journal* from Economist and Professor Anne Osborn Krueger, where she contended that Bangladesh had an outside chance to follow in the footsteps of South Korea in terms of its development. Intrigued by this comparison, Badiul wrote a paper titled "Economics of Growth and Stagnation: Korea versus Bangladesh" in which he noted that Korea and Bangladesh were in a similar state of development in 1971, with both countries having similar per capita income, exports, and investment share of GDP. Yet by 1988, South Korea's per capita income had grown to $4,700 while Bangladesh's stalled at $258. A similar pattern was evident in comparing GDP: In 1971, the GDP for both countries was $9 billion. Yet by 1988, South Korea had increased its GDP to $200 billion, while Bangladesh's languished at $26 billion. South Korea didn't have any resources other than some low-quality coal, while Bangladesh had significant resources, including fertile soil and fresh water. Why then had Bangladesh's advancement stagnated?

Answering this question about his county's stifled potential would define the next stage of his life. He noticed that the poverty that beset his nation had captured the imagination of the generous people of Western countries, and a lot of aid and assistance flowed to the newly liberated country. Yet he was troubled, and the words from Rabindranath Tagore's poem "Crossing," verse 47, spoke to him deeply: the more the West gave from their "careless abundance," the more Badiul felt the "beggar's bowl." He realized there had to be another way.

When Henry Kissinger called Bangladesh a "basket case," and Norwegian Economist Just Faaland characterized it as a "test case"—if Bangladesh can get out of its abject poverty, anybody could—Badiul's sense of pride was hurt. He strongly believed that a nation which could earn its independence by shedding blood—lots of blood—deserved better. His people should be able to fend for themselves. He believed that after the Liberation War, Bangladesh lacked the right kind of leadership to keep them united and focused on fighting hunger and poverty together. They forgot what they had learned, namely, that people matter, and people, if they take responsibility and action, can make anything happen.

He was inspired by Amartya Sen's ideas around capability and freedom, which Sen later wrote about in his seminal book "Development as Freedom", particularly the idea that people are not created poor nor must remain poor. They can be awakened and mobilized to change their future. The poor are not the problem, rather they are the solution to their own hunger.

Badiul believed that if the commitment and determination that the people demonstrated by confronting and defeating the formidable Pakistani army could be mobilized, the country's dream of "Sonar Bangla" (Golden Bengal)—could come true. The valiant Freedom Fighters showed that nothing was impossible for a people who were determined and were willing to make the necessary sacrifice.

These things were percolating for many years, and his restlessness was getting stronger.

In his twenty-one years spent living in the USA, Badiul achieved more than he could have ever imagined. He had an incredible family. He earned the highest academic degree possible from a well-known American university. Now he was a professor, teaching kids in the richest country in the world, and was successful in his research and scholarly work. He had worked for NASA, doing something meaningful with significance for humanity. As an advisor to the Saudi Royal family, he'd had the opportunity to rub shoulders with a lot of important dignitaries from around the world. These experiences had shaped his character, and Badiul was confident about his abilities and potential. He could rest on these laurels, but deep down, he was not satisfied.

In 1990, it was time for his sabbatical leave given to tenured faculty after six years. The university would pay his full salary for one semester, or half salary for two semesters, with the intention that he would be able to travel, produce some worthwhile scholarly research, and come back renewed and reenergized.

Badiul had quite a few options for spending his sabbatical year, including offers to go to Maastricht, Netherlands, to work at a school of international business; work at McKinsey and Company, the famous consulting house; or work with the legendary Economist and Nobel Prize Laureate Robert Solow. But another option presented itself. One that he couldn't ignore.

It is sometimes said that one loves a country more once you leave it. This was more so in his case because Badiul had a small role in creating the country—Bangladesh, by playing a leadership role in the 1969 movement, and in the period leading up to the war of liberation. He'd helped mobilize American public opinion in favor of liberation, including lobbying the American congressional leadership against the Nixon Administration's support for the brutal atrocities of the Yahya regime in East Pakistan.

Thus, the birth of Bangladesh was a dream-come-true for him and he always harbored the yearning to go back and do his part to truly liberate the people of Bangladesh. But as he had learned from his mentor Peter Drucker, true liberation meant more than achieving independence. Badiul had been restless, waiting for the right opportunity to return to Bangladesh.

And now that time had come.

CHAPTER THREE

At a Crossroads

During his two decades of living in the United States, Bangladesh had stagnated, held back through war, famine, political instability, and poor economic decisions. Upon returning home, Badiul had no specific plan for his sabbatical, other than trying to find a way to assist his country in the most meaningful way possible. The agreement between him and Tazima was they would return to the United States after twelve months. Yet Badiul harbored a secret dream in his heart, not shared with anyone, including his wife, that he would not be returning to his old life in America, and in fact would never live there again permanently. Badiul hoped this sabbatical would afford him the time to turn his dream into reality.

In Dhaka, the family, except for Mahbub, who was at MIT for his undergraduate studies, moved into his in-law's house. Initially, everyone was happy to see them. But when all the relatives heard that Badiul hoped to stay for a longer period, everyone was up in arms. Tazima's uncle, H. T. Imam, was a cabinet secretary of the government, and the guardian from her family's side traditionally entrusted to protect her interests. He was the one who was most upset that Badiul was contemplating returning to Bangladesh permanently and leaving behind a tenured full professorship in America. Others also thought he would be wasting his time. Tazima herself was the decider. While preferring to live in the USA, she didn't resist the idea of staying in Dhaka, and agreed to remain there for the time being. It would prove to be a pivotal decision, for without her support, Badiul would not have been able to remain in Bangladesh.

The country Badiul had left as a young man in 1970 was no longer the same country he returned to in 1991, and he felt the strong need to reacquaint himself. He wanted to understand the changes that had taken place, their implications, and what was really going on in the country. On the surface, there were things to glean, through reading newspapers and having conversations with friends and family. But he wanted to know the people's thinking, and what had happened to the broader community during his twenty-one years away.

To discover this, he began traveling throughout the country. At that time, he didn't have his own vehicle, so he took public transport buses and traveled by train. Sometimes he would stay with relatives who were still living in small villages and towns. He visited different institutions and sought out people who had made a difference in Bangladesh through their leadership.

Badiul met with people from different walks of life, from high-level government officials and policymakers to village farmers and daily wage laborers. In his period of exploration, he didn't know quite what he was searching for, only that he needed to shed any preconceived ideas of his country, including romantic notions of his youth about what rural living was like. More and more, he was aware of his outsider's mindset—that he was both from—and not from—the country. He was determined to set aside his judgement as much as he could, and truly see what was before him. He needed both the analytical mind of a professor to be able to understand the country as it was, and the love of a patriot who would not turn away despite the challenging conditions he observed.

What he observed throughout the nation shocked him. While sitting with and interacting with the poor in the villages, he noticed time and again that the skinniest person in a family was the woman, and they generally ate last and got the least amount of food, even if they were pregnant or breastfeeding. Sometimes there would be nothing left for her after feeding everyone else in a family with limited means. One of the outcomes of this was stunting, with the height of Bangladeshis getting shorter each year.

The poor also married their daughters off early, when they were in their lower teens, usually to a man much older. Early marriage had been common when he was a young boy, but it shocked Badiul to see how prevalent it still was so many decades later. Often those daughters, abandoned by husbands, came back with their children, creating additional burdens for the parents. Men smoked or chewed tobacco. Family sizes were large. Water-borne diseases were rampant: unclean water fetched from a dirty pond was not boiled before drinking, and even if latrines were present, they were not often used. Diarrheal death of children was widespread.

The rural poor that Badiul met worked harder than anyone else. Some were peddling rickshaws eighteen hours a day for very little money. Others were working in the fields as laborers and not paid much. They were farm workers doing grueling work under the boiling sun, or they were women who, after a long day of hard work, sewed late into the night by the flicker of a small candle to make the handicrafts they hoped would sell at the market. Yet, no matter how hard people worked, they could not make ends meet. They were going round and round in the poverty cycle. The services and support they needed to create an enabling environment for them to succeed were missing.

This time he spent traveling brought home a belief that became foundational to his thinking—that every human being—rich or poor, black or white, Bangladeshi or American, woman or man—is created to be self-sufficient, with similar physical and mental abilities to become self-reliant. He believed that irrespective of where one was born, nearly everyone had a powerful thinking machine sitting on their shoulders, giving them the ability to think and respond to life. Being dependent on handouts for survival represented to him a denial of what it meant to be a human being.

In this Badiul did not agree with the neo-liberal exhortation "pull yourself up by your bootstraps." Quite the opposite. He believed that his fellow citizens could be fully active and responsible in the matter of their own life—and—that the environment they lived in—enabling or disabling, was every bit as important as a person's own determination.

Unlike the popular narrative that saw Bangladesh as a "basket case," Badiul knew that there was nothing wrong with the people of his country, poor and destitute though they may be. He saw beyond the prevailing view that these people were hopeless, helpless, and pathetic. He knew them to be hardworking, resourceful, resilient, and creative, able to survive with so few means, and flourish, given the opportunity. Like his own mother managing with very little, he knew they were no different than him, only the circumstances and conditioning had been different.

In the U.S. Badiul had well-known intellectuals like Peter Drucker, Bela Gold, and others as his teachers. They helped develop his conceptual abilities—to think, and reason. Yet these months of traveling and getting to know his country widened his perspective even further. Across Bangladesh, he found a new band of teachers who helped him use his conceptual abilities to derive new understandings. His new teachers were uneducated villagers, who were dismissed by everybody, but they helped him see things differently with a fresh set of eyes.

These travels were transformational experiences for him, and in later years, even when he had been working in the field for decades, this growth and learning continued. While the poor continued to be his greatest teachers, making him a different and stronger person, it was an unexpected encounter with a parrot that proved to be a seminal moment that was to shape Badiul's thinking for the next three decades.

One day, he was sitting on the sofa at a friend's house drinking tea. When he put the teacup down, he heard a noise under the table. Looking under it, he saw a parrot walking around. He was immediately very curious and asked his host: "Doesn't the parrot fly away?"

The friend said no, so Badiul became even more curious. "How come? Is it sick? Have you clipped its wings?"

"No. It is a healthy parrot. We did not clip its wings. This is a parrot which cannot fly."

Badiul was fascinated. The bird looked like a parrot, walked like a parrot—in every way it was a parrot, but it lacked the essential ability of a parrot—which is to fly. He asked a series of questions, finding out that his friend had bought the baby parrot for their child for ten takas. They looked after it, rearing it with great care and affection, providing it with a beautiful cage situated in the corner of the room.

His friend picked up the parrot and put it on top of a bookcase in another corner of the room. The parrot walked around for a few minutes and jumped down, flapping its wings. Badiul was excited! He challenged his friend, "you said that the bird can't fly, but I see it is flying."

The friend stopped him and said, "it can jump down by flapping its wings, but it can't fly away."

Badiul asked what they fed the parrot. He was told that initially they used to feed it hot peppers and star fruits, but as time went on, they introduced other foods, including human food.

Badiul was very surprised: "Does it eat all the food that you eat?"

And his friend responded that "yes, it eats some of the food we eat, except it has discriminating tastes. It will not touch any food that is cold." Moreover, due to the parrot's favored status, it received its meals immediately after food was cooked, even before humans had a chance to eat. The parrot had grown accustomed to consuming only hot food.

Badiul thought about this parrot long after his visit to see his friend ended. He reflected that the inherent ability of a parrot is to fly, to find its way, and to survive. But this parrot wouldn't survive even five minutes if it were freed. The cat next door would eat it up! It dawned on him the reason it couldn't fly was because it had never used its innate ability to fly. Muscles in its wings never developed because they were not used. And wasn't that like Bangladesh? The country had been created from a bloody war of liberation. Millions had died through that, and from the famine that followed. The world responded with compassionate aid, initially serving as a lifeline. However, over time, the generous support transformed into a dependence, and the people and government of Bangladesh grew accustomed to receiving assistance and being taken care of, much like the parrot. Badiul realized that, even two decades later, he was witnessing the harsh reality of this dependency.

It became very clear to him that a deep sense of dependency had taken hold. People had become conditioned to rely on external aid and support, hindering their ability to thrive independently. This was a debilitating condition, from which came mindsets of hopelessness, resignation, and helplessness. Like the parrot's unused wings, so too the potential of his countryfolk remained untapped. The ability to become self-reliant was there for most people, but if this ability was not used people become dependent like the parrot. You lose it, if you don't use it!

The essentialness of the enabling environment became clearer for him. Place that same Bangladeshi family struggling to make ends meet in a different context, one where access to education, labor rights, health care, and other services are a given, and you would see them thrive. An environment that supported the health and well-being of the nation was fundamental, and this included laws and policies that gave everyone equal rights and freedom, instead of just the privileged few. It required people to interact proactively with the functions of government, and those functions had to respond appropriately. It included the provision of basic services, like clean water and safe sanitation for every person. These were the foundations upon which his people could strengthen their wings and fly.

This reminded him of the lines from a famous Tagore poem:

> "No: it is not yours to open buds into blossoms.
> Shake the bud, strike it; it is beyond
> your power to make it blossom."[3]

The implication was that one cannot make a flower blossom no matter how hard you try—pull the petal or hit the bud—only the flower itself has the inherent ability to blossom. You can only support the environment it has to grow in: you water and fertilize the plant and put a fence around it so that no one breaks its stems. Badiul began to understand the importance of the gardener and creating an enabling environment—when this happens, the plant will do the rest.

Giving handouts or alms as the strategy for improving a society was as limiting as the cage the parrot was confined to. Notwithstanding a crisis situation, such as famine and war, charity was not good for people's dignity and agency. It reminded him of a health care center in a village where people lacked access to essential elements for well-being—good livelihood, education, safe sanitation, etc. The health center became a revolving door where people came in sick and left well, but without attention paid to the quality of people's lives outside the center, they were doomed to get sick again. This encapsulated the futility of the typical aid approach, which provided one single element but ignored everything else that was needed.

From all these experiences, strategies began to take shape in

---

3 *Fruit-Gathering*, XV111 By Rabindranath Tagore [Translated from Bengali to English by the author] New York: The Macmillan Company, 1916.

Badiul's mind about how to confront this mindset of dependency and create the enabling environment for people to succeed. It informed his understanding of human nature: if you do things for people because you believe they are helpless; if you take care of them because you think they cannot take care of themselves; if you don't support them as they strive to reach their goals, then whatever you do will not empower them. It will not be sustainable. This further inspired Badiul to create pathways to put these realizations into practice.

Meanwhile, Badiul needed to find work to provide for his family now that the twelve months of his sabbatical were up. He'd spent decades studying, teaching, and applying economics in the U.S. and felt he could use these skills to contribute to the growth and development of his country. Badiul was particularly interested in industrialization and removing some of the regulations and restrictions that shackled private initiative. He believed deregulation would foster innovation and be a means of developing a vibrant private sector. He thought his knowledge and experience in these areas might make a positive impact.

So when Badiul was offered a job by a bilateral donor's contractor to be the head of an industrial deregulation project, he gladly accepted. As part of the compensation package, his three school aged children's tuition fees were to be paid by the company—this was important to Tazima as she didn't want their children's education compromised by the extended stay in Bangladesh. Mahfuz, Shahirah, and Rozana were enrolled at the American International School, where tuition fees were steep, and Samirah went to pre-school.

To begin, Badiul hired some competent staff to get the project off the ground. As the office became operational, he found himself unwillingly drawn into the shady side of Bangladesh business that he had not directly confronted before. When he began the process of procuring a vehicle and other supplies, it was "suggested" by a senior colleague that he buy a reconditioned Japanese vehicle and record it as a new vehicle in the accounts, pocketing the difference in price. Badiul pushed back vehemently, and the matter was dropped. But this was only the beginning—his naivety and values would soon prove incompatible with how business was conducted there. In that first year, some former government officials wanted Badiul to give them a kickback in exchange for giving him a contract. He didn't want any part of it and told them so, unwittingly alienating powerful people. It didn't stop there. A bureaucrat with a reputation for dirty dealings invited Badiul to dinner at Hotel Sonargaon, which Badiul declined as he knew nothing good would come of it. The man then came to his office and offered Badiul a bribe to hire a firm as a local counterpart. When Badiul refused, another senior government official tried to pressure him to accept the offer. Badiul was shocked at the blatant corruption, especially from within the government.

Worse was to follow. Badiul was at a seminar where the Planning Minister, Zahiruddin Khan, was giving a lecture about the government's commitment to transparency and accountability to combat corruption. Badiul was impressed and went up to the minster to share the pressures he was under to accept kickbacks. The minister seemed sympathetic and asked Badiul to put it all in writing, which he ingenuously did.

A few days later, he received a written communication from the former government official who had offered him the bribe, and it took him to task, writing that "the aspersion on one government official was an aspersion on all." Badiul realized too late that he had been sucked in by the rhetoric of a commitment to good governance. He'd been out of the country for too long and was naive to the scale of entrenched privilege, power, and corruption that had become commonplace.

Not long after, Tazima and Badiul invited the representatives of the bilateral agency and a few other close friends to dinner. The donor representatives failed to show up and did not answer their phones when he called to follow up. The next day, he got a letter from the contractor terminating his contract. Instead of supporting him, the government functionaries had pressured the donor to take action against him by firing him.

Badiul felt embarrassed and ashamed, but also indignant. This was not fair! He was not indulged by family members and friends who blamed him instead of the minister. "What did you expect?" they said, shaking their heads in bemused disbelief. This was a shocking development. He was fired for the first time in his life, punished for not partaking in the endemic corruption in Bangladesh. He was furious that his employer succumbed to the pressure and did not stand by him. The financial implication of Badiul being fired was also serious. His children were no longer eligible for free schooling, which meant Badiul and Tazima had to find a way to pay for their tuition. This was a significant financial burden they hadn't anticipated, and it left them feeling overwhelmed and uncertain about the future. In the end, their children had to withdraw from school.

It was a low point for Badiul, and he started to question whether returning home had been the right decision. Should he have stayed in the United States and pursued his career there? Should he have listened to the people who told him that he was foolish to come back?

A physical attack compounded concerns that he was on the wrong track. On a hot afternoon in September, Badiul and Tazima were in a rickshaw when three men suddenly approached them from three sides—one with a knife in his hand. Instinctively, Badiul kicked out at the attacker coming at him, and he stumbled and fell to the ground. But another man came from behind and grabbed Tazima's necklace and pulled it off, while the man on the left tried to grab her bag. Badiul screamed and yelled for help, but the bystanders just stood there and watched. He got off the rickshaw and started to chase after the attackers, but they quickly disappeared into the crowd. He was shaken and angry, and it took some time to compose himself. They reported the incident to the police, who took their statement.

A few days later, Badiul took a walk to the Parliament area, which was not too far away from his in-law's house. A stranger stopped him to ask about the status of the police report he'd filed after the mugging. Badiul was startled as he did not know the man. He had shared the incident with some of his friends, including a former senior police officer, but no one else. It was not public knowledge. The man told Badiul he should be careful because the muggers may be following them. He suggested that they should probably leave for the U.S. because their safety may be in danger.

While Badiul refused to be intimidated, he knew he had some hard decisions to make. He had come back to Bangladesh in 1991 to do something useful for his country, and two years later he was feeling beaten. Badiul didn't know what to do. He thought very seriously about his future, and whether this marked the end of the road in his idealistic dream of helping his country. He and Tazima spoke at length, considering their options. Maybe they should give up and return to the U.S. in the summer to teach summer school. The university wanted him back, and they both knew what to expect from life there and it was comfortable. While it felt like a backward step, in the end they reluctantly decided to move back to the U.S.. Badiul felt defeated and thwarted, but he needed to make the right decision for his family. Returning to the U.S. to resume teaching at the university made sense—he felt he had not made any difference during his time in Bangladesh. It was over.

Then fate intervened.

PART TWO

NURTURING A REVOLUTION

CHAPTER FOUR

Breaking New Ground

In the middle of March 1993, when Tazima and Badiul were reluctantly planning their return to the United States, he was invited to a meeting by his friend Mr. Gias Kamal Chowdhury, a prominent journalist. He told Badiul that two people from the U.S. would be meeting with some Bangladeshi youths and asked if he would like to join them. Being fired, frustrated, and about to leave the country meant Badiul had nothing better to do, so he went.

He entered a small room where about a dozen mostly young people were in conversation with two foreigners, who he learned were Joan Holmes and Dr. John Coonrod, President and Vice President, respectively of the international non-government organization (NGO), The Hunger Project (THP). Little did Badiul know they would become two of the most important influences in his life.

Coming from academia, Badiul was unfamiliar with The Hunger Project. Chowdhury explained that it was an international NGO committed to ending hunger and had been founded in

1977 in the aftermath of the 1974 Bangladesh famine. It had recently been incorporated in Bangladesh by a group of young volunteers, who were part of the Voice of America Listeners Club. Chowdhury himself was chief advisor of the new organization.

It was a lively meeting that Badiul walked into, with the young men passionately and relentlessly, in Badiul's opinion, demanding money from the two Americans seated at the table. They wanted to know from Joan and John what projects they were going to initiate—in those days, the perception, and reality were that NGOs were all about money and projects. The group urgently wanted a number on how much money THP was going to give. Badiul heard the group go on and on, pressuring Joan and John—who seemed caught off guard—for funding, resources, and help. He listened to the demands and, after a while, became tired of this badgering. So, he opened his mouth and told them to stop it.

All eyes were on the man who had interrupted, and for Badiul, the floodgates opened, and all his experiences of the past few years poured out. Even though he was supposed to be an observer, he spoke forcefully and without hesitation to the young volunteers, telling them they needed to think about how to help the country and what actions could be taken locally by themselves. He told them that Bangladeshis needed to take ownership of their own future.

This perspective was a 180-degree shift from what Badiul had learned through his studies. Badiul was trained as a neoclassical economist and had been taught that people played an important role primarily through supplying labor into the production process. For decades he had believed that labor and capital working together were the source of economic growth and the well-being of the people. Hunger and poverty were "problems" that needed to be solved through the "trickle down" process of stimulating more production and higher economic growth. People's participation in achieving economic development was not viewed as important. People only needed to be involved at some stage, especially as consumers.

In this traditional view of economists, human drive, initiative, innovation, entrepreneurship, and their mindset played little, if any, role in creating a better life for people. In fact, people, especially the poor, were viewed as the target of poverty eradication rather than as the solutions to poverty. The belief was that they needed support and handouts as "beneficiaries" of government, NGO, and individual largesse. Thus, charity became the overarching development paradigm.

From his time in Bangladesh, Badiul felt strongly that this prevailing view was wrong. Based on his experiences and observations, it was clear that charity only created a sense of dependency which conditioned human beings to think in ways that perpetuated them needing outside help, such as; *we are poor, please give us more*. Badiul shared all this and more in the meeting. He knew the charity paradigm needed to be challenged, and he didn't hold back. After all, he was leaving the country in a couple of months and had nothing at all to lose.

Unbeknownst to him, The Hunger Project shared his views. It advocated that hunger was not inevitable and that it could be eradicated—but it would not be solved by traditional charity. After the African famine of the 1980s, it became clear to the organization that what was missing in the international response to hunger and poverty was not just more top-down aid, but rather local leadership and strategies in each country that would put people in charge of their own development at the grassroots level. This is what THP set out to do, and a new approach called "Strategic Planning-in-Action" was launched by the organization in India in 1990 and Senegal in 1991. They were hoping to implement the approach in Bangladesh also.

Upon hearing Badiul share this philosophy, John Coonrod wrote something down on a piece of paper and passed it to Joan Holmes. The note said *Hire This Guy*.

The Hunger Project global leadership was having a difficult time in Bangladesh—they were committed to working in the country, but there was confusion about how to make it happen. The young, enthusiastic volunteers wanted funding for their own initiatives they would do under the THP banner. They were passionate but not fully aligned with THP's approach. Moving forward without any effective, experienced leadership was not tenable for Joan Holmes.

Joan and John were in Dhaka to break through this impasse. In listening to Badiul, Holmes knew she had met the next leader of The Hunger Project in Bangladesh. The more he spoke about his vision only reinforced her understanding and perception. It was a relief because she had been looking for a country leader to run Strategic Planning in Action in Bangladesh for some time. Unaware of her plans, Badiul joined Joan and John after the meeting to share further thoughts on transforming development. The conversation went on late into the evening. Badiul felt alive and excited for the first time in a long time. They were speaking his language.

The next few days were spent working together on a document that would become the primary strategy for the next decade for THP Bangladesh. The backbone for it was a two-pronged strategy that firstly mobilized communities to take self-reliant actions to end hunger, and secondly engaged the "movers and shakers" of the country to promote reforms which would be pro-people. It was clear that tools would need to be developed to awaken and mobilize the people. In a world that believed the poor were helpless and hopeless, and that things needed to be done FOR them and given TO them to alleviate poverty, the pathway to shift mindsets and activate leadership at the grassroots level was not there. It needed to be created.

Badiul then went with Joan and John to the Tangail District to meet others interested in The Hunger Project, which gave them the opportunity to observe him further. This also offered Badiul further opportunities to share his views and learn more about THP. He was intrigued by what he was hearing. The more he heard, the more attracted to it he became. It was like a love affair and grew stronger as he discovered they felt the same way.

Before leaving for THP's global board meeting in Madras (Chennai since 1996), India, Joan Holmes met with Badiul and offered him the role to lead the organization in Bangladesh and execute the strategy they had all created in the last few days. Joan's invitation was simple: "Badiul, I am not a negotiator, but I would like you to join The Hunger Project."

Badiul was startled—he was not expecting her offer. He had been stimulated and inspired by the conversations and shared perspectives, but in his mind, he was always still going back to the United States. However, with this offer on the table, he was very interested—excited even. He told Joan he needed to consult with his wife Tazima before saying yes and suggested a meeting between Joan and Tazima.

The next morning, very early, Tazima and Joan met in the

lobby at the Hotel Sonargaon. Joan shared with her how important and critical it was that Bangladesh had an authentic, intelligent, visionary leader. This was essential to achieve the end of hunger in Bangladesh, but strategically it was also necessary for its role in the bigger vision. Global hunger could not be addressed fully if it was not being addressed in Bangladesh.

Joan was really committed to Badiul leading THP, and yet in meeting with Tazima, she held back her increasing conviction that Badiul must say yes. She knew she was asking someone to make a big life decision that would be a huge disruption to their plans for the future. Tazima listened calmly to Joan's pitch. She was gracious and interested while asking questions. Even in that early meeting, both of them felt like they were on the same team. Tazima didn't say yes right away. She needed to confer with Badiul.

That conversation was brief. Tazima told Badiul that she liked Joan and was interested in what the organization was about. She also knew, more than anyone, how deeply unhappy and disillusioned her husband was. If this was a chance for him to use his experience to help their country, then she would not stand in his way. She told him she would commit to staying in Dhaka as a family with Badiul working at The Hunger Project "for one year only."

With Tazima's partnership, Badiul hit the ground running. Before formally joining THP, they accepted an invitation to join the Global Board meeting in Madras, which was to happen in a few days. They scrambled to get the visa for India, and once there met some of the leaders of The Hunger Project, including then COO Hugo Cardona, with whom details of the contract were discussed and finalized. Badiul found the experience of joining the Global Board meeting very rewarding. The more he learned about the approach of the organization, the more he felt it was in line with his own thinking. He had hope for the first time in a long time and was moved by this opportunity to make the difference he had yearned to do for so long.

Badiul returned to Dhaka as the newly minted Global Office Representative to Bangladesh, and the work started immediately. Finding a new office was one of the first things to do. At this point, THP-Bangladesh was made up of a few volunteers and little else. There were no staff yet, so hiring people who were excited about the two-pronged approach to ending hunger also became paramount. The first hires were young activists, Rezaul Karim Belal, Ahsanul Kabir (nicknamed Dollar) who is still on staff to this day, Rashedul Karim Munna, and an accountant. The salaries were small, only about $202 per month, and they would each be working long days at the office.

Even with a new team, Badiul did not have a clear runway. Although he had the imprimatur of the global organization, he was not starting with a blank slate. Unfortunately, those young, impassioned volunteers he had met at that first meeting were not happy with his appointment to the leadership position, and they did not agree with his ideas. Where Badiul was committed to mobilizing the mindsets and leadership for the poor to be the authors of their own future, these early originators of THP-Bangladesh wanted something quite different. They were stuck on the international aid model, where projects were designed and funded by NGOs, and the people living in poverty were targeted as aid beneficiaries, to receive services they'd neither asked for nor possibly even needed. The board members and original volunteers also wanted the fancy office, high salaries, and other financial benefits that went along with the traditional aid industry.

However, Badiul knew this approach was counterproductive. He had seen how destructive the "they will do this for me" mindset was on the ground. He initially tried to work with the founders and help them understand that THP was not a money-centered and staff-driven service delivery organization, but they were not interested in hearing any of this.

Badiul also faced resistance from some members of the local board who wanted The Hunger Project to be a vehicle for making money and as a way to dispense goodies and favors to their cronies. Badiul, of course, vehemently opposed this. The founders' discontent increased, and they tried to complain directly to Joan, which Hugo Cardona did not allow. Hugo told them in no uncertain terms that THP was not a run-of-the mill NGO, and they were on the wrong bus.

Gradually the resistance became very strong, to the degree that there was a contract placed on Badiul's life. He was quietly informed by some people in his circle that death threats had been made against him that would be carried out unless he agreed to stay on the path of traditional development, as that was where the money was. He wasn't convinced the threats were real as it seemed such an unlikely escalation, but he nonetheless took extra precautions, traveling to work in different ways and being more observant about what was happening around him. He even tried to cajole the old guard to find a solution to resolve this high-stakes impasse, but to no avail. It was a scary time for Badiul, but the idea of quitting made him furious. He would not cave in to thuggery.

In the end, Tracy Howard, a formidable negotiator, and former staff member of the global THP, came to Bangladesh to troubleshoot. She was forthright, with a no-holds-barred communication style. She called Badiul "a chicken" for tolerating the unworkability—and he realized she was right. Badiul was trying to please everyone and get them all on board. He was being too nice, hoping the dissension would go away. He wanted to focus on the actual work, which he was so passionate about, so he had let this toxic and potentially dangerous situation drag on too long.

Tracy's ability to cut through the rhetoric and come to the heart of the matter was the circuit breaker everyone needed. All the big boys became afraid of Tracy, and finally, with the support of Gias Kamal Chowdhury and Nurul Amin, a board member, the Board was disbanded, and the THP's registration with the Directorate of Social Welfare, which required having a board, was also canceled.

Badiul learned a lot from this experience. Hesitating and not addressing complex relationship and ideological differences early and directly, had meant lost focus and diverted energy. This ineffective approach always costs more in the end, and given the enormity of the work ahead, this price was not one he wanted to pay. Badiul's forthrightness, his conviction in his understandings, and his stand for a new type of development he later termed "the empowerment paradigm" were all strengthened as a result.

During these early days, he was not alone. Joan Holmes was his mentor and advisor, and John Coonrod was his close partner. Tazima was the chief volunteer, working by his side every day, often in the office till midnight. The family had moved into her parents' downstairs apartment, which meant the children could be cared for by their grandparents who lived on the floor above. Badiul was also fortunate to form a close bond with Lalita Banavali, the Country Director for THP India for nearly a decade, and her experience was invaluable for him.

CHAPTER FIVE

Awakening a Vision for Change

From his travels around Bangladesh, his breakthrough realizations from seeing the parrot, and his engagement with THP, Badiul's belief had deepened that the mindsets of resignation and dependency needed to be confronted as they prevented people from taking action. But how? This was the question that consumed him. Without figuring this out, he knew nothing else would work. He did not want to launch initiatives over the top of people's resignation and fatalism. Finding a way to overcome them became his top priority.

Equally committed to this was John Coonrod, who was Badiul's constant companion. They worked as a very close team, speaking every day, with John coming to Dhaka many times. In trying to work out where to start and to test the hypothesis, they went through an exercise, an informal inquiry if you like, to find out *what is missing*. What's missing, that if it were added, could end hunger and poverty in Bangladesh?

The concept of *what is missing* was an essential Hunger Project tool. Usually, the world is set up to answer the question "what is wrong?" and its sister questions "who is to blame?" or "whose fault is this?" This right/wrong paradigm only entrenches positions and doesn't move one toward creating a new approach.

To uncover *what is missing,* they talked to many people, including important thinkers and community builders like Mohammad Yunus and Fazle Hasan Abed. They canvassed both the who's who of Bangladesh, as well as people who were not as well-known but were equally passionate about making a difference.

This process and what was revealed verified Badiul's belief that confronting the mindsets of dependency, hopelessness, and helplessness was a priority. To begin to change these, he conceived of a workshop where people would come together to address mindsets for ending hunger. John Coonrod offered to come up with a draft outline of a method that could work.

Working with John was a real meeting of the minds, and the process proved constructive for them both—they learned from one another. John shared his observation that Badiul was often driven by reality rather than vision, with Badiul caught up in trying to figure out the process and remove obstacles before giving himself permission to step into the vision. This resonated for Badiul and became something he watched out for. Badiul was equally forthright with John, especially to ensure the approach they took was as culturally relevant as possible. He was adamant that John be sensitive to the unique cultural attributes of the country, including understanding that people in Bangladesh are subtle rather than direct. For example, there were things one doesn't say directly to another person without much consideration. Badiul knew they couldn't just impose a Western idea and expect it to work. After having lived in the West for two decades, Badiul understood that what would work there would not work here. John was his complete partner in tailoring the workshop for this context.

Soon they had the outline of a three-hour workshop that would eventually be delivered to millions of people—not just throughout Bangladesh, but around the world. They named it the Vision, Commitment, and Action Workshop—or VCAW for short. The purpose was to call forth people's leadership and commitment to create a vision for a better future and take action to achieve it.

Badiul strongly believed that the three components of Vision, Commitment, and Action were equally essential and that they all needed to be elicited from attendees. Like a three-legged stool—miss one of these three and the thing would collapse.

For vision, a guided visualization was written where people would be led through an imagined Bangladesh that was safe and clean, with fresh water, safe sanitation, girls and boys in school, healthy children, healthcare centers with staff and medicines, and enough income generated to meet daily needs. People would then analyze the vision by asking, "what will it take to achieve that vision?" "Who must do what?" "What must I do?" "How much money would it cost, and what must the government do?"

To evoke their commitment, people would be guided to realize that this vision is not a pipe dream. It won't just happen. It must be acted upon with a commitment to make it happen. Commitment is what gives humans the power to transform vision into reality. Badiul wanted them to understand that commitment keeps people motivated for the long haul. Even when what you are trying to do is difficult, you do not give up—the power of commitment can overcome most hurdles.

For action, participants would see that they had a part to play. Based on the analysis of the vision, people would then design the actions and next steps to achieve it, using their own resources. They would not wait for donors— instead, they would start with whatever resources they have. It would be through taking action and not just dreaming about it, that the results will happen.

This was the theory—it was now time to put it to the test. Badiul decided to run a pilot workshop and find out.

To start, a small group of six friends and family were invited to do the VCAW in his home. There were only a few staff members at this point, and they came too. Tazima was in attendance, both as host and as collaborator. She was as eager as Badiul to see if this new approach could work in Bangladesh.

As people arrived and Badiul greeted them, he felt nervous. These were people who knew him in both a private and personal capacity, and as he gathered them together to take their seats for the workshop to begin, he felt anxious. *What would they think? Did he look like a fool? Would they think he's lost his way?* Self-consciously, he started the presentation. It was unfamiliar territory; he was presenting something which was professional and beyond the social niceties of family relationships. However, he pushed through this discomfort, as he was determined for the VCAW to work.

For the most part, the participants were happy to play along with him, curious about their friend and his new "charitable endeavors." However, during the vision exercise, people "got it." The room palpably shifted when Badiul led them through the guided process, where they imagined a new reality of what could be possible. People, with their eyes closed, were visibly moved. No one present had previously thought there could be a different Bangladesh. They had each been trapped in the belief that "*that's just the way it is*" and they had never realized this before. It was a wake-up call and prompted a lot of questions and real engagement. This new vision was enticing to them. They wanted to know "how are we going to do it? How are we going to achieve it?" It raised problems too: "This is a Bangladesh. People want things to be given to them, they want money. How are you going to deliver the vision without the money?"

Badiul did not have the answers to these questions, but he didn't feel defensive or worried. He knew the answers would come. The first part of creating change was for people to see that the change was possible and worthwhile.

He also knew he was experimenting with something that hadn't been done before. Badiul had studied a lot of the literature on rural development and knew that most attempts to uplift the poor didn't succeed. Even his hero Rabindranath Tagore's trials didn't bear lasting fruit. Tagore had set up many experiments to alleviate poverty in East Bengal, now Bangladesh, from which Badiul learned a great deal. While initially these efforts showed promise, in the long run, they fizzled out because people were still the beneficiaries of their landlord Tagore's efforts. True ownership, equal partnership, personal autonomy, and the leadership of the poor had not been established, thereby cutting people off from being the owners of their own future, a critical ingredient for any sustainable development.

After this first workshop, Badiul led it a few more times in Dhaka to audiences of about twenty-five people, mostly middle class, with a mix of ages. Rather than the awkwardness he felt with friends and family, Badiul felt enlivened and empowered. This was working! People leaned in to listen. As a professor, he had credibility. Again, the vision exercise shook people awake and similar questions were asked: "what do we do? We want a better Bangladesh our Freedom Fighters gave their lives for. But how?"

The questions the VCAW posed, and the invitation to imagine a better Bangladesh, captured people's hearts, minds, and imaginations. There had been so much loss and struggle. People had felt their country was doomed. The VCAW gave them an experience of looking at their own thinking and beliefs, and how those beliefs fostered cynicism and despair. It invited them to dare to dream that something else was possible.

The response was incredibly encouraging. At the end of the workshop, people came to the conclusion that "I am the key, and that unless I take the action, nothing will happen." They realized, many for the first time, that they could act individually and collectively, to make the country better, and to even hold institutions and government accountable. The beauty of the engagement showed that many of the actions do not need any money. Changing attitudes, behaviors, and habits can solve many of the problems.

It was now time to take the workshop outside Dhaka, into the rural areas where most of the poor lived. A number of the organization's supporters, themselves having done the VCAW, got involved, setting up meetings in some villages for Badiul to present to.

This was a critical moment for the VCAW's relevance. It was one thing to confront the mindsets of those relatively well-off people living in the cities—it was another thing entirely to engage illiterate and very poor people in these same concepts. Things were very hard for most people living rurally. It was not uncommon for people to eat only one bowl of rice a day—hunger and poverty were not conceptual; they were real.

The first VCAW Badiul led in a village community had about twenty-five attendees, subsistence farmers, mostly men. They sat around him in a small building, with the sun beating down on the tin roof. This was a village similar to where he had grown up and Badiul personally knew aspects of the daily grind each person faced. Everyone had been invited to attend a discussion about ending hunger, and most came because they thought they would be provided with food or something material.

Badiul initially found trying to explain concepts of vision, mindsets, and leadership to be very difficult. People's exposure to big-picture-thinking and imaginative ideas were limited. Most attendees had not been to school past grade two and at least 60 percent of the group were completely illiterate. The language comprehension was also hard to grasp. The group's concerns included, "what does 'self-reliant' mean? Are you going to give me food? Am I going to be fed? Will this help me send my children to school?" Just as a person who has lived their whole life in a prison cannot understand what freedom is, so too the villagers struggled to understand that their lives and their community could be improved.

Badiul found leading the first few village VCAWs confronting. When faced with suffering, sickness, lack of education, and hunger, the normal human response is to do something specific and tangible about those things; to give people things. This was not the purpose of the VCAW. Staying the course was hard, yet even though the questions people asked were challenging, deep down Badiul knew that just giving people handouts wouldn't make any long-lasting change. His country had been used to this charity approach for a long time. Despite government and NGO services, which were patchy and badly provisioned, people's lives had not improved. There must be a better way. And more than that, he believed in the potential of the people in the VCAW to lead this change.

Again, the vision exercise created the turning point. Listening to a detailed and compelling vision—of dreaming of things not yet done, was transformational. People had never dared imagine what life could look like without hunger. A life and a village with clean water, babies not dying of simple things like the common cold or diarrhea, enough money for food—this moved some people deeply. Some cried softly.

At the end of these trial VCAWs, the participants had come alive. They were making plans for the next steps and working out what to do. The difference was stark and undeniable.

Despite his initial apprehension, the message of the VCAW resonated in the rural areas. People wanted nearly all of what the vision of a self-reliant village offered—safe water, sanitary latrines, more income, etc. A sticking point for some was getting behind the role envisioned for women as leaders and co-contributors to that vision. Badiul experienced resistance in each training from those who were satisfied with the traditional roles women currently played of mother and wife. Shifting such deep cultural conditioning would take more than a single attendance at a three-hour workshop, but Badiul was satisfied that at least a window had been slightly opened for this idea to take hold at a later date.

Despite the cultural issues, most of the participants came

out of the workshop inspired. Many of the Muslims related the message of the VCAW to their religious belief that Allah created human beings as "ashraful mokhlukat"—the best of His creation. They also could relate to the well-known Quranic verse that Allah only changes the conditions of those who take initiatives to change their own conditions. Some of them even articulated that they were not "cursed"—they were not created poor to remain poor. The workshop appeared to have reinforced their religious beliefs that their future depended on them, not on others—a teaching that got lost in prevailing policies and practices of poverty alleviation.

Badiul was very encouraged by the reactions and feedback received during the rollout of the pilot VCAWs in the villages. He was convinced that the program would work to shift mindsets, and he was pleased that it was not in conflict or inconsistent with people's religious beliefs. There was nothing in the workshop, which was troublesome to anyone, other than the occasional pushback about the role of women and the deeply entrenched dependency mindset.

Badiul was largely satisfied. Even though people had told him villagers wouldn't be able to understand or meaningfully participate in the process, he had seen that with the right approach they could awaken their leadership and inherent human abilities. Word spread and soon invitations were coming from all over the country to try this new approach. Badiul happily took up the mantle, traveling the length and breadth of Bangladesh to lead the VCAW.

One of the first visible successes of the VCAW was a literacy campaign The Hunger Project initiated in partnership with the district administration of Gazipur district. The initiative, called

Auronuzzal Gazipur, was so inspiring that all the government officials of the district contributed one-day's salary to finance it, and the Deputy Commissioner of Manikganj set up VCAWs in every *Upazila* (sub-district) in his administrative region for Badiul to inspire people to take action to improve their conditions.

The twelve months Badiul had agreed with Tazima to stay in Bangladesh came and went without either of them noticing. Right from the beginning, they were both heavily involved in the work of the organization. Tazima was the Number One Volunteer and by Badiul's side doing whatever was needed, so continuing that work seemed natural to them both. While Badiul had always harbored a desire to remain in Bangladesh, it hadn't taken long for Tazima to share Badiul's commitment. She was inspired by the potential they were creating for their country, and so going back to her old life became irrelevant, and not a consideration. Tazima had realized at her first meeting with Joan Holmes that what Badiul was embarking on was not a year's job—it would be "never-ending." While she had given him the yearlong ultimatum, it was more to give herself space and permission to adjust to what their lives would now be like. It didn't take long for her to give up thoughts about leaving the country.

Over these first few years as an activist, Tazima gained a larger purpose in her life that had been missing, and she did not want to give that up, even for the comforts of America. Her only prerequisite for staying was a stable living arrangement for the family. She was tired of "camping!" The children were enrolled in the American International School which meant they were getting a U.S. education, and her parents were on hand to support with the childcare as Tazima traveled to the field constantly, sometimes joining her husband, but often in the pursuit of her own volunteer activism. She was passionate about the rights of women and there were some villages she returned to weekly to support them; the visible progress deeply gratifying.

The decision to remain in Bangladesh wasn't all smooth sailing. The two younger children were happy to remain in Dhaka as they had moved there when they were still very young, but Mahfuz and Shahirah struggled. They had left America and their friends when they were older and found it harder to adjust to the new life. It was also difficult for the children to have both their parents working around the clock; while they were lovingly cared for by grandparents, they missed their baba and mom. However, Badiul and Tazima were both aligned—the family would be staying in Bangladesh.

Over the years, the VCAW morphed and changed as more people attended the workshop and the team were able to gauge its effectiveness. Badiul was also a conscientious innovator; he wasn't attached to how it was and instead saw the workshop as a living process, open to input and new information. He integrated feedback from his own observations, his team, and from the participants themselves, which meant fine-tuning happened frequently.

One early change happened quite quickly. Initially, the decision was made to pay the participants a very small amount of money for snacks, as this was what other organizations did, and it was expected. However, Badiul observed over a matter of months that some people were only coming for the money for snacks—they were not active after the workshop, and they never would be. Badiul stopped the payments, and not giving participants money to attend became a governing principle going forward. People would not be paid to participate in their own liberation.

Another change occurred: after presenting more than thirty VCAWs, something was bothering Badiul. The awakening was happening, but that wasn't enough. People needed a bridge between their current reality and the vision. They needed to know "how." Breaking down how to achieve the vision was necessary. In the VCAW, people agreed to a self-reliant and Hunger Free Bangladesh, which was a breakthrough as previously no one thought this was possible. Yet the questions remained: "Is it a pipe dream? Is it achievable? Is this even possible, given the state we are in? How do we get there?"

To begin to bridge this gap, Badiul thought adding a visual analysis of how the vision could be achieved would be useful. Guided by decades of adult education, and understanding the need to make the complex simple, he believed analyzing the vision would not just make it desirable—people would start to see a pathway for how to achieve it.

To do this, he drew columns on a flip chart that had the elements of the vision written on the left-hand side, and the responsible players along the top. This flip chart or butchers' paper was used in every workshop. He would stick it to walls in a schoolroom, on a tree in the field, or on a post in the courtyard—no matter where he was leading the VCAW, he found a place to secure the paper so people could see this analysis for themselves. The way he structured it (see below), meant that even those who could not read could still follow what was being revealed.

VISION ELEMENTS	INDIVIDUAL	COLLECTIVE	GOVT/NGO	NEEDS MONEY?	IS IT POSSIBLE?
Education	√	√	√		√
Girls in school	√	√			√
No child marriage	√	√			√
Good health	√	√			√
Income generation	√	√		√	√
Women	√	√			√
No dowry	√	√			√
No litigation	√	√			√
Functional local government	√	√	√		√
Youth	√	√			√
Harmony	√	√			√
Nutrition	√	√		√	√
Safe water	√	√			√
Sanitary latrine	√	√			√

After the vision part of the VCAW had been imagined, Badiul would turn to the flip chart and asked participants "What are you going to do? You want to achieve this vision—how will you do it? Who will be involved?" He went through each of the elements, questioning, "Whose responsibility is this? Will it take money?"

Starting with education, Badiul asked, "who is responsible for children going to school?" In the discussion, it becomes clear that in areas where there are schools, this was an individual effort mainly, but also included the collective because when everyone makes a commitment to sending their children to school, it normalizes education and cuts down truancy. All agreed it didn't require much money, and that it was possible.

Next was sending girls to school. This was an individual decision that they could make as parents, and also one the village should commit to. This took some conversation, because a common mindset was that educating a girl was a waste as she only left her home to go and live with another family once married. Parents were also concerned that if their daughter was educated "no one would marry her," and that putting her in school meant they had less help around the house and in the field.

Badiul listened to it all, knowing this is how people process new ideas and get their head around what it could mean for them—people sometimes become defensive, trying to justify their decisions or situations rather than focusing on the possibilities. He facilitated this process of adjustment by asking insightful questions that might lead to a new perspective. "Do you think it works to have an uneducated girl raising children? Can uneducated mothers ensure their children are educated? How will she provide best for her family? How will she read the labels on the medicine bottles?" He goes on: "When girls are educated, they lift the whole community. It's like a bird having two wings to fly—when girls get educated and women can speak and move freely, everything is better for everyone."

Next is the element of stopping child marriage.

"We want to stop child marriage. Whose job is this? Who

needs to make sure this happens?" People agreed it was an individual's responsibility. Each family had to make that decision, and it was on them to keep their daughters unmarried until they turned eighteen. It was also a collective responsibility because when young girls married too soon, it was not good for anyone—babies were born malnourished, children were unwell, and girls did not have the opportunity to be educated. It was agreed that having a village that was child marriage free was not a government responsibility. In fact, child marriage was already against the law—although it was not fully enforced. It was also agreed that outside money was not needed to stop child marriages. In working through the analysis, it was clear that the main players for ending child marriage were the people themselves. They were the key.

Badiul went through this process for all the elements, and for each one, the single common denominator was the responsibility of the people themselves. Each item required their own personal leadership first, with collective responsibility coming second. The main power wasn't in the hands of governments, or with outside agencies giving them money. In fact, most activities did not even require money! Laying it out like this visually, the penny dropped, and he could see the change in the people's responses. They got it. *It starts with me and it's up to me. I am the key.*

The Action part of the VCAW became more structured and well-defined too. At the beginning, people would think of things they could do to help but never declared them in an actionable way. Over time Badiul observed that the lack of clarity on actions and follow through wasn't serving anyone. He wanted people to leave with specific tasks to do to further the vision and have a way of holding each other accountable. From what he was seeing every day in the villages around the country, he knew that small wins built momentum for the road ahead. In an area mired by failure and false promises, it was critical people experience the accomplishment of a quick win, of creating movement and progress toward a goal they had long felt was impossible and believed would never happen.

Applying this took care, respect, and patience, like in Cumilla where he led a VCAW in a village that struggled with tainted drinking water caused by the endemic arsenic in the groundwater that poisoned the tube wells. During the workshop, people committed to doing something about this and Badiul asked what the plan was. One woman stood up to tell him they will need to test the water all throughout the *Union Parishad* (lowest level of local government). Badiul asked who would take responsibility for testing, and two people said they would. Badiul looked around the room quizzically and suggested they'd need more helpers, ideally one person from each of the six locations. Six people then came forward.

Other priorities were treated similarly in the workshop, so at the end the whole village had a roadmap of next actions, the reasons why they were important, and who would do it.

But this was not enough for Badiul. He asked them whether these actions would happen on their own or if people needed to keep coming together to move it forward—by asking this, he created awareness for collective accountability to create progress. People agreed to meet again, and Badiul got them to set a date and time that worked for everyone, including women who had additional chores, a religious festival for the minority Hindu community, and evening prayer.

Even then Badiul focused their thinking by asking them the

date the work would be finished. He reminded them they were making the commitment to themselves and their community. The meeting concluded with clarity and alignment by all attendees.

Bringing this level of specificity to a VCAW was not initially easy for him to do. It required Badiul to be quite pernickety to help people boil down the action steps that would move the vision forward. At first, he felt clumsy being so persistent about what needed to happen, by when, and by whom, but he knew that clarity wasn't just for inspiration or to tick a box—it had real consequences. Done right, it would start a process of cultivating leadership and change that would affect the village for generations.

For VCAWs to work, not everyone in a community needed to participate. In fact, even those who did not attend were often caught up in the flow from other people's commitment. One of many examples of this was when Badiul stayed in a village in Kishoreganj for a week to run a series of VCAWs. He'd been asked to go there by a determined young volunteer because it was a very conservative area where women were raised traditionally, which limited both their access to education and their ability to move about freely. The volunteer was not having much luck convincing women to attend, and was also obstructed by some men who wanted to keep the status of women as it was.

Badiul's approach was more accommodating. Rather than trying to get the women to attend the VCAW, which from what he'd heard was an improbable task, he set about finding ways to talk to them informally, hoping this might begin the process of including them in The Hunger Project activities.

Most of the houses in the village were made from bamboo, with a thatched roof. There were large gaps between the bamboo poles, which served as the structure, upon which women hung scraps of material to create a privacy shield. Walking among the homes, Badiul nodded to the occasional man he passed, but saw no women on the street, in the market, or in the field. It was like they had vanished. Then, while remaining at a respectful distance, he was called to come closer to one particular hut, where, through the gaps in the walls, he could see a number of women gathered behind a curtain created with old saris. The women agreed to talk to Badiul because his grey hair gave them comfort their husbands and fathers-in-law wouldn't object.

He entered the hut where half a dozen women gathered. These were women who, at the time, had very little exposure to anything beyond the confines of their homes and small village. There was no television and visits from people outside their area were infrequent. They each had their faces and head covered, but that did not limit their curiosity.

This invitation to talk with them started off a series of conversations that shaped the community over time. Badiul noticed that many children were sickly, and the women thought that was "just how they are." There was no understanding of the role nutrition played in their child's well-being. They weren't aware of the importance of sanitation. They didn't know the risks of child marriage, such as by marrying early, their daughter's bodies were not developed enough to birth healthy babies. He had several other conversations with the women and gently made these links for them, underscoring the power they had to take matters into their own hands to change what they could. Sometimes the men would stop by from the field and lean against the door to listen. Badiul was conscious of showing them respect and inviting them into the conversation.

While this was happening, people who had done the VCAW

in the area created a plan to expand the fish farming cooperative, which would provide each person with some income and a source of protein. Badiul included the women in the ideas behind it and encouraged them to get involved. Over a number of months, Badiul's team spent a lot of time supporting the volunteer leaders in that community, with Badiul personally making a number of visits. In time, he noticed changes had occurred. Some women he had spoken to in the huts did get involved in the fish farming project. Over the coming years, women from adjoining areas attended the VCAW, with many becoming Hunger Project trained volunteers. Eventually these women would join the Hunger Project network called Unleashed Women Leaders, who helped educate and activate their own and nearby communities to end hunger. This whole process was very instructive for Badiul. It was one of the first times he directly involved himself in working only with women, and it became a source of inspiration for the work he would do in the future to build a dedicated and trained network of women leaders.

The issues people faced in their communities were immense and while he intellectually understood that change would be slow, Badiul was often confronted by just how difficult sustained social change could be. He was impatient for things to change, and meeting people like twenty-one-year-old Prabhati Yasmin Borsha both hastened his desire for progress, and provided an unexpected counterbalance.

Prabhati lived in a village in Gangni that faced many challenges, especially related to dowry (the illegal yet widespread practice where money, goods, or property is brought by a woman to her husband or husband's family upon marriage). Prabhati had done the VCAW with Badiul and dowry was at the top of the list of priorities for her. In her community, if a woman's family was unable to pay a sufficient amount of dowry, they were unlikely to get their daughter married to anyone from a good family. Such practices caused a severe financial load on the parents, which was the case for Prabhati. Without a good dowry, which was not possible for her family, her only options for marriage were to a man who was much older, or a man with a known problem like drinking or gambling.

Even if families could pay the requested amount, it often didn't stop there. The issue of husbands "torturing" wives for more dowry was very common, and happened to a close friend of Prabhati's. After they had been married for only three months, her husband's family beat her severely to exhort more money from her parents. The girl's parents paid the money, but it kept happening, and eventually they could not afford to keep paying. The girl was then killed, hung by the husband, who made it look like suicide. The whole community protested after her death, and in a rare victory, the husband was charged. Dowry violence against wives is so widespread that police often don't get involved.

Prabhati had felt powerless about the situation. She shared that before the VCAW, "I thought I should focus only on my family, my studies, and not concern myself with other matters. Mainly because it's not my responsibility, it's the government's, or the job of other families. But also, because I didn't think I could do anything—I'm from a poor village, and a woman, so what can I do?"

When Prabhati attended the VCAW, one of her biggest realizations was that "to solve the problems we face, the individual must take action. Without this, nothing will change. I have a responsibility to my community, and I can also set the trend for others to follow."

Activated by the VCAW, Prabhati mobilized her community to exert pressure on families and husbands not to tolerate dowry violence. She gathered together other young people and got them involved, then the young people invited their parents to attend follow-up meetings. Supported by The Hunger Project, Prabhati would explain to the assembled group how dowry kept the community poor, and that women were not "a cash cow in-laws could keep milking." She was very brave because there was a lot of resistance to this idea. For every family that suffered financial losses and was plunged into debt and poverty to provide a dowry when their daughter married, there was another family that reaped the benefits when their son married. Change was slow to happen, yet this did not deter Prabhati from doing what she could.

From taking part in the VCAW, Prabhati gained a bigger vision for her life, and an ability to stay the course for longer term change. She told Badiul that this was something she personally wanted to work on to bring about change. She told Badiul: "I realize that I am capable of leading and can play an important role in solving the problems in the community. This village is my responsibility. A better future is not a dream. If we work together, we can solve our challenges, and this makes me feel very happy."

Prabhati and women like her inspired Badiul. She was on the frontline of massive social change, dealing with horrific situations, and he was moved by her courage. It brought home to him that the vision people created through the VCAW might not be achieved quickly, but the way people engaged with it empowered them to act. It also contextualized his own huge vision for a hunger free Bangladesh. He realized he needed to be ok with balancing the purity of his vision with the realities on the ground, instead of letting the latter tarnish the former. There was enough fatalism and despair in the country, he would not add to it. This brought him a kind of peace if not to settle, then at least to soothe his questing, driven nature. Even with his best efforts, his vision may not be achieved in his lifetime, but he could make a grudging peace with that as long as progress was being made.

The VCAW did not only make ripples in the lives of the poorest people. The success and attention it received caught the interest of the highest authority of government. In 1996, a VCAW was organized by the Ministry of Youth and Sports, and the Directorate of Youth Development, and held in the constituency of the newly elected Prime Minister Sheikh Hasina. Rafiqul Islam Sarkar, a senior journalist with BTV, helped arrange the workshop. Badiul was excited about the prospect and less nervous than one might think because he personally knew many politicians in Bangladesh from his days as a student activist in the 1960s. Still, he realized the opportunity to influence the Prime Minister was a big thing, and he prepared carefully for it. Hasina had invited bureaucrats and political leaders to attend, and while she listened to the entire workshop, it was the vision exercise that moved her. Sitting with her eyes closed, she shared afterwards what she had seen in her mind—her father Sheikh Mujibur Rahman's "*Sonar Bangla*"—the Golden Bengal.

The Prime Minister asked Badiul to work with her to mobilize her Gopalganj district, and he gladly agreed. Badiul requested the Prime Minister assign one government official for each sub-district to work with his team to help bring government services to the people. She brought Mr. Nasiruddin as the new Deputy Commissioner of Gopalganj from Gaibandha, where he worked with Badiul and his team to organize a district-wide campaign for the use of iodized salt. The Hunger Project team, guided by a dynamic staffer, Naimuzzaman Mukta, began to hold VCAWs to mobilize people in the area at the grassroots level. It was an exciting time for Badiul to have The Hunger Project's approach taken up at the highest level, and to have the prime minister of the country share the vision of a future free from hunger. Hasina met with Joan Holmes, John Coonrod, and Badiul several times, discussing what might be the next steps to take this further. She even assigned her Private Secretary, Yahia Chowdhury, to get the initiative off the ground.

However, the partnership did not last. The bureaucrats did not cooperate, possibly because an approach that awakened and mobilized the people contradicted the patronage system they upheld and enjoyed. Services promised to the people—safe water, health clinics, and schools—services the government leaders were obliged to deliver, did not materialize. In the end, Hasina, bogged down in political turmoil, was not able to deliver her part of the bargain.

Sometimes the transformation people were able to bring in their life from the VCAW surprised even Badiul, and Shanti's journey from broken woman to entrepreneur buoyed both him and Tazima, and it began at Ramna Park.

Every Friday, when possible, Badiul led a VCAW at Ramna Park in the center of Dhaka. Numbers would vary, but there would usually be between fifty and one hundred people attending, sitting on the faded mats that covered the grass. Women in bright saris, men in business attire or with orange hennaed beards wearing lunghis, and university students all sat together under the hot sun, listening and participating in the training. Many highly influential people, such as Dr. Atiur Rahman, who later became the Governor of Bangladesh Bank, attended the Ramna Park workshop.

Shanti Ribaru also attended. She was from a slum near Rayer Bazaar and her outlook was bleak. Her area was full of garbage, and to walk anywhere she had to plow through thigh high rubbish that was crawling with rats. Destitute and regularly beaten by her husband, Shanti had no education and was not literate, but despite this, she had heard of others attending the VCAW and was curious. She came and sat at the very back, not sure she even belonged there, and she listened carefully. What she heard lit a fire within her.

Every Friday for weeks Shanti went back to Ramna Park to redo the VCAW, trying to understand what this gray-haired man was saying, and wondering if it could apply to her. One day she gathered up her courage to visit The Hunger Project office and hid in the kitchen, refusing to come out. She did this for days on end. Tazima noticed her, of course, and would talk to her, gently encouraging her. This connection between them gave Shanti confidence.

Under Tazima's thoughtful and loving guidance, shy Shanti, who was too fearful to show herself at first, transformed her life. Instead of viewing her garbage infested living situation as evidence of her low status, she turned it into a successful business. She saved the little money she earned from her sewing and handicrafts business and bought her first cart to collect rubbish and recycle it for cash. Initially, she went through the slum collecting and sorting the rubbish herself, but it soon became so profitable that she was able to buy more carts and employ local youths to collect the rubbish. Her success meant that Shanti's children were educated, and she bought a home for the family. Even her husband changed his view and stopped beating her, eventually joining the business as her employee.

Shanti was formally recognized as a leader in her community when her project was inaugurated by the Minister for Local Government and Rural Development, Mr. Zillur Rahman, who later became the President of Bangladesh. She even ran for Parliament twice, although unsuccessfully. Her story was so impressive that Badiul wrote a case study about her initiative for the World Bank.

Badiul never took this type of transformation for granted. It still stopped him in his tracks and brought a huge smile to his face when he saw the change people created when they engaged with the ideas he was spreading. He also gave great credit to his wife. Through her leadership, women like Shanti were learning how they could end their poverty. Working with the women in Rayer Bazaar slum became a big passion for Tazima, and every week she could be seen talking to women there, helping them set up handicraft businesses and encouraging their daughters to go to school. Tazima's leadership was formidable, and Badiul delighted in seeing how the same changes that were happening in his country were also happening for him and his wife. They too were growing.

CHAPTER SIX

Igniting a Movement

In the first six months, Badiul delivered more than forty VCAWs all over the country, and he and his team could see how effective they were. Reports came in every day of some exciting new action taken in the field. People contacted the office by phone and fax to share what was being achieved, and eagerly ask him to return to their communities. The demand for VCAWs grew; participants shared the information with others, not only in their village, but with family members and friends across the country.

The experience of leading the VCAWs convinced Badiul of their effectiveness. More importantly, he was confident it was the tool he had been looking for to foment a nationwide movement. The next challenge was to roll it out in a big way. He could not continue to lead them all, and now that the pilots were complete, he knew he needed to hand this part over to others. Yet to whom? The traditional answer was to hire staff and train them to give the workshop throughout the country, yet this was a daunting task, especially considering the potential costs. Such an undertaking would be prohibitively expensive. To reach as many people in the country as possible would take a staff of thousands just to deliver the training.

He needed to think differently, so he turned to his favorite tool in economics to solve the problem: the principle of leverage. The VCAW unleashed passion and commitment that even money couldn't buy. Thousands of people had attended the workshop at this point. Could that energy and inspiration be the key resource? Could this be leveraged through developing a cadre of volunteer leaders to lead the VCAW? Such activities built social capital—an underappreciated yet necessary resource that well-functioning communities cultivated. Badiul, having lived in the United States for a long time, knew that volunteering, be it for civic institutions like Scouts and Rotary, or in the community, was a normal part of life, so for him, this idea seemed feasible.

Others weren't so sure. The accepted view was that Bangladesh was different and no one would do anything if they were not paid. The ideas of social responsibility, community building, and civic-mindedness were deemed dead after the war. Every single NGO paid people just to come to a meeting, and this expectation ran so deep that if the money wasn't offered, people wouldn't come. Badiul's idea of building a national body of volunteer leaders was outside that paradigm.

Yet he believed the sense of community and the spirit of social responsibility weren't dead, but merely lying dormant. He wanted the VCAW to be available in every part of the country and this bold vision needed bold thinking to match it. Despite steep opposition from almost everyone around him, Badiul wanted to give it a go. He wanted to build a movement of leaders across the nation who would animate others to take actions to end hunger.

So, he consulted with John, who immediately said, "Yes. How can I help?"

Designing the training for people to lead the VCAW was a more complicated affair than creating the VCAW. Due to what was at stake, John called in the help of former Hunger Project UK Managing Director, Andrew Davies, and Global Hunger Project former staff member, Lawrence Flynn. Both were experienced in creating a space of learning where something transformative could happen—something that would catalyze change and not just be informative.

Together Badiul, John, Andrew, and Lawrence developed the framework, with Joan Holmes regularly giving her guidance. They were all in agreement the training needed to *animate*—bring to life—people's sense of possibility, and so it was named the Animators Training. It also needed to provide enough space and time for people to really grapple with their own mindsets and beliefs, because in Badiul's mind, this would be the vehicle to galvanize a level of leadership that had not been seen since the war. Part of the training must also include teaching people how to deliver the VCAW. This wouldn't be easy as the workshop material needed to be brought to life—one couldn't just read a manual out loud and expect people to change their communities. Everyone leading the VCAW would need patience to listen and to leave their ego at the door. After a few weeks of discussion and co-creation, an outline for the Animators Training was finalized which Badiul was satisfied with and felt addressed the purpose.

To pilot it, Badiul and his small team invited people they

knew, most of whom had participated in the VCAW. Details were kept to a minimum: people didn't know specifics on what they were attending, other than it would be motivational and give new perspectives and insights. Everything shared about the Animators Training was immediately different and intriguing. For instance, it was highly unusual for a training to be held where people weren't paid to attend. And to have it be four days long—this was not common.

Andrew and Lawrence agreed to come to Dhaka in December 1993 and lead the first one, using it as an opportunity to support Badiul and adjust the format if necessary. Badiul was immensely grateful for their help since, although he was confident to lead the three-hour VCAW, he had no experience delivering a longer and more intense training. In the days leading up to it, Badiul, Tazima, and the team contacted the participants to make sure they had the details and were coming. It was a time before mobile phones, but also many residences didn't have home phones either, so this piece took a lot of effort.

On the morning of the first day of the Animators Training, Badiul arrived early at the government building in Dhaka where it was being held. Even though Andrew and Lawrence reassured him that the training would be successful, he felt very nervous. As soon as he entered the room, he noticed there were immediate issues. The chairs had been set in the typical theater style formation, so he and his colleagues moved things around to make the seating U-shaped, which meant people could see one another better, instead of just looking at the facilitator. There were other logistical issues to contend with, including a broken tea urn and a malfunctioning microphone. Badiul was there as emcee, trainer, cleaner, and fixer. There was a lot to juggle.

Soon 150 participants filed in, and looking out at the sea of faces, Badiul's nerves skyrocketed. *Would they get value from it? Would this be considered weird? Would they stay for the whole four days?* Yet even with these opening day nerves, he knew the training had to proceed—there was no going back. The need to activate more people to lead the VCAW overrode other concerns. They had to find a way to expand the work, and he hoped the Animators Training would be that way.

The training began with Badiul welcoming everyone and getting people settled. He introduced Andrew and Lawrence, and then the program began. It didn't start smoothly. The language barrier proved difficult, as Andrew's English accent was hard for some people to understand. And Badiul, who was doing the translation when he was not leading, found it a clumsy task. He hadn't translated in real time much and found switching between the two languages challenging.

But over the four days, all of these obstacles proved inconsequential. Every day Badiul saw the change in the mood of participants. Their willingness to explore ideas of self-reliance, and to engage with the material got him excited. They were asking deep questions and participating energetically. It was working. People were guided to think about some profound concepts for the first time, including "What do I believe about my leadership?" "Why are we hungry?" and "What new future could we bring about for Bangladesh?" They grappled with how complicit they were with the status quo, and how resigned they had become. The vision for their country that their compatriots had fought and died for only two decades earlier seemed a dream and unattainable—but was that true?

One man stood and, holding back his emotions, cried out:

"My father fought in the liberation war; he was a Freedom Fighter. Today I stand in his place as a new generation of Freedom Fighter, for my country to be liberated from hunger and poverty." People were genuinely moved. The Animators Training was proving to be a gateway for expressing both the loss of the dream they had all once had, and the rising hope that all was not lost. A new future for Bangladesh was not only possible—it was achievable—and they were the key. There was still doubt, of course, with people asking: "We have so many daunting challenges, and most NGOs are giving away money—are we really going to succeed?" Badiul understood these considerations as he knew they came from a place of wanting to figure out how to make this work—it indicated the depth of people's commitment.

Midway through the training people were taught how to lead the VCAW. This was very challenging for some of the participants who were not comfortable with the idea of speaking in front of people. It was a learning space for everyone and the reason for the Animators Training in the first place. If this worked, these people would take the messages they learned back to their communities and lead the VCAW. Badiul wondered how this section of the training would go. *Would people be able to lead a workshop confidently? Or would it fail and be left to him and a handful of others to soldier on*? As he looked around the room at who was there, his nerves returned. Could this group of mostly students, social workers, businesspeople, and bureaucrats learn to lead a revolution?

The printed VCAW manual in Bangla was handed out for people to read. Most had experienced the VCAW at least once. This was now the time to get intimately acquainted with the material. People practiced in small groups, standing in front of others to lead sections of the VCAW, while Badiul, Andrew, and Lawrence walked around offering them coaching. The hardest aspect was encouraging people not to lecture like a schoolteacher or an authority figure. It was critical since this "I know, and you don't know, so I will teach you" mindset was not how this material should be shared. The key to the VCAW's effectiveness was in participants realizing things for themselves as an inner truth, rather than just agreeing to some information they were given. The whole day and part of the next day were spent on this. People would always have the manual with them when leading the VCAW in the future, so they didn't have to memorize the material, but they did need to be leading with curiosity, respect, and love, and be engaged with the participants.

The last day came, and people were transformed. They had come to know in their bones that they were the key to a better and prosperous Bangladesh, and that creating such a future would not take an arm and a leg—they could start the journey with the resources they already had.

There was a lot of emotion and energy, with people talking amongst themselves about the next steps to take. They proudly declared themselves Animators Batch One, and this started the tradition of animators introducing themselves to one another, stating their batch number. Particularly moving for Badiul was when he looked into the audience and caught the eye of his old university professor and mentor, Professor Habibullah. He was suddenly back at school, anxious as to what his mentor would think of him, but Habibullah held his hand and declared loudly, "Badiul Alam was my student. From today onwards, I have become his proud student." At the close of the training, people lingered to talk with each other and share ideas.

Badiul was rapt and he and Tazima continued talking late into the night about what had happened, reliving some of their favorite parts. The next morning the team came together to debrief, and everyone felt similarly—exuberant and with a great sense of accomplishment. They had done something they hadn't quite believed could be done, and they were on fire for what was now possible as a result. They identified some changes to fine-tune the program, and one of these was realizing that the emotional energy people expressed at the end of the training should be grounded in something more solemn and meaningful. They introduced a section at the very end where participants would sign a written declaration that stated, "I'm an animator. I stand for a self-reliant Bangladesh, and I am the key to bringing this about," and then stand and make this declaration to a room of their peers. This would become part of all future Animators trainings.

In the months that followed Badiul traveled to the areas where the new animators lived and saw them leading the VCAW for their community. He gave some coaching where it was needed, but for the most part was happy to let people figure out their own way of delivering the workshop. As some of the participants had come from different parts of the country, an idea for how this could spread beyond Dhaka also came into clearer view.

Running that first Animators Training took a lot of effort, preparation, thinking, and cautious planning. At the time Badiul imagined the team could run four a year, at most, and indeed it would take a few years before even that was possible. By 1997, there had been six batches in total, creating 801 animators. Yet by 1999 there were more than 2,500 animators from twenty-six batches, and by 2005 more than 79,789 animators from 873 batches were mobilized across the country. What started as an experiment with some friends and supporters would become a national movement that would change the country.

At an Animators Training in Bogura, the famous economist and writer Anisur Rahman was in attendance and was incredibly moved by a letter a woman read out loud, addressed to her husband. Her letter was in response to an exercise in the training where people wrote to someone they wanted to be their partner in ending hunger.

The letter, which Rahman, with her permission, later published as part of an article in the leading newspaper, *Prothom Alo,* said:

> "*Dearest, you didn't want me to come to this training, but I defied you and came anyway. You do not know what a mistake you made by not allowing me to come. You'll see when I come back how much I have changed, how self-confident I have become. You'll see when I come back that I'll work not only for my family, but to bring everyone in the village to work together. You must take this training and be with me in this work. All my love, my dearest.*"
>
> *16 December 1998.*

Rahman's article that included this letter was called "The Fire That Is Burning," the title in reference to his influential 1993 book "The Lost Moment: Dreams with a Nation Born Through Fire" in which he lamented that the fire which sparked his country's liberation had been snuffed out. What he saw and heard in the

Animators Training seemed to him a rekindling of that same fire. It gave Rahman immense hope.

In response to Rahman's article, there was a letter to the editor that said:

> *"I've become very happy to read this column. I, a 70-year-old retired teacher, along with eleven of my young friends, travelled to Bogura to participate in this training. The fire that was simmering in our hearts caused an explosion. It was here I became familiar with a different development philosophy, which is unlike the traditional foreign donor-controlled model which creates beneficiaries. The training sparked the commitment within me to create a self-reliant, respectful and dignified future for Bangladesh. It aroused in me the same emotion which was present during the Liberation War. I am asking the government to hold this training throughout the country with the help of local government bodies. This will prepare us for a second liberation of economic self-reliance and financial independence. Sincerely, SM Waliur Rahman"*

Anisur Rahman was a hero to Badiul, and it touched him greatly that he would write about both the Animators Training, and the new possibility emerging for the country. The courageous and deeply personal note the woman had written to her husband, and the passionate response it elicited when published, seemed to Badiul to encapsulate what was so unique about what was happening. The Animators Training wasn't only about helping others; it also enlarged and empowered the animator's own life. It embodied the meaning of the proverb "*I build the road, and the road builds me.*"

Noticing unifying themes in the work of The Hunger Project, Badiul asked John Coonrod for a copy of the organization's principles and was surprised to hear they didn't exist! Badiul believed it was crucial that these be articulated as a foundation upon which his mobilization efforts could grow, and he also thought the global movement would benefit if the same principles could be observed wherever The Hunger Project operated. John agreed and mapped out the key principles upon which THP operated, largely informed by the learnings from the Strategic Planning Action approach Badiul was pioneering in Bangladesh. Ten principles were drafted under the guidance of Joan Holmes, and these Principles became the framework to align the movement of volunteer leaders in Bangladesh.

Badiul included them in every Animators Training and each principle was discussed at length, with Badiul not moving on until there was alignment within the group. These were not something to be just read out and agreed to, like a rote exercise to check the box; sometimes it could take a whole day for people to understand them and make them their own. Badiul was fine with that—the principles laid down a new mental framework for how people could lead themselves and others to end hunger, so he always gave participants sufficient time for the concepts to settle and take root. They became the Rosetta Stone, which guided new volunteers as they started their work in their communities and they created a coherence in what would become a huge, non-hierarchical, national movement for ending hunger.

The first principle was Human Spirit, which recognized that

the essence of humanity is creative, resourceful, connected, and productive. The Human Spirit is the inherent animating source that people are born with, and when awakened and amplified, it is a power that can solve any problem, big or small.

The second principle was Interconnectedness, and this spoke to the idea that "no man is an island"—societal change won't succeed if the focus is only on the individual getting ahead. What Badiul saw in the field was not only do people impact one another with their actions, their well-being depends on the actions of all other people, in concert with the natural environment. Talking this through with Joan Holmes clarified something essential for him: not only do we affect each other, at a profound level *we are each other*.

Vision was the third principle, and of course, it was no surprise that something so foundational to Badiul's approach became one of the organization's principles. People act based on their vision; and be it an empowering vision or a limiting one, a person's vision sets their path. Animating one's vision was critical to leadership. Badiul believed a human being without a vision was like a dead body, their life an empty vessel.

The fourth was Commitment which allowed individuals to encounter obstacles, frustrations, and failures on the road to achievement and still keep going. It recognized that achieving the future they envision will not just happen on its own, they must make it happen, and this will take immense commitment. Badiul used the example of the Freedom Fighters who liberated their country through their extraordinary commitment. They were relentless; they didn't stop in the middle of the struggle but carried through to the end. Commitment can turn an ordinary individual into an extraordinary one; a person not honored by birth, but by deeds.

Transformative Leadership was the fifth principle, and this recognized that ending hunger required a new kind of leadership at all levels of society—from the village to the district, state, nation, and the international community. Traditional top-down leadership won't cut it. Instead, there must be local leadership that reawakened people to their agency and selfhood, called forth their vision and commitment, and mobilized them to take effective action.

Strategy and Action was the seventh principle, and called for new approaches to ending hunger that were led by local people themselves, instead of by a parade of outside experts. Any path forward should create new avenues for progress, with bold and creative actions that achieved maximum results at minimum cost.

Enabling Environment was the eighth principle, and it affirmed that hunger and poverty were not "accidents." They were consequences of deeply entrenched social conditions which systematically denied people—particularly women—the opportunities they needed to build lives of self-reliance and dignity. Those systems must be challenged and dismantled, and new ones created in their place. Poverty wasn't caused by a lack of riches or money, but by the lack of an enabling environment. Badiul reminded the animators that they cannot make the community self-reliant, but they can bring people together and foster the enabling environment for people to thrive. Their role was to tend the social soil within which a healthy community could grow.

Empowering Women was not initially the ninth principle, (self-reliance was, and it got absorbed into the Leadership principle when the shift to gender occurred), but became so in the late 90s. Engaging participants in this principle was complex:

it wasn't widely understood that women bore almost the entire responsibility for meeting the family's basic needs, yet were systematically denied the resources, freedom of action, and voice in decision-making to fulfil that responsibility. To ground the animators in this principle, Badiul would ask; "Before taking any step you must first ask—will it empower women? Will it restore her to her own dignity? Will it recognize her agency?"

The final principle was Global Responsibility, which meant that hunger was a global issue, not a regional or local one. Therefore, a global response based on partnership was needed to end it. This principle reverberated around the world: whether one was an activist in London or Dhaka, the principle of shared responsibility was central. Money should not be given as handouts steeped in pity, but in honest recognition of the role each person could play to end hunger, no matter which country they lived in. Bangladesh was not interested in a donor/recipient relationship. They wanted investment, not charity.

Badiul's recognition of the importance of articulating these principles was prescient, and the impact on the organization cannot be overstated. That the principles were crafted from what was being learned on the ground, rather than from a lofty theoretical framework, gave them resonance and power. For them to be adopted globally, Joan Holmes spent four days in San Francisco with Hunger Project staff, activists, and investors from around the world to share them, so they too took root in the hearts, minds, and actions of the organization. Using the Principles as the measure against which decisions were made brought cohesion and connectedness to everyone involved. Wherever The Hunger Project operated, the singularness of these principles was felt. Badiul's keen insight that this was needed was validated.

The concepts introduced in the Animators Training were completely new to people and encouraged them to think about things they had never really thought about. This included the idea of "citizenry," and what it meant to be a good citizen. Badiul's experience in Saudi Arabia a decade earlier, where he saw how feudal style governance stifled progress and inflicted further hardship on the poor, had not left him. He noted something similar at play in Bangladesh and he wanted to address this in the training. He hoped to shake up the mindset of passivity in national affairs that he'd witnessed, which inadvertently rewarded inept policy and unaccountable governance. In a country with rampant corruption, and a tossing back and forth of power between two opposing families, the difference between subject and citizen was crucial. The country's constitution was founded on the principle that all power belonged to the people, and Badiul sensed this had been forgotten, with people neglecting their responsibilities as citizens. Many of the policies that directly led to the poverty in people's villages were created by governments not being held to account. He saw this as critical to be addressed in the training and agreed with Louis D. Brandeis, a former US Supreme Court Judge, who said: "The most important political office is that of the private citizen."

Badiul believed that one of the most critical preconditions in a democracy was for people to realize they were citizens with rights and responsibilities, and not subjects dependent on the whims of the overlords. In an undemocratic country or colony, people were subjects rather than citizens. In a colonial setting, everything was owned by and belonged to the colonial power. People were forced to be compliant because whatever was given to them was given only through the generosity and mercy of the colonial power. When a colony becomes independent and takes a democratic path of governance, an emancipation of the people must follow.

Bangladesh became emancipated twice; in 1947 from Britain, and in 1971 from Pakistan, yet Badiul believed this process from subject to emancipated citizens never took place. Successive Bangladeshi governments treated their people like subjects, and the people also acted like subjects. Whatever was received from the authorities was through the largesse and generosity of the people in charge and came from a culture of patronage. Ruling party leaders and the government functionaries were the patrons, and common people were the beneficiaries. Without a sense of citizenship, rights and responsibilities were alien. With a subject mindset, people received benefits only through the goodness of the benefactor, which meant common people were deprived, denied the services and support they were entitled to by the state. To access these resources required a shift in consciousness from subject to citizen.

Badiul took special care in how to introduce this concept into the Animators Training and make it relevant to people. He didn't want it to be theoretical; he wanted it to come alive for them—this knowledge would sharpen their activism and help them advocate for themselves and their villages more effectively to ensure basic needs were being supplied by government bodies.

He began the process by asking what it meant to be a citizen. Typically, answers included things like "abide by the constitution" and "follow the law." Badiul would remind them that the biggest law in the state was the constitution, which said that everyone was equal, and all power belonged to the people. In using this power, people elected others to run the functions of government for them. His point was that citizens are the owners of the country, and they must be responsible, vigilant, and not stay silent, for when they say nothing, the state can decide anything, even if it's not good policy. Misuse of power happened when people were passive.

Through this discussion, mindsets started to shift from "I am getting a favor" to "It is my right." People began to realize that to have a functioning democratic system, everyone must step up to do the right thing, including voting for clean candidates, instead of who pays you to vote for them. By the end of the discussion the penny had dropped—hunger would not end if the nation remained beholden to vested interests that treated the population like subjects. Animators committed to playing a role to empower active citizenry.

This early emphasis on democracy and a rights-based approach to development was the beginning of Badiul's focus on the second part of the two-pronged approach for ending hunger which had been outlined with Joan Holmes and John Coonrod before he even joined the organization. The first phase, mobilizing people and shifting mindsets, was underway. The second, which was about good governance, was now beginning. This would only get stronger throughout the years, as Badiul laid the groundwork for promoting ideas of good citizenship that would be spread nationwide.

In the early days of the Animators Trainings, an important lesson was learned about the role of money as a spoiler. When animators began leading VCAWs in their villages, there was huge excitement—they were going to alter their lives and mobilize and transform their communities. As projects and initiatives sprung up, it was assumed that seed money would be available from The

Hunger Project to get them started. This was consistent with the norm for development work, as most organizations offered money. While Badiul was clear about not paying people to attend the trainings, he had not really thought about the role of money in helping locally based projects get started. The business professor in him was open to the idea of providing some seed capital as a stepping-stone toward becoming self-reliant.

Parameters were set so that money given by The Hunger Project could only be used to generate income for the village, like buying fingerlings to start a fisheries pond, or plants to start a nursery. This was agreed to, however things soon changed; once the project was established people then wanted more money to hire someone to look after the water bodies or build dikes or purchase machinery and tools. Soon it became apparent that whatever money The Hunger Project invested, people wanted more next time. The organization was soon paying for ongoing costs of the original investment. Initially, Badiul agreed to bear some of these costs, but soon villagers and even some animators wanted the cost of all the activities paid for. This was in line with the current thinking around small loans to start ventures, but Badiul was becoming concerned. Something about this didn't sit right with him and it came to a head during an interaction at an Animators Training.

Toward the end of the third day of the training, one of the participants stood and shared enthusiastically about how his eyes were being opened to something he had never dared imagine—his village hunger free. He talked about the ways he would contribute toward making this a reality, and how inspired he was to begin. People around him nodded their heads. They felt it too. He spoke about the principles and how they made complete sense to him.

"For years," he said, "I felt like a failure. My father and his friends had risked so much to give us freedom, but before now, I have never known how to continue this legacy. I now have my pathway, as an animator. I know I am the key to making changes in my village." People cheered, including Badiul, who had a huge smile on his face. "Yes," he said to the man, "you can. And you will."

Then the man's tone changed.

"To do this, I need your help. I need money. I am a poor person, and my village is very poor. I want to be an animator and do these things, but I need you to help me. I have a budget and what I need is this amount of taka." He pulled out a piece of paper from his pocket and showed it to Badiul. "I am so poor; anything less is not possible for me. I can't achieve my vision if you don't give me this." Badiul noticed how the group responded to his entreaty. A few seemed sympathetic, nodding their heads, while others looked annoyed with the pleading.

Badiul responded, "This is not a traditional NGO, our work is not about giving you microcredit. This is about the resources you already have and how to think about them differently. You are a capable person. You have the same physical and mental attributes as anyone else. You were not created poor, nor are you meant to remain poor. If others can make it, so can you."

The man responded, "But you don't know my situation. I'm really poor. I have no money and no income. I have children and in-laws to take care of. I don't have a job. I need this money to achieve my vision."

Badiul was not swayed. "A person with an unleashed spirit is not poor," he said. "If you get this money and use it, then what? You'll soon be in the same situation as you are now. Money is not a solution." He quoted the Quran, "You are created 'best of creation.'

You are endowed with everything a person needs to become self-reliant. Self-reliance is the normal thing, the natural thing. You decide what future you want to create. If you come to the Animators Training for money and we give you money, you will use that and then come back again. It will go on and on—and to what end? You're not better off. You're stuck in a cycle of poverty."

Badiul was speaking to the man, but also addressing everyone present because this mindset was not unique to this one person. It was a deeply conditioned perspective, reflecting the sense of dependency that needed to be rooted out. Badiul was also getting clarity for himself about where he stood in relation to giving money. His position was coming into view. He realized that money given this way would not be the help he and the community thought it would be. Bangladesh was awash with available money through loans, but it had not made enough of a difference. He also knew a person's identity as "poor" hindered their ability to see beyond their current circumstances.

Badiul turned to the larger body of people and asked them, "Why do you think you are poor? What resources do you have? What resources are there in the village?" He could see thoughts churning.

He continued, "Money is not the only resource. As animators and as a community, you can pool your resources—both financial and non-financial and create opportunities. You can do a lot of things together. When people come together and work shoulder-to-shoulder, a different type of capital is created. And that is called social capital. Where economic capital is scarce, social capital can make up for it." He pressed on. "With the knowledge you now have, you can find your way. For example, are there fishponds that can be desilted? Can your village plant a small vegetable garden, then sell the surplus vegetables for a profit which can be used for your projects? Most of the challenges you face can be solved without money. Change your behavior and the way you look at things and your condition will change. A lot of these old ways of thinking and old ways of doing things are contributing to your poverty and keeping you in this situation. It's a trap."

Badiul returned to the man, putting his hand on his shoulder and regarding him with affection. "What the Freedom Fighters achieved against the odds, so you, too, can do this. We can achieve the vision together."

The man sat down, a bit disgruntled. Yet over the following day, something seemed to click for him. A shift in his bearing was noticeable. He seemed different. At the end of the training, he stood up to thank Badiul for what he now realized. He broke down. "I understand," he said. "I can do this." With this realization, he changed the future he thought he would always be burdened by. He could fulfil his vision through the ideas he had and the network of support from other animators. His identity around being poor shifted. Badiul could see that others in the room had also come to this same realization.

Something also clicked for Badiul. This interaction brought him intense clarity. It had been the first time in the Animators Training, where the expectation of money was vivid and up front, and Badiul now understood how this undermined the essential principle of self-reliance. He realized his error in contributing seed money. It meant some people came to the Animators Training expecting money and framing themselves as poor and hopeless to get it. It took away the ownership of initiatives in the villages. It confused who was accountable and where the true power lay—namely, with the people and their yearning for a better future.

On reflection, he was not surprised. In 1976, in Bangladesh, Muhammad Yunus was the "Banker to the poor," and had pioneered lending money to people with no financial means as a way for them to access capital to start businesses and develop economically. More than 95 percent of all borrowers were women. Grameen (which means *of the village*) Bank started as an experiment and went on to be recognized by the Bangladesh government as an independent bank in 1983. (Yunus himself was awarded the Nobel Peace Prize in 2007.) Grameen Bank pioneered the use of social mobilization for giving loans, by which women in groups rather than individually, borrowed money. This meant women were guarantors for each other's loans.

In Yunus' attempt to cultivate the social consciousness of borrowers, each person had to make commitments (called the Sixteen Decisions), to be able to borrow money. These commitments included promising to educate their children, install and use sanitary latrines, and refuse to offer or accept dowry. Unfortunately, these were rarely upheld or monitored, yet the Grameen banking model still proved that lending to groups of women could lift some people from poverty, and with that success, more organizations like BRAC and ASA came along offering small loans. However, a side effect of the proliferation of microloans was that people came to associate money and loans with mobilization.

What became clear to Badiul was that money should not be a primary pillar for social change. He was reminded of the old adage, "When money talks, everything else is silent." He was convinced an integrated approach to ending hunger was required, and not one that led with money. He reflected that poverty was more than a lack of money, and that focusing on money as the only way out of poverty further entrenched the scarcity mindset.

As the great Bengali poet Tagore had once said, “No, it is not the want of money that is the cause of our suffering; its cause is the poverty of our heart.”

After this experience in the Animators Training, Badiul stopped all seed capital for VCAW projects. This was understandably an unpopular decision, with significant ramifications: in most cases the projects didn’t survive when the money was withdrawn. This was devastating to the team and the animators who had been excited by the results in their villages. They keenly felt the loss, as many activities ceased when the money dried up. Even worse, in some places where initiatives were abandoned, it was more than a decade before a new group of animators could mobilize successfully in those same areas.

In retrospect, it was not a big surprise for Badiul to realize that despite what people had learned, when money was added to the mix, the mindset shifted from “This is our initiative” to “This is a Hunger Project initiative.” Through this process, the ownership got transferred. It was a hard lesson for him to learn—that the corrupting influence of money and handouts was stronger than the realizations some people had come to in the trainings. The message in the VCAW and Animators Training was that *you can play a key role in ending hunger*, yet the subtext that came with giving even small amounts of money was “*you can’t do this without us doing it for you*” or “*The Hunger Project does not give handouts, but here are some funds you can use because you won’t succeed without it.*”

This was a difficult yet formative time for Badiul and his team. Even with its noble intention, the introduction of outside money had thwarted the deeper message of self-reliance. It undermined the major shift of mindsets that Badiul wanted to see, namely, steering participants away from hopelessness and waiting on outside forces to save them, and toward their own capabilities—both individual and collective. Anything that did not challenge dependency and resignation—even when it was popular and fueled initial actions—had to be abandoned. It would only spoil future efforts.

Badiul was left with a choice between doing what was popular and coasting on some initial wins that funding projects had given them, versus doing what was deeply unpopular and, in the short-term at least, would set things back. He chose the latter, and although he didn't have proof at the time, his conclusion was correct. Over the next few years, this decision would more deeply align the volunteer leaders to the spirit of self-reliance, with "no ifs or buts." As a result, people became more committed and daring, and the movement grew exponentially. Understanding that there was no shortcut to liberation gave people the determination to become who they needed to be to bring about the end of hunger.

Once the door was closed on using money to fund activities, a bigger possibility emerged that would lead to the sort of wildfire spread of leadership and activity Badiul had hoped for. Lyjoo was one of many leaders who exemplified this for him. She had grown up in a small village near Kolkanda, Rangpur, and like most women with limited means, she held no authority and felt hopeless about her situation.

Local animators held a VCAW which she attended. There she heard for the first time that it was possible to put an end to hunger and poverty in her village, and that she could contribute to the activities to bring this about. She learned that if she wanted to change her life, there was no point waiting for a miracle or sitting on the sidelines. It would have to start with her.

She then joined a self-help group, started by The Hunger

Project animators, where women came together to offer support for each other to be able to live better lives. Self-help groups are informal gatherings of between ten and twenty-five women that are self-governed and peer controlled. In villages like the one Lyjoo was from, women come together to help one another, save money, and dispense credit on their own terms, and The Hunger Project does not collect or oversee the money. This way, the savings created locally stay local, unlike traditional microcredit operations.[4] Economic independence was one of the pillars of Lyjoo's group and to achieve this, each member committed to putting aside a fist full of rice before cooking their (sometimes) one meal a day. Over the course of a week, every woman had saved a growing mound of rice, which she brought to the weekly self-help group meeting. The rice was collectively pooled and sold at the market, thus providing a small amount of capital to lend to a different member each week for her to start an income generating activity.

When it was her turn, Lyjoo bought some chickens, and over time those hens multiplied, providing her with eggs and chicken meat to sell. Soon Lyjoo was making enough money to expand her small enterprise, so she bought a small cow and added dairy to her business, selling the milk and making yogurt. With this economic empowerment came confidence.

All along, she was supported by the women in her group, and by the local animators. No outside money was ever given to her. Everything she had was gained through taking courageous actions which developed her self-belief; learning new ideas in

4 In 2023 there were nearly 2,000 self-help groups that THP has catalyzed throughout Bangladesh, with over 32,000 members and 232 million takas of accumulated savings.

the different training courses she attended; and the supportive environment the self-help group offered.

After two years, Lyjoo was financially stable, and she began to think more about how to help others in her village. This came into sharp focus when she heard that her twelve-year-old female cousin was getting married. Already educated about the ills of child marriage from her participation in The Hunger Project, Lyjoo set about stopping the marriage. She first approached the family, demanding that the marriage be stopped. The family refused, lying about the girl's age, saying she was eighteen. When Lyjoo asked to see the birth certificate, she was marched out of the hut.

Lyjoo then went to see the Imam, the religious leader in the village. The Imam went to talk to the family, and couldn't persuade them to abandon the marriage, so resignedly informed Lyjoo that—"there is nothing I can do" and the marriage was to take place.

In response, Lyjoo mobilized a dozen women from her self-help group and went to the police. This was a bold move in a country where corruption is rife, and police are not normally sympathetic to "domestic" issues. However, Lyjoo was formidable in her commitment to stop the child marriage. In the end, the police went to the hut and got the marriage stopped.

Lyjoo grew in her leadership endeavors. She built a small home for herself but did not get complacent. She never forgot that it was up to her to keep working to end hunger in her village. Over the next fifteen years, she personally stopped more than thirty child marriages.

Badiul admired Lyjoo's achievements all the more because while they were extraordinary, they weren't singular. She was one of thousands of women who were unleashed by local animators, propelled into economic independence, not through handouts, but through accessing resources and support, including the money their self-help group had generated together through their own leadership, to achieve their goals. They attended trainings, collaborated with others, took risks, and cast off the old constraints and beliefs that kept them hobbled. For Badiul, women like Lyjoo redefined the meaning of leadership, and he did not lose sight of this.

After only a handful of Animators Trainings, it was clear to Badiul that he had a winner in awakening and mobilizing people. He saw how the Animators Training deepened the vision people had gotten in touch with in the VCAW and cemented their commitment to help make ending hunger a reality. After the four-day training, people felt ready to conquer the world! They could do anything; it was like an explosion! A transformation. And they were taking action.

Through the process of deeply questioning unexamined beliefs and assumptions, the Animators Trainings revealed to people that a new future was possible. It gave them control over their lives. It was a mindset shift from the poor viewing themselves as victims. Badiul took to heart these words from Anisur Rahman in his book "People's Self-Development"[5]:

> "Development is the liberation of the creative energy of people. The (leaders') task is to open the door on which the spirit of humanity is knocking. Let the spirit burst in, lift it high so it can see its perspective, and then let it surge forward."

5 People's Self-Development: Perspectives on Participatory Action Research, Anisur Rahman, 1993

It was a profound time for Badiul to see what was emerging from his stand to make a difference. He had known real change was possible conceptually, but to see it happening with the poorest of the poor was something else. He confided in Tazima privately that perhaps now he could exhale. This was bigger than him. Now all he had to do was not mess it up!

Badiul continued to travel across the country, leading trainings and providing support and encouragement to the volunteer leaders. Something big and inspiring was bubbling up in places where previously hunger and despair reigned. This was reflected in what Abul Basher, an animator from Kishoreganj, told him: "Before the Animators Training, I thought I'd move to Saudi Arabia. But now I will stay here. I have discovered why I was born—I will first remove hunger from my village, then my district, then my country, and then the world. No family anywhere should be hungry." This was echoed by others, like Nurul Islam from Jessore, who shared "I know I am not alone in this work to end hunger. I feel Bangladesh is connected with the whole world."

These feelings of hope and optimism swept people into Badiul's orbit. Many wanted to work with him personally—his intellectual curiosity, integrity, and indefatigable energy were compelling. A brilliant group of leaders became part of his team, and even though he couldn't offer them much money, or an easy life, the two things he did offer were irresistible to them—the chance to play a meaningful role in the next frontier of liberation for their country—and the opportunity to make a difference with their own lives.

CHAPTER SEVEN

Keeping the Fire Burning

Four Animators Trainings were held in Dhaka within the first few years, each with around two-hundred participants. Badiul led them all, with occasional assistance from foreign trainers who were supporting the delivery of the program. With the promising outcomes reported from the field, there was soon mounting pressure to train more animators, and while the animators concept looked like it was working, Badiul resisted the idea of an accelerated expansion. He just did not have the capacity to offer more trainings, support the movement, lead his team, and continue to hold VCAWs each week in Ramna Park. He also didn't think his team could manage organizing more trainings, follow up with existing animators, and provide the support they needed to make serious gains in their villages.

He was also hamstrung by not having other trainers to draw on, so this too needed to be resolved before scaling could properly be considered. Training new trainers was a slow process, as it depended on trainer candidates attending multiple trainings to learn through watching Badiul. This was a limitation: holding enough Animators Trainings for candidates to learn how to lead the program was challenging, and it became an unhelpful cycle—more trainers were needed to expand the pool of facilitators, and yet the mechanism to do this, namely Badiul's time, was a limited resource. But slowly, over the following years, the group of trainers grew; first they were given sections of the Animators Training to facilitate, which was critiqued and improved with Badiul's guidance, and eventually they were able to lead a whole Animators Training on their own.

What was initially a slow process began to bear fruit as the cohort of trainers started to increase cumulatively—by leading an Animators Training, each new trainer would double, then triple the opportunities for others to build their own competency to run the whole training themselves. This methodical approach, while frustrating in its slowness, did pay off; by the early 2000s there were more than a dozen people running the Animators Training, which lifted the previous constraints and made it possible for The Hunger Project to offer more than ever before.

There was no issue with finding people to attend, as the demand to become an animator was immense, fueled by word of mouth. People had seen or heard of the results from family members or friends and were excited to be trained to produce similar results in their own villages. Demand for the training also came from the government. Bangladesh Civil Service Academy added a new training unit titled "Catalyzing Self-Reliance" in its training curricula. Badiul and his colleagues led these trainings, which allowed hundreds of young government bureaucrats to receive the Animators Training. In addition, the Ministry of

Local Government arranged Animators Trainings for the faculty and staff of the premiere rural development academies, BARD and Rural Development Academy (RDA), and the specialized training institute NILG (National Institute of Local Government). Later, nearly two dozen special seven-day Animators Trainings were given to mixed groups of local government representatives and government functionaries of the *Upazila* (local government) level.

This was all enormously satisfying for Badiul. He increased the number of staff to take some of the workload, and the enthusiasm he witnessed wherever he traveled within the country motivated him further.

Soon, an exciting initiative burst forth from the grassroots, which pleased Badiul immensely. Initially, actions taken by villagers who had done the VCAW were individual, like planting seedlings with a view to increase shade, or starting a small fisheries project to provide additional income to feed the family. But very quickly, and beyond anything Badiul could conceive, animators began to mobilize more broadly. Rather than focusing on initiatives one person could do individually, or with a small group within a village, animators started to organize on a larger scale as they realized the power available when the community combined their efforts. This organic, bottom-up process became known as creating Hunger Free Zones (HFZ), and it meant the whole village worked together toward the same vision, taking action collectively, which compounded the impact. Hunger Free Zones were based on an understanding that self-reliance wasn't just an individual responsibility, where only a few people could break out of poverty if they took action. Instead, it advocated that the community as a whole could create the enabling environment which allowed for everyone's condition to be uplifted, and this was as important as a person's own self-determination. Soon village after village began declaring themselves to be a Hunger Free Zone.

Badiul was thrilled with this growing ownership and leadership of the animator network, and he enthusiastically supported it. The Hunger Free Zones strategy gave Badiul hope, because what he saw every day in his work was very challenging. He had confronted many troubling incidences of suffering and destitution, but nothing had made him angrier than a visit to a health facility in the Sherpur district in the late 1990s.

He was in a hospital waiting room when a young couple came in carrying a small child. They were looking for help to get him well. The family was very poor and had traveled long distances to get there, and this was at a time when roads were bad, and transport options were few.

Observing the trio, Badiul noticed how thin and frail the parents looked, and saw that the child was severely malnourished, looking like a skeletal baby seen during the African famine. The baby was so still, and so small, that Badiul feared the child might not even be alive. The parents tried to get the doctor's attention, but the doctor would not pay them any heed, ignoring them completely.

Eventually he glanced over, and without examining the child, or taking the family into a private room, announced that the child was dead. He showed no sign of empathy or a "human expression" in delivering this devastating news. He was dismissive of the parents and told them to go away. Even in their confusion and loss, the doctor berated them—"Why did you come this far?

Why did you bring him? He's already dead." The doctor told them to "go back (with their child) to where you came from."

Badiul, watching all this, was furious.

The parents, already devastated by the loss of their child, were now being intimidated by the doctor. They started to walk back toward the door while holding their child. They looked bereft and bewildered. It was a case of utmost cruelty.

Badiul stepped in to support the family, commiserating with them, giving them some money, and calling for a nurse to assist with the wrapping and correct handling of their child. Once this was done, Badiul took the doctor to task, and he did not hold back. He reminded him that it was his responsibility as a doctor to help everyone, and to treat people with dignity and respect. The doctor was unmoved by this exchange, but for Badiul, it was a searing example of how widespread the mindsets and attitudes of superiority were toward the poor. There was a perception of the poor as being less than human. A belief that they were stupid, and their poverty and suffering were somehow their fault. The concept of service and compassion was not there for them.

So a few years later it was especially moving for him to visit another health center opened due to the organizing efforts of local animators in their Hunger Free Zone. Badiul was impressed as he wandered through a clean, functioning, and inclusive health facility which treated all members of the community equally. This had all started with VCAWs, when people declared access to health care as their main priority in making the village a Hunger Free Zone. At the time, most people were waiting in vain for government funding and support to materialize.

To break that cycle, the animators gathered the village to identify what was missing that would bring health care workers to their area. Once this was determined, they would then work together to figure out a way to provide it. To start with, the nurses' accommodations were substandard, with broken windows, doors that didn't close, and parts of the roof were leaking. No one wanted to stay there. So the village came together, and using their labor and resources, they fixed up the accommodations by painting it and making the repairs to make it attractive and welcoming for professionals to come and stay.

Then they did the same to the existing health center that wasn't being used. They started by cleaning it out and erecting a porch with a veranda to make a waiting area that was out of the sun and prevented crowding the interior of the clinic. With these efforts, the government was prepared to supply a doctor and nursing staff and pay for the dispensary to reopen. Badiul spoke with the medical staff and found their attitudes to be professional and motivated—a complete change from the doctor in Sherpur a few years earlier. It was another indication for him of the myriad shifts that happen when local people take responsibility for their community. It elevated the respect and interaction between all parties.

Literacy was another big focus for Hunger Free Zones. In a visit to Gaibanda, Badiul met Rhada, an animator who ran a free adult literacy class for women from 3 p.m. to 4:30 p.m., six days a week. Before she started the class, literacy rates for women, especially older women, were less than 30 percent in her village. Gathered in a small tin shed were about twenty-five women, all excitedly learning to read and count numbers.

Rhada's passion for education was given wings through the

Animators Training. As part of the Hunger Free Zones strategy, her village had committed to be illiteracy free within the next six months, and Rhada was motivated to be involved. She told Badiul, "These women are never going to go to university or to school. But this does not mean they should not know the joy and the dignity of being able to write your own name and understand the written word."

One of the women overhearing this shared emotionally, "I never knew how much pleasure reading and writing would give me. I can now read, but even if I only knew one word, this would mean everything to me."

A deeply personal initiative was led by Badiul himself, where he set up a school in the village where he had grown up. Called the People's Initiative Girl's High School and College, as the name suggested it was truly a people's initiative. Local animators, particularly Syed Omar Ahmed, and Golam Rabbani Mazumders with Badiul's guidance, mobilized the community as part of the Hunger Free Zone strategy. People contributed to the construction of the school by donating their labor and materials to spread girls' education in their rural community. As the school grew, Tazima and Badiul later contributed to the construction of a three-story building to pay back his debt to the community where he had lived with love and affection for his neighbors until he left for Dhaka in 1964.[6]

Hunger Free Zone activities were not limited to a village or local area—some were district-wide campaigns whose influence spread nationally. One of these was promoting the use of iodized

---

6 The school now provides educational opportunities for over 1,200 mostly impoverished girls, from grade six to twelve, and is the best institution in the entire sub-district.

salt to counter the widespread incidence of goiter among the people of the Gaibandha district. Badiul, in partnership with government functionaries and under the leadership of Deputy Commissioner Nasiruddin, mobilized hundreds of volunteers to reach each household of the district of about two million people. The animators and volunteers also undertook growing fish in open waterbodies, and this spread like wildfire with whole communities owning fisheries projects. People invested money to buy shares, and those without cash donated labor in exchange for a financial stake, thus receiving ongoing income for themselves and their family. Many dignitaries, including ministers, visited those fisheries projects and Professor Abul Bayes, the former Vice Chancellor of Jahangirnagar University, wrote an op-ed in the largest circulating newspaper of Bangladesh, giving it national fame. Soon, these types of initiatives were happening in other parts of the country.

It was a very exciting time, and Badiul kept abreast of the achievements and activities as he crisscrossed the country. Countless times he would be urged to deviate from a destination to visit a small community where people were committed to making their village a Hunger Free Zone. Badiul would be thrilled to see functioning health centers that people had mobilized for, income-generating activities, and social campaigns. On one occasion, he was with some of his international colleagues on their way to a large gathering when he was urged to stop at a rural *Upazila* (sub-district). His guests wanted to know what was happening and Badiul didn't know. Leaving the car to see what the delay was about; he was met with passionate animators who had gathered the whole village together. Everyone got out of the car and en masse they were led through the village, proudly shown the new latrines people were now using, and the once silted and disused fishponds that were now clean, full of fish, owned by the village, and providing nutrients to everyone. They heard about the united stand to not marry girl children before the age of eighteen and met with a number of students who were not married because of this commitment. Badiul had no idea that any of this was taking place in this area. It was not planned by the Dhaka office. There had been no external resources allocated to these projects or any management of the process, yet these committed human beings were ending hunger in their community. As Badiul and his guests got back into the car to continue to their destination, he felt deeply moved.

This was happening across the country. It was completely outside the scope of the usual service delivery paradigm, where staff do things, donors pay for it, and the people themselves are the beneficiaries. This was different. Rather than the traditional approach of successfully delivering planned interventions, the only investment that had been made was in developing people's vision and leadership, and the ongoing support of the animators. Empowerment—not financial input—drove the outcomes.

The more Badiul reflected on these contradictions, the more improbable it seemed. Yet he couldn't deny it was working and this prompted him to think about what else was needed to keep the fire going. Monthly gatherings for animators were piloted, for people to come together to share ideas, learn from each other, and figure out solutions to obstacles or problems. These took off and became critical to deepening the level of leadership the organization was able to deploy. This was people activating people, and it was unique for its time in Bangladesh. It was the beginning of a national movement.

To facilitate this movement, Badiul wrote a set of criteria or characteristics for the Hunger Free Zones movement based on his discussions with its leaders and the principles of THP. These included:

- People taking action themselves
- Active participation of women
- Must be a volunteer-based movement
- Grounded in a rights-based approach
- Come from creating a phenomenon and not implementing projects
- Be centered in local leadership and responsibility
- Include local level planning
- The actions must be based on self-reliance
- Must promote a sustainable environment.

These criteria were enthusiastically taken up by animators across the country and helped bring continuity and coherence to the diverse HFZ movement.

One important manifestation of the volunteer-based movement was a bottom-up initiative to address the issues of hygiene, water, and sanitation in Patnitola Upazila of Noagoan district. In partnership with the Hysawa Company, animators mobilized the households of all eleven Unions of the *Upazila* (230,000 people), to install handpumps and sanitary latrines, and raised their awareness to improve hygienic practices. The households also collectively decided the locations where the community latrines and water points were to be installed by the Hysawa company. External evaluators found this integrated social movement approach extremely effective.[7]

The success of the Hunger Free Zone strategy had one surprising casualty: the impact on Badiul's intellectual world view. The unleashing of people's leadership and the wildfire nature of how activities spread had not come out of a scientific laboratory. It was completely experimental, and a conundrum as it challenged Badiul's professorially held beliefs around management. He was learning that you can't manage a movement. There were so many unplanned variables because the source of the activity was people's own vision and the individual actions they took to fulfill it. Badiul could steer the movement, and he had certainly set the context for it, but there was a highly chaotic nature to what was happening that could not be contained. Like most economists, Badiul had learned and then taught Peter Drucker's theory "management by objective" which Drucker first outlined in his 1954 book "The Practice of Management." Management by objective was standard management fare, yet this seemed at odds with the emergence and scale of activity and leadership that came from the Animators Training and found expression through the Hunger Free Zones movement.

The process of managing by objective had five parts: establishing goals based on the company's mission and strategy, this was being done by managers; establishing specific objectives

7 See Badiul Alam Majumdar and John Coonrod, "Social Mobilization: An Innovative Approach to Meeting Water-Sanitation Related MDGs in Bangladesh," in *Peace and Sustainable Development in South Asia* published for Sustainable Development Policy Institute (Lahore: Sang-E-Meel Publications, 2012).

to be achieved to further the mission—these being set by managers and employees together; managers developing action plans which allow employees to achieve identified objectives; appraising results, whereby managers evaluate specific performance of individuals, comparing what was expected against what was delivered; and corrective action, when managers use the appraisal to help reorient or motivate the employee, so they are more on track to deliver work based on the set objectives. In making sense of the process, Badiul loosely imagined The Hunger Project staff in the role of "managers," and animators were in the role of "employees."

None of what was occurring in the field in Bangladesh fit Drucker's parameters, which meant Badiul's management theory went out the window. The activity and impact as a result of the Animators Training could not be contained. Ideas around planned and measured interventions leading to desired results were obsolete. And despite this veering from management canon, huge outcomes were being produced miles away from the Dhaka headquarters. Badiul sought to find a way to reconcile this dichotomy. He wanted to quantify and report on what was happening and see how he could try to manage the process. If it was growing so brilliantly without much structure and reporting, surely the addition of these tools would only contribute to more accelerated growth? In addition, the global leadership team, inspired by the breakthroughs, wanted to understand it further to see how it could be replicated. Data and evidence were needed.

Badiul started looking for ways to quantify inputs and outputs and track progress. Besides being useful for him, he believed it would also empower animators to set up their Hunger Free Zones. It was on a train ride from Kolkata to Delhi with Tazima and their three daughters that he landed on what became known as the Forty-Point Plan. It was based on eight key elements, broken down into forty subsections that comprised a healthy, functioning village. The eight key elements were Education and Literacy; Primary Health Care; Children's Health Care; Income and Self-employment; General Well-being of People; Community, Responsibility and Organization; Social Consciousness of the People; and Conditions of Women and Children. The idea was that animators, with the people in their community, would set targets for the forty points and follow up six months later to measure progress towards them. The instrument included both qualitative and quantitative targets and indicators.

At follow up leadership trainings, animators were taught how to use the system to plan and track developments made in their communities. What was so ingenious about this was that people themselves set their own targets and were able to see what progress they were making toward their goals. Typically, targets were set by an organization, and they dictated what people had to focus on, whether or not it was an actual local priority. Instead, choosing what to focus on and what the goal over the next six months would be created transparency and ownership. Badiul loved attending the tracking meetings in a village where sometimes a hundred people would be gathered to work through the forty points, with the information drawn up on sheets of brown butcher paper for everyone to see.

If the goal was under Education and Literacy, they would hear data on the current status (for example, the percentage of children aged six to ten who attended primary school); what their target had been; and then decide together what the goal for the next six months would be. Under Children's Healthcare, they would see, for instance, the percentage of children (birth to two years old) who had their height and weight measured in the previous six months; and what percentage of children below the age of five were given deworming medications. Where progress was not as high as they had hoped, there was then a thoughtful discussion about what was needed to be able to hit the goal for the next reporting period.

Badiul was hearing from animators everywhere how motivating the forty-point plan was. When goals were met, there was immense pride, and when they weren't, it only spurred people on to achieve them next time. Local empowerment was the main aim of the process because, in reality, very little of the local forty-point data ended up in the Dhaka office, and that which did overwhelmed the small staff's ability to categorize and input it into systems. But for Badiul, this was a lesser concern. His priority was to give people the tools to set their objectives and have a way of measuring when they were on the path to achieving a hunger free zone. His philosophy wasn't to let management dictate what was needed on the ground.

Badiul regularly brought together animators who were leading the charge for the Hunger Free Zones movement. At one such meeting in Gaibandha, he gathered nearly thirty animators at one of the government outposts dotted across the country. The venue had a dormitory, which meant those from further afield could stay for the whole day. It was winter and cold. Breath frosted the air and shawls were tightly gripped. Yet eyes were shining, and voices spirited as the group explored what characterized a leader of the Hunger Free Zone movement, and what made one successful. This was a typical approach for Badiul: to set the context for discussion but to leave the exploration and discovery to the group. He found this offered a richness that rewarded everyone present.

From the conversation, five key elements for a successful Hunger Free Zone catalyst emerged, the first one being the belief that this was about people doing it for themselves and not waiting around for someone else—including The Hunger Project staff, to fix it for them. To succeed as a leader for a Hunger Free Zone one must believe that people—even the most marginalized—had inherent power and could do this themselves. The paradigm of development where people were made "beneficiaries" of a leader's activism cost human dignity and would not be supported.

The second element was this was a volunteer movement—Hunger Free Zone animators were not hired help. The people gathered felt strongly there should not be a mindset of "what's in it for me" or being paid to be the driver for taking actions. What gave them their power in mobilizing their community was that they too were doing this as volunteers, taking action because it was the right thing to do and because the outcome for the village was achievable.

The third element spoke to the commitment to building a movement. Hunger Free Zones were about creating a phenomenon—a movement—not implementing projects. Additionally, two or three stand-alone projects would not make an area a Hunger Free Zone—there needed to be an upswell of initiatives across the community. One young man made a wise analogy. He said, "just as two or three successful countries won't make a global transformation, neither will a handful of projects in a village."

The fourth was that local leadership and responsibility were fundamental. For a Hunger Free Zone to be achieved, unleashing local leadership was a must. Leadership must come from that area. This made the best use of local resources as well as underscoring the mindset of "We can do it," which parachuting in external leadership would undermine. Local leaders also enabled collective leadership to emerge. They saw Badiul's role as helping to change people's mindset so they could become change agents.

The final element was local level planning, with the main feature being it must emerge bottom up. Any pre-made plan, including plans out of the Dhaka office, would mar the emergence of local leadership. The forty-point instrument helped people make their own plans and monitor those plans themselves.

Aside from these elements, which became pillars for the Hunger Free Zone movement, Badiul wanted to determine the difficulties animators faced in setting up Hunger Free Zones, and seven main obstacles emerged out of the discussion. The first was illiteracy coupled with religious superstition. When people have had no access to education, it made logic and reasoning hard to follow. For example, understanding germ theory and the need to wash your hands was often seen as counter to the belief that everything is "the will of Allah."

The second obstacle was how much the equality of women was lacking. Animators' experiences were that too often women's husbands or parents needed to be on board for women to succeed, and these family and social barriers kept women from participating. One animator shared that, when speaking to families, the most common response was "a woman's place is inside the home."

Thirdly, a lack of collective participation and an unwillingness to organize made the work hard going at times. Breaking through sentiments like "I should only think about myself. Why should I help others work for their own gain?" was more difficult than the leaders had expected. Individually, people mostly thought only of themselves and the mindset that accompanied that was often "how will I benefit and what will I get from this?"

The fourth was dealing with the dependency mindset, created through decades of charity and dependence on government and NGOs. The Hunger Project animators knew people could do things for themselves, but it took time for people to understand this philosophy. Additionally, as The Hunger Project didn't give loans, people found it hard initially to understand what the benefit of the organization was as they saw other development groups giving handouts.

The fifth obstacle was lack of resources, and it was agreed that even though most Hunger Free Zone's projects included creating funds through local savings such as in a self-help group, this wasn't enough. As one animator explained, "literacy programs are run under trees, and they need help. It's not good enough. It's too hot and there are many distractions."

Lack of trust in the community was the sixth obstacle. People had been promised so many things in the past from politicians and the government, and little of it was delivered. Trust had been betrayed and people had been deceived a number of times. They wondered how they could be sure The Hunger Project would not also deceive them. They were wary of getting their hopes up and putting in the time. That also made it difficult to bring people together, as the time spent in a workshop was seen as a waste.

The last obstacle was lack of momentum which would happen when there were only one or two animators in a village. Alone, they could not create a miracle. As one of the participants shared, "We need lots of animators, collectively, collaboratively, united. Other organizations have regular and full-time officials, but The Hunger Project has volunteers. This is a benefit in the long run, but it makes it harder to get going and build momentum."

This discussion was very helpful for Badiul and the animators, and it helped him develop his thinking on what was needed to break through these obstacles. He used the analogy of "catalyst" to describe their leadership, and told them "In science, a catalyst does not change the character of something, it hastens the reaction."

He asked them what made them leaders and if there were qualities they all shared. Responses included "I am self-confident and make others self-confident." "I identify problems and transform them." One woman proudly called out, "If you light a candle it burns, it lights the surrounding area, but it will burn out. A catalyst does not burn out. I will spread light around me, but I will not be burned out!" Another shared, "A catalyst may be invisible, but nothing would have started if they hadn't been there."

As Badiul traveled home that night, tired but energized from the day's conversation and analysis, he reflected on the enormous depth the volunteer leaders around him brought to their shared mission. They demonstrated real ownership, standing with him to make this better and not looking to him for answers. They were his full partners. The discussion that day helped him design the next phase of expanding the leadership to continue moving toward ending hunger.

With such rapid expansion,[8] quality control was paramount. Badiul knew he couldn't manage a movement, but he needed to ensure grassroots activists had the support they needed to succeed. He was aware how hard it was to make inroads toward ending hunger, and the obstacles were enormous. He didn't want these bright, passionate, and deeply committed people burning out when it inevitably got hard.

In training people to become animators, the team at THP needed to stay the course with them. This meant following up with them through regular local meetings, listening to them, and even staying in the villages with them. This was a constraint because there were not enough staff to do this and hiring additional people would be exorbitant. Badiul did not have a big enough team to support the growing body of leaders in the field. But there had to be another way.

To overcome this challenge, Badiul created Volunteer Trainers who took on part of the workload. Volunteer Trainers were successful animators who received additional training to better supervise and empower the local animators' delivery of mobilization projects; they were key to ensuring a phenomenon was unleashed. They already lived in the villages and took it upon themselves to mentor animators and others toward fulfilling the vision. They would also report back either through tracking the Forty Point Plan, or with a staff person who was assigned to support them.

This whole strategy of relying on volunteers to lead and foment a nationwide movement confounded leaders of other

8 From 2001-2012 more than 1,800 Animator Trainings took place, with more than 145,000 people leading the grassroots movement as animators. To keep up with the demand and continue the momentum, in some years there were four trainings held every weekend. By 2023 there were 184,102 animators in Bangladesh.

organizations. Once, when Badiul was showing members of USAID the efficacy of his approach in Khulna, an official asked him why people did this for free. Badiul decided to have the volunteers answer for themselves. The answers were sometimes deeply personal; one woman was married too young and wanted to stop this from happening to other girls. But mostly there were answers like "We want to make a difference with our lives," or "We are the new generation of Freedom Fighters" or "We feel a deep sense of social responsibility." Unlike other organizations, what was happening in the villages around the country was not contributing toward some business model. It was an ideal, a vision that propelled them.

Volunteer leadership toward lofty goals had a rich history in Bangladesh, and this was something Badiul drew upon. It was rooted in the liberation war, which was a people's war. The "Father of the Nation," Sheikh Mujibur Rahman, famously exhorted his people in March 1971 to give what they had for their liberation. "Be ready with whatever you have to face the enemy. Turn every house into a fortress…Having mastered the lesson of sacrifice, we shall give more blood. Inshallah, we shall free the people of this land." This idea of a bottom-up resistance, something that was at the grassroots level, where you gave of yourself for a noble cause, still rang true in people's hearts. The enemy had changed from the Pakistani Army to poverty and hunger, yet the principle still held.

While the expanding movement was immensely gratifying to Badiul, it didn't come without a cost. The Hunger Project had always felt like a family—he had once known all the animators, recognizing faces at least, if not names, and knowing which area the person was from. Badiul was very personable and friendly with people, generous with his smile and affection, and he loved this feeling that they were all comrades in arms. But there came a point where THP had grown exponentially, and with others leading Animator Trainings and supporting the volunteer leaders, Badiul could not possibly know even a fraction of who was now involved, and he really hated that. Losing this family feeling also concerned him; he was worried it might grow so big that the social capital and sense of solidarity that fueled the movement could be lost.

It was with this in mind that Badiul decided to hold an Animators Reunion. He wanted as many people as possible to come together to share, learn, and celebrate their leadership and achievements in ending hunger. This was a huge undertaking and given the numbers of people expected, it was held in an indoor stadium, with a prominent group of dignitaries participating to cheer the animators on. People traveled there using their own money, some saving for months to afford the bus rides and accommodation to be able to attend. Due to THP's budget restraints, each person received only a meager lunch with some rice, an egg, and a piece of chicken to eat, but it did not matter. The whole day was spent singing and sharing stories—it was pure inspiration! Badiul's face ached from smiling all day. Hearing how much the animators had personally grown, and what they had achieved to end hunger in their villages on the strength of their own vision, commitment, and action, was intensely moving. His heart was bursting—these were his people, and he was theirs. At the end of the reunion, the animators traveled during the night to their homes, often spending eight or twelve hours on the bus.

With the success of this first one, the Animators Reunion became something Badiul was committed to continuing. The second Reunion was held on the grounds of the Dhaka Police Headquarters. An enormous tent was constructed with bamboo sticks and more than 10,000 animators arrived from all over the country for the day. The Minister for Local Government and Rural Development and several other distinguished Bangladeshis participated in the event. The third Animators Reunion was held on the Grounds of the Physical College, where 12,000 volunteer animators participated. Sir Fazle Hasan Abed, the founder of BRAC, the largest NGO in the world, came, and he was so inspired by what the animators shared that he publicly made an offer to work with them. This led to a subsequent partnership with BRAC to implement THP-Bangladesh's "MDG Union Strategy."

Badiul knew the power that was present when people came together to celebrate what had been achieved and to gather fuel for the road ahead. The reunion also personally inspired and energized him. He realized he too needed this type of gathering to keep him empowered—such moments of joy and reflection helped him make sense of the hard work, time away from family, and pressures he often felt. It was a hard life he had chosen for himself, with little comfort and many sacrifices. He knew intellectually it was worth it, but the Animators Reunion fed his soul. As a man of the people, he loved nothing more than being amongst other committed humans.

Right from the beginning, Badiul was passionate about sharing the impact of the VCAW and Animators Training and he would be quite the evangelist at the regular global staff meetings he attended in New York City. He was convinced other countries could benefit from using this approach, especially countries in Africa where THP was working. Initially, this rubbed Ambassador Fitigu Tadesse, the Ethiopian head of Africa programs for THP, the wrong way. Badiul invited Fitigu to Bangladesh to see it for himself. That visit changed everything.

Fitigu went to Bangladesh to immerse himself in the programs and approach Badiul had created. In both the VCAW and the Animators Training, he immediately saw possibilities for the African context, but it would need to be adapted. He assessed that the widespread movement approach in Bangladesh would not work in Senegal and other countries, and instead a two-person per village approach would work best. Badiul thought this was unnecessarily limiting but also respected that it was Fitigu's call. He was very happy to share as much as he could to give the VCAW and Animators Training the best chance in Africa.

The Global Office was thrilled with this development, and VCAW was delivered for the first time in Senegal in 1998, and in Ghana in 1999. When Joan was in Ghana working on the African Woman Food Farmer Initiative, she asked the Ghana team how the people liked the VCAW and Animators Training—they were over the moon about it. Badiul beamed when he heard this.

The VCAWs and Animators Training have become core pillars to the Epicenter Strategy approach THP uses across nine countries in Africa. Over time, individual countries have adapted the structure to suit their specific needs, for instance, different animators are trained specifically for HIV/AIDS activities, or microfinance. But the content of the trainings is similar and the ethos unchanged. Through this approach, the poor themselves play the leadership role in ending hunger.[9]

The fire Badiul had lit now burned around the world.

9 By 2023 across nine countries in Africa, 2,214 Animators Trainings have been held resulting in 42,778 trained volunteer animators taking catalytic action in their communities. These programs have been the cornerstone of the African Epicenter Strategy, which is ending hunger across a number of regions in Africa. Remarkably, fifteen percent more women than men have been trained as animators.

CHAPTER EIGHT

Unleashing the Leadership of Women

The Hunger Project had built a global reputation for approaching the issue of hunger and poverty in a pioneering way wherever it worked, and this was equally true in Bangladesh. Badiul's insights on people's development and the way he had turned addressing them into a widespread grassroots movement, were recognized at home—even the Prime Minister had attended a public VCAW in her constituency. Badiul was riding a wave of confidence.

Yet his work was to undergo a seismic shift when it became clear in development circles that even the best programs in the world would not succeed without the empowerment and inclusion of women. Women needed to be brought forward to the center of development activities if those activities were to be effective and sustainable. Taking this on became the number one priority for The Hunger Project globally, causing soul-searching amongst its leaders, and a transformation for all programs on the ground.

Badiul was not immune to the change this would bring to him and his organization. The following years would cause a reckoning with his own blind spots as a man in a patriarchal society, and a profound change in the work he and the team did.

The Beijing Women's Summit in 1995 was a global clarion call for women. Over 17,000 women attended, with a further 30,000 activists participating in a parallel forum. Women, including Tazima, traveled from across the globe, from grassroots organizations, large bilateral agencies, businesses, or as private citizens and activists. Beijing's Summit was remarkable for the sheer number of women who came together to speak, be heard, and connect with one other. Even the First Lady of the United States of America attended, with Hilary Clinton famously declaring, "Human rights are women rights, women's rights are human rights." There had been previous international conferences for women, but 1995 was a real moment.

Joan Holmes was also there, and in deeply listening to the pain and anguish of women's stories from the Global South, something irrevocably shifted within her. It wasn't that she hadn't stood for women and women's rights and inclusion before. That was something she believed in and had spoken about. But in Beijing, she *became* it. For Joan, it was a completely different experience than talking about it.

A few months later, in 1996, a landmark report from UNICEF called *The Asian Enigma*[10] was published, and it sought to discover why the health of children in South Asian countries was so much

10 Ramalingaswami, U., Jonsson, J., & Rohde, J. (1996). *The Asian Enigma.*

worse than for children in economically poorer sub-Saharan Africa.

The study looked at common explanations: differences in purchasing power, agricultural performance, logistics, extreme inequality, food availability, etc. But its startling conclusion was that "the exceptionally high rates of malnutrition in South Asia are rooted deep in the soil of inequality between men and women."

It described it this way: "However much a mother may love her children, it is all but impossible for her to provide high-quality child care if she herself is poor and oppressed, illiterate and uninformed, anemic and unhealthy, has five or six other children, lives in a slum or shanty, has neither clean water nor safe sanitation, and if she is without the necessary support either from health services, her society, or from the father of her children."

In showing that even the best development initiatives would not succeed if women were not positioned at the forefront of initiatives, the report sent shockwaves through development circles and crystallized what was already coming into focus for Joan Holmes. In response, in August 1997 in Bangalore India, Holmes convened a meeting with stakeholders and global board members to read through and focus on the findings from the *Asian Enigma*. The Hunger Project board of directors at that time included the "father of India's green revolution," Dr. M.S. Swaminathan; United Nations Under-Secretary-General and Special Envoy on Women and Development, Gertrude Mongella; and Former Secretary-General of the United Nations, Javier Pérez de Cuéllar, and it was here that the organizational decision was made to focus on the empowerment of women. This decision would change the face of The Hunger Project, including Badiul's work in Bangladesh.

The Asian Enigma outlined five key areas to be addressed to empower women, and Badiul critically examined these to see how to apply them to Bangladesh. The first recommendation was maternal healthcare, which included access to quality services, good pre- and post-natal care, and skilled birth attendants for healthier pregnancies and safer deliveries. In determining how to apply this in Bangladesh, it was clear that not only should services be available to women—something that was not guaranteed at the village level—but women should also make use of these services. This meant confronting mindsets similar to what one man told Badiul: "I'll get the vet if I have to for the cow, but I won't spend money on my wife. She can deliver the baby herself, and if something happens, well, then I'll get another wife." A societal shift was desperately needed that acknowledged women were humans deserving of medical attention, and that maternal care meant better outcomes for everyone.

The second key was accessible and widespread health knowledge and practices, which included education on nutrition, hygiene, and disease prevention. Having these meant increased vaccination rates, proper nutrition, and safer drinking water. In analyzing this, Badiul realized that achieving this outcome would require community education, and then mobilization for local solutions. There were limited safe water sources for drinking, as well as a lack of understanding of why it was important. People thought disease and illness were part of life and not something they could prevent.

In most villages there was no sanitation facility, so people defecated in the fields, near crops, and where people lived, spreading disease. The need for safe sanitation was also highly gendered—assaults on women and girls often happened when they went to relieve themselves. Without a safe and private space to go, women would wait all day, past the point of discomfort, causing bladder and other issues.

Improving nutrition also meant education, specifically around critical micronutrients available from varying the diet with the addition of greens. The more Badiul looked into it, the more he saw that accessibility to nutrition was also a gendered issue. It was women and girls eating last and least, even when pregnant, due to societal subjugation. In people's homes, women first fed the husband, then her sons, and with whatever was left, she fed her daughters. Only at the end would she eat herself, sometimes only the scrapings from the pot as nothing was left for her. This was normalized and part of the conditioning people shared about the role of women, and consequently, the thinnest and the most malnourished persons in the villages were women.

The third area was giving women decision-making authority on issues that affected them and their children, and this was one of the hardest changes for Badiul to figure out how to make happen. Women making informed choices regarding their own health and the health of their children meant they could advocate for their children's needs, and actively participate in discussions and decisions relating to their children's health and well-being. This included the age their daughters were ready for marriage and deciding to send girls to school.

Yet women had so little say in decisions that affected them, and this was built into the social and family structure. Men made decisions in public and domestic spheres. They were the politicians, the decision makers, and the arbiters of what—and who—were important. Within the home, a woman's life was dictated by the whims of her husband and in-laws. He had the power to constrict her movements to their small hut, decide whether she went to the market, and even if she spoke. Women were conditioned to accept this, and mothers-in-law, having faced the subjugation that came with marrying young into a family with no rights themselves, often exercised power by dominating their daughters-in-law. Badiul could see that giving women a say in decision making would require transformation in social, domestic, and individual domains. Empowering women to use their voices and access power would have a huge benefit to the society, but it would be treacherous terrain to navigate. Picking through the minefield and finding a way forward would not be easy, but he was convinced it was necessary.

The fourth intervention was economic empowerment, which made immediate sense to the economist in Badiul. Having both women and men engaged in productive activities that made money, with both deciding how it should be spent meant the benefits of money could be used more equitably. Supporting women in income-generating activities meant more money was available for their children's health and education, as well as better nutrition. Research was clear that when women made financial decisions, money went to outcomes that improved the condition for the whole family, versus men who would spend it mainly on what they wanted and not necessarily what would be best for the family.

The last area to address was a big one, breaking intergenerational poverty cycles. The research was clear; malnourished children come from malnourished women and focusing on the child only after birth was not sufficient. A woman's malnutrition affected multiple generations through "fetal programming," where the future health of a person is determined by the nutritional status of that person as a fetus in the mother's womb. If the mother is malnourished, the fetus' normal protections against certain diseases are lost, and consequently the incidence of diabetes, stroke, and heart disease in Bangladesh was among the highest in the world, even in rural villages and despite these being diseases of affluence. The cycle must be broken. Again, the answer to this was empowering women. An empowered woman makes better decisions, secures better resources, and gains the behaviors, knowledge, and skills needed to be healthy herself, and raise a safe and healthy family.

The Asian Enigma was especially relevant to Bangladesh, where 50 percent of babies had a low birthweight, compared to 25 percent in India and 17 percent in sub-Saharan Africa. By any measure, this was unacceptably high. Badiul understood that for women to improve the health and well-being of their children, a shift in approach was required. The outcome of what needed to happen was clear—but the pathway was not. In a country where many women could not freely leave their own home, and where movement and education were highly restricted and often monitored, mobilizing women seemed a pipe dream. Forging a way forward would not be easy, yet Badiul knew it must be attempted.

And one of the biggest obstacles in the way was his own patriarchal mindset.

In the aftermath of the organization's shift in direction, global staff leaders were called to the New York headquarters in what became a multiyear conversation on how to orient the work of THP toward empowering women. Joan Holmes knew that what was required was nothing short of a transformation. It wasn't just about changing some of the programs and tinkering around the edges so that women were included. It required a complete confrontation with the structures of privilege and power men were afforded, as well as the individual work women and men must do that accompanied this. Change wasn't only going to happen *out there* in the programs on the ground. It needed to happen *in here* as well, in the hearts and minds of the leaders of the organization.

It was difficult for everyone, especially the men, to explore how perhaps their position and success in the world were determined less by their own efforts as previously thought, and more from being born male in a world designed for and by men. For many, this was a painful realization, but a necessary one, and this was true for Badiul, too. He was a typical man of his generation, and blithely unaware of his own limiting beliefs about women. Even though he considered himself a "good man" and considerate of women, he had been raised to have his way of doing things be the way things were done, and he hadn't questioned this before. In both his marriages, he had made the financial decisions, and while he liked to think he included his wives in them, on reflection he could see he truly did not. Whatever opportunities he had wanted to pursue, be they educational or vocational, Badiul had seized, not fully accounting for the cost to his family—the turmoil and instability—that his choices caused them. To make the leap fully into empowering women in their leadership, he had a lot of old ideas and behaviors to examine and transform. All of this was intensely uncomfortable for him, but he committed himself to it, and Joan and Tazima were his uncompromising partners in this awakening.

There was also the enormity of how to translate this shift in approach to the actual world where people lived—in villages and homes across Bangladesh. Many practical and heartbreaking questions were raised in these global meetings: "How do you empower women when they are not even able to leave the four walls of their hut? How can they be encouraged to speak out when they had been conditioned to not voice their opinions?" In trying to reconcile this, a transformative and very tough conversation occurred between Badiul and Joan.

Joan asked him for the number of women attending VCAW and Animators Trainings versus men, and Badiul reported that on average each had about 10 to 20 percent female attendance. He outlined the reasons why: Women couldn't travel freely. They don't have autonomy and are beholden to the husband. Even if they wanted to come, they are prevented. They have to attend to family chores and domestic duties. Everyone listened, nodding their heads—what he said tracked and made sense. But Joan would have none of it. She challenged Badiul to increase the number of women and said that if there were not at least as many women as men participants, then the trainings should not be held.

Things got quite heated. Badiul said this wasn't possible. He outlined the reasons again. The best he could hope for over time would be about 25 or 30 percent, but even those numbers would take years to achieve. Joan stopped him there, telling him it must be 50 percent. "If that means you can only get three women to an Animators Training, then you have a training for six people. This is not negotiable. You need to find a way." Her unequivocalness astounded Badiul, and the exchange didn't sit well with him. He thought Joan was being unreasonable and unfair. How could she possibly understand the constraints he was up against in his country? And working toward 30 percent female attendance wasn't bad—in that context, it was incredible! No other organization was managing that. Badiul was overwhelmed by the circumstances, realities, and difficulties in the way of making this shift. He knew how conservative and patriarchal Bangladesh was, and that things moved slowly. He was a man who grew up in that society, where women take the back seat. It wasn't easy for him. However, he also trusted Joan, who had been his longstanding partner, and he was aware that she might see something fresh and new precisely because she wasn't caught up with the intricacies, norms, and "realities" of his country. She wasn't beholden to the old ways. He knew Joan was fiercely committed to ushering in what was most effective for ending hunger, and he couldn't deny that empowering women was crucial.

By the end of the back and forth with Joan, and the discussions with other leaders in the organization, Badiul found a place to stand. He acknowledged to himself that his background as an educated male gave him greater prestige and respect than others, especially women. He could see he too had inherited an unconscious limiting view of women, and this held him back. Something shifted for him—he would find the way. With this settled for him internally, he was resolved. The issue now was strategic. Badiul needed to figure out how to make this shift happen within his team in Dhaka, and then in the field.

Badiul started by inviting Joan to Dhaka and arranged a series of meetings for her to assess women's status in Bangladesh and assist him to design the best approach to implement the program changes they both were committed to. In one of those meetings, Holmes met with the who's who of Bangladesh, and one after another these distinguished individuals spoke about the respect and esteem with which all women were held in Bangladeshi society, and in unison they denied the conditions of subjugation, mistreatment, deprivation, and violence against women of Bangladesh. Although Joan listened politely to speaker after speaker, she saw this as indicative of the monumental challenges that lay ahead.

For Badiul, a visit to a museum in Mohastangar, Bogura helped him understand how embedded these views were. There he saw a sculpture from centuries ago in which a man was beating a woman with one hand while holding her by her hair with the other and pushing her down with his knee. It shocked and repelled him to see the beating of a woman by a man depicted in a cultural artifact. He reflected on how widespread a practice this has been for centuries, and that the mistreatment of women was part of his culture, deeply ingrained in his forefather's blood. Patriarchy was thus inherited, and to overcome this, Badiul knew he and other men would have to fight against their inherited and deeply ingrained prejudices.

Badiul and Joan decided the first thing to do to begin this process was to create a shared understanding about the organization's shift to empowering women with the other Hunger Project leaders in Bangladesh, and so Badiul convened a gathering of the staff and key animators—people who were already deeply committed to the goal of ending hunger in Bangladesh. Looking out into a sea of faces, Joan, and Badiul saw that 90 percent of them were men. They knew they were asking a lot for men to shift the focus of their work to include and empower women. Badiul knew from personal experience that it would require a confrontation with who they thought they were. But both Joan and Badiul knew that whether or not these people took it on, empowering women would be the priority for THP-Bangladesh going forward.

Joan spoke first, and though it was tough going, it marked the beginning of a pivotal shift. Many subsequent conversations and discussions were held in open and private forums. More than a few men felt as Badiul had, that this was nice in theory, but it absolutely would not work in Bangladesh. Some spoke with Badiul privately, questioning whether this course of action was even possible. THP was already making a name for itself, and the programs were gaining traction—why risk a good thing?

One of the main mindsets that needed to be changed was a belief that women just weren't capable of the leadership and activity that being an animator required. "They are too busy in their homes and with their families." "Women don't have the education." They can't think like we do." Badiul knew these prejudices were in the way of women being empowered, and while he had some small empathy for these antiquated positions—after all, he once believed some of this—he was not deterred. Both he and Joan knew that this inner wrestling wasn't in the way of the work. Changing these mindsets was the work!

Privately, Joan acknowledged Badiul's courage for taking this difficult new direction on so fully. She knew that the evidence from Bangladesh on why this couldn't happen was immense—any objective look at the reality would view the task ahead as almost impossible. Having witnessed the resistance amongst the country's intellectuals as well as some animators, she was determined to support Badiul wholeheartedly. But at no time did either of them waver. There was a respect and an understanding between them for how difficult it would be, but that had no bearing in terms of what they were going to do. What Badiul was setting out to do was completely "unreasonable" in the context of George Bernard Shaw's insight from his play "Man and Superman" where he wrote: "The reasonable man adapts himself to the world: the unreasonable one persists in trying to adapt the world to himself. Therefore, all progress depends on the unreasonable man." Being unreasonable was an asset when it came to ending the subjugation and marginalization of women in Bangladesh.

Badiul didn't build the movement for women or figure out the crucial steps in a vacuum. Right from the beginning, he had a fierce advocate and partner in the work, his wife Tazima. She fully supported this direction and gave Badiul advice and counsel on how to proceed. Tazima had become close to Joan Holmes and had also spent a lot of time in the field speaking with women—she knew more intimately than him the life women led. She had easier access to the private domains of a family compound, and her compassionate nature lent itself to women unburdening themselves to her. Tazima took her commitment as an animator seriously, and as she too was profoundly impacted by the Beijing Summit for Women, her focus from the beginning was women.[11]

Through the VCAWs and Animators Trainings, thousands of people had come to a profound reckoning with their own resignation, and underneath that, their deep love for their country. It unlocked leadership and determination in people

11 Tazima mobilized women who lived in slums in Dhaka to generate income, organizing sewing circles and handicraft groups. She used the global network of The Hunger Project as a market for these women by selling their wares at events in New York, San Francisco, and London. She and Badiul traveled everywhere with suitcases full of hand stitched garments, tapestries, and jewelry the women had made, setting up stalls at conferences and gala dinners to sell these to The Hunger Project investors and activists. Tazima had also started a school for girls in the slum near Rayer Bazaar that ran for nearly three decades, only closing because of COVID-19.

everywhere. One of these was Nasima Akhter, or Jolly as she was known, who attended the second ever Animators Training. Jolly had her master's in accounting from Rajshahi University and a Diploma in Human Resources from Bangladesh Institute of Management, Dhaka, and at the time was working as the Assistant Director, Women's Empowerment and Finance with TMSS, one of the country's largest national NGOs which had a primary focus on loans for women. Jolly was concerned that in the name of "empowerment," poor women were getting caught in a net of increased debt day after day, increasing their poverty. Loans on their own were exacerbating the cycle of poverty, and this led to questions in her mind prior to doing the Animators Training.

Her Animators Training took place at the Planning Academy in Dhaka, and its impact was immense. For the first time in her life, she imagined a country with no poverty, where all children are healthy, and women are empowered. The training changed her mindset and "shocked my consciousness"—she wanted in and soon joined The Hunger Project. Her addition to the team, and her leadership as Badiul's close associate, became crucial to the breakthroughs in women's empowerment the organization was able to catalyze around the country.

Jolly was at that pivotal meeting with Joan Holmes in 1998, and she took on cracking the code for how to involve women who were traditionally locked out of public spaces and discourse. In this process, she and Badiul noticed something intriguing: over the course of many Animators Trainings, women rarely participated, often saying nothing at all, and no coaxing by the trainer to draw them out shifted this dynamic. In talking privately to the women, Jolly heard over and over again that while they were pleased to be there, they didn't feel comfortable speaking in the mixed environment. While there was a section in the four-day training dedicated to empowering women, it wasn't enough—the immense subjugation women faced in every aspect of their daily life wasn't conceptual for them. They lived it, and unpacking what this was and how to break free was something the training didn't cover.

As a woman, Jolly could speak more freely with village women, and she understood the difficulties they faced. Women shared openly with her. One profound early experience she shared with Badiul happened when she was in her home district of Bogura for a training. There in a small village, she met a woman racked with sobs who told Jolly she had been divorced by her husband and that she and their son had nowhere to go. The woman had visited her parents and bought some biscuits to share with them. When the husband found out she had bought biscuits without seeking his permission and approval first, he burst into a rage, beating her and shouting at her. "How dare you take it upon yourself to do this without my consent?" In the violence that ensued, he told her he would divorce her, and he did. The woman was wailing in deep anguish and shame at her wrongdoing.

Jolly was incensed on her behalf. The source of this calamity was rooted in the woman's abject disenfranchisement from her rights. Far too many women across the country truly believed they were at the beck and call of their husbands, who were their masters. They were convinced that not getting permission was a big offense and wrong of them and, therefore, the beatings and violence were justified. They had no understanding that they too were human beings, with autonomy and rights. The passion to support women as they learned these rights, and developed their own agency as human beings, burned through Jolly's core, and this encounter became her touchstone. Jolly knew for a fact that if this social dynamic didn't change, and if women and men could not work together in true partnership, nothing would change for her country.

Abdul Aziz, a young volunteer animator, was also grappling with how to include and empower women in his village. Aziz had been at that seminal session with Joan Homes and knew firsthand how marginalized women were in his rural village in Kishoreganj. It was difficult to get them to attend VCAWs as his area, in the northeast of the country, was more disadvantaged than most, and the situation for women was more acute. Everywhere there were visual cues of women's subjugation, from the gaunt faces of women not eating enough, to the paucity of girls staying in school past grade three, to the number of twelve, thirteen, and fourteen-year-old girls getting married. Adding to the difficulty was a high observance of purdah, which restricted women's personal, social, and economic activities outside the home. Purdah involved secluding women from the public gaze, with only male family members and other women able to see them without them being fully covered. At a minimum, purdah meant women could only go outside in full burqa (veil), but it sometimes meant women could not leave their huts or compounds at all.

Aziz realized he needed to work within the current context, so he approached Badiul and Jolly about holding a female only VCAW. They were immediately onboard, so he spoke to his female relatives in the village—his mother and aunties—to identify and approach women about attending. He sought out male family relatives too, the husbands, sons, and brothers of the proposed attendees, to explain what the VCAW was about, and gain their approval. Aziz secured the use of the local primary school and installed a cloth partition to visually separate the women from any men, including him and Badiul, who might see them.

All this took time, but eventually the workshop day dawned, and Badiul, Jolly, and Tazima set out early for the drive to Kishoreganj. They had decided not to alter the content of the VCAW too much, thinking that the female only audience and their shared experiences would provide the context needed. Badiul was curious about how it would go; he had never led a VCAW with participants he could not see. How would he gauge whether the messages were being received? What if he was just going on and they weren't following any of what he said?

He and Aziz stood on one side of the partition, and Tazima, Jolly, and thirty-five women, most still wearing their burqas, sat on the other side. Throughout the workshop, women thoughtfully engaged with the concepts, doing the deep work to apply it to their own situation. Badiul had no doubt it had succeeded—the women's sharing, animation, and fresh understandings were clear to everyone there. At the end, more than a dozen women crossed the partition to meet Badiul and talk to him directly. Already this was a bold step. They were excited, and so were the members of the team. Aziz had tears in his eyes. This was a way to reach women where they were at.

Badiul seized the strategic opening this offered, and over the next two years, more than ten female only VCAWs were held. These workshops not only reached women who couldn't attend a mixed training, but also provided useful information from the women themselves about what was needed for them to truly step forth as leaders in their communities. The individual work was important, but it was equally clear that more focus was needed on the men in the communities in order for women to step forward.

The movement needed more men like Aziz, who stood for this societal shift. Like the work Badiul had done to confront his own bias a few years earlier, men needed to examine their own conditioning and mindsets and unlearn old beliefs about the role of women. And this included his key staff leaders.

Badiul knew he needed help bringing about this reckoning and invited John Coonrod to assist as they had both grappled with this inner work together a few years earlier. John came to Dhaka and convened a discussion of the unspoken beliefs men held about women. Fifteen men gathered in the conference room at the office, and for Badiul, this was one of the most important meetings he had ever organized. Even though these were all good men, kind and well educated, old mindsets about women were stitched into the fabric of Bangladeshi culture and their impact should not be underestimated as they resided out of view. Badiul knew platitudes and reasoning would not be enough to shift outdated and harmful notions about women. They needed to be excavated from the hearts of his team so they could be examined and transformed.

At the start of the meeting, the men did not readily accept they might hold "backward" opinions about women, but Badiul expected this—after all, he had resisted the same notion about himself a few years earlier. These views were very, very hard for anyone to admit to. To achieve the transformation, Badiul knew it was vital that the "container" for the conversation be one of safety, vulnerability, and respect; he did not want his team to feel so ashamed that they stopped engaging in the inquiry, or be so full of bravado and denial that the discussion would be useless. He and John thus set the tone by sharing their own journey in a way that was immensely personal and courageous. In the space of such honest reflection, the group began to open up.

It started timidly, with men disclosing some common and negative sayings about women that they too (even partially) held, like "women are just emotional" and "women are irrational." The discussion gathered steam with comments like "They say A and do B," "They can't manage money," and "They need men to guide them." During the process, there was a profound realization that underneath all the rhetoric of empowerment, the men mostly regarded women as weak, pitiable, and helpless. There was a long, uncomfortable pause as John wrote everything on a flip chart which filled multiple pages. After some more time in silence and with great courage, the group opened up to more sinister beliefs, including "a woman is like a drum; more you beat her, the better she sounds." With this stated out loud, they looked at each other in the room. *Do we really think this? Is this what we believe when all is said and done?*

Once everything was out in the open, and received without judgement by Badiul and John, the second step was to examine whether these beliefs were actually true. They analyzed them and concluded the opposite was the case. John and Badiul then discussed the paradigm of patriarchy that had passed these same thoughts and beliefs down through the generations, and then the men explored together what the cost of these beliefs was for them, women, and the country. In this rich and courageous space, deep wisdom was unearthed. Some men shared about the fear men had of women, and whether putting women down might come out of that fear of women's power.

At the end of this long and emotional session, Badiul's team dedicated themselves to making sure that "women are the key" was integrated into all The Hunger Project's programs, and they committed to this fiercely and authentically. They became the guardians of this out in the field and calling out comments or behaviors they might have overlooked before became a new standard for them. Profound and life-altering changes had been made. The work was not over—as Badiul knew, this was the work—but the shift that had started with Badiul in New York had rippled outwards.

With this newfound commitment to empowering women, aspects of the Animators Training were tightened, and a rights-based approach to development was added to all the trainings. It was crucial that people understood that empowering women didn't just make social or economic sense. It wasn't just critical for hunger to end. It was also about women becoming fully human in the eyes of their community, having their agency recognized and their rights respected and upheld. Even more important than being a wife or a mother, women were citizens and human beings first.

Out in the field, women animators took the lead in bringing this work into the domestic sphere. Instead of holding larger mixed VCAWs, which was how male volunteers were mobilizing communities, they held smaller and more intimate courtyard sessions. Women flocked to these, eager to understand their situations differently, and discover how to step out of the constraints society had imposed on them. Learning their rights caused the biggest shifts. It was both shocking and liberating for women to know they were citizens. They could choose how to vote. By law, they had the authority to make their own decisions.

These courtyard sessions kindled a fire as women shared what they were discovering with other women. Soon many were attending Animators Training and learning how to run VCAWs themselves, and for Badiul, this was when the movement for women took off.

This was not to say women didn't have their work cut out for them. They absolutely did, and numerous interactions highlighting the precarious situation for women brought this home for Badiul.

On one occasion, he was in a village near Rangpur at the invitation of the animators who were beginning their work there. Many people had not heard of The Hunger Project, so the animators had planned to use Badiul's visit to introduce the concepts. Everywhere there were children, and hovering around the edge of huts were women, sometimes ten or more, curious about what was happening but not engaging themselves in the discussions. This was a region of endemic poverty and deep subjugation of women.

Looking out over the field, Badiul spied a young girl walking back from the water pump. Her head was covered by her veil so only the center of her face showed. She looked like a child, but as she came closer to him, he got a shock. The girl was pregnant.

Badiul knew the reality: a staggering 74 percent of Bangladeshi girls were married before the legal age of eighteen, and early marriage entrenched poverty and powerlessness. Girls were at risk of increased birthing complications, including fistula, obstructed labor, and death, as their young bodies had not yet matured. Those who became pregnant before the age of sixteen were three to four times more likely to die while giving birth than women in their twenties.

In his very gentle way, Badiul approached and started talking to her, as she carried the water back to her hut. Her name was Rahima, and she was thirteen. Until recently, she was at school, enjoying her classes when she could attend, though she missed a lot of days because she had to take care of her younger siblings and help in the field. Then one day nine months earlier, she was married to a thirty-five-year-old man. She had no say in the matter. She was now six months pregnant.

Rahima's story was not an anomaly. In her area, 60 percent of the girls were married before they turned eighteen, and one of the drivers for this was dowry. In many places, dowry was lower for girls who were uneducated and young, which made it a financial decision for parents to marry their daughters so early. Of the girls who did get married, 50 percent became pregnant within that first year. This meant that children were giving birth to children. With girls being fed last and least in the family home, they were also malnourished, in turn giving birth to malnourished babies in what experts call the "cycle of malnutrition."

Badiul confronted this gross injustice every time he was in the field, but there was something about Rahima's smallness and piteous situation that made his blood boil. Rahima's desperate sadness was palpable, and looking around the village, he saw other young girls whose fate would be similar without intervention. Both compassion and anguish were in his eyes.

Not long after meeting Rahima, another interaction solidified the path he was committed to for women's empowerment. Badiul was in a nearby area observing a woman animator deliver her first VCAW to about a dozen women, all sitting on colorful mats and shaded by a large tree. Badiul loved this part of his work, seeing women leaders who were now proud and confident after a lifetime of subjugation and belittlement. He watched as the animator helped other women understand the role they had to keep their families clean, safe, and fed.

In the distance there was a disturbance—the loud voice of a man calling out and his words were jeering and mocking, directed toward the women. He shouted that women could never be anything other than what they were, domestic and sexual servants to men. As his obscenities got louder and more vulgar, Badiul took off, his stride lengthening and quickening as others followed in his wake. He reached the man who was standing outside his hut with his wife behind him.

The man pointed to his wife with a grin on his face and shouted down to Badiul and all the other people who had gathered. "I can do what I want to her." Waving his arm to include all the other men there, he continued, "We can do what we want. There is nothing you can do to stop us." His wife cowered nearby.

Badiul stood there, furious. He wanted to chastise the man and speak to him at his level. But he also knew that this was a teaching moment. Laid bare were attitudes that were prevalent in the community. Attitudes he was committed to changing. Yet it hit him like a gut punch, this depth of diminishment that women were held in by men. He knew he wouldn't change this man with a single conversation, so he spoke more to the audience, especially the women gathered who were now listening intently. He told the man. "This is your wife. Your partner. You do not own her. You cannot do whatever you like to her."

The man just laughed, but Badiul continued. "Do you realize all she does, from giving you children, to looking after them, feeding them, all the household and laboring chores, as well as catering to you and all the needs of members of your family?"

Badiul turned to speak to the crowd. "This is why Bangladesh cannot move out of hunger. As long as women are mistreated, we will not have a better country. It is necessary for women to have a voice and respect. They must be educated. They must get the food and nutrients they need."

"We wonder why our country is so poor. This is why. In countries that have gotten rid of this type of poverty, women are educated, and her children are well nourished and have opportunities. She can make her own decisions. Countries that have given women a voice and empowered them, prosper. Bangladesh will always remain poor if we treat women like this man treats his wife."

He then turned to speak directly to the women who had drifted out from their huts to see what was going on. He told them, "The day will come when you can move freely, where you will be respected and able to contribute to the whole community. A civilized society does not mistreat its women and children. It does not. This is our biggest shame as a nation, and one all of you can change. When you do, you will have healthy children, more income, and life will be better for everyone."

People listened intently. They could see that he meant it, and it came from a place of deep truth and empathy. Badiul was one of them, raised in a village—and a man—so to hear him talking about what was no longer acceptable had an impact.

Badiul left that man and his wife and went back to the gathering place. He sat in the circle and spoke with deep respect to the women attending their first VCAW. Badiul acknowledged their many challenges, but focused on the power they did have. He encouraged them to take action together. When he left, they committed to work closely with the woman animator to lead the change in their village.

Encounters like this and the one with Rahima could have closed his heart as a protective mechanism, but instead they fueled the flame that was lit within him. When asked about this, he replied, "When the day comes that I am not moved, not saddened, not angered by the toll the poorest keep paying for the hunger and poverty in Bangladesh, then that is the day I will step down. I never want anyone to be considered just another statistic. Each person matters—and each person is also the key to the end of their own hunger." On another occasion, he declared his commitment before a global audience, "I do not want to die until hunger ends in my country."

Badiul's greatest influence was always his beloved mother Anjumennessa from whom he learned just how capable women were, and the obstacles they faced in trying to improve their lives. He knew that had she been given access to education instead of being married as a child, she would have achieved great things. Although he was busy traversing the country, he always made time for her, calling when he could and visiting a few times a year. Each of these visits filled his cup—he never lost sight of how his life and the impact he was making would not have been possible without her belief in him.

So it was worrying for him to receive a call while he and Tazima were in Germany for some meetings, that his mother, who had a severe case of osteoporosis, had fallen from her bed and broken her back. Relatives thought she was sick and were giving her liquids typical of a "sick person's diet," and this caused her to deteriorate. In response to the decline of her health, their son Mahfuz brought her to Dhaka. By this time, Anjumennessa had fallen into a semi coma only to sink into a full coma when the senior doctor in the hospital prescribed regular food rather than tubal feeding.

Badiul and Tazima reached her bedside in a state of deep concern in the evening. Tazima's brother, who was a doctor, had come from Saudi Arabia to be with them at the hospital. He was shocked at her condition and arranged with the hospital physicians to put her on tubal feeding, however this intervention was too late. Anjumennessa died the next morning, perhaps waiting until Badiul and Tazima were able to get there.

Her death was a huge blow to Badiul and created a despondency and malaise that took many months to recover from. Although he soon returned to his duties, he was devastated, and this grief was compounded by the poor state of health care people received in his country. It only inflamed his desire to do more for women and strengthened his refusal to give up.

While progress was being made in the villages, and more women were attending the Animators Training as a result, Badiul was still concerned about how little the women participated once they were there.

He spoke about this to Andrew Davies, who was still supporting Badiul in leading Animators Trainings, and Andrew suggested involving a woman in the training process who was experienced in creating spaces of transformation. He recommended Deborah Protter, who at that time was leading leadership programs in the UK and was also a passionate investor in THP's work. She happily agreed to lend her expertise pro bono, and soon found herself in

Dhaka for the first time. Also playing a critical role at this time was Elisabeth Roelvink, a Dutch national, who spent a year in Bangladesh volunteering for THP, and who learned Bangla so she could communicate and work with rural women.

Deborah and Elisabeth believed an intervention to support women's full participation was needed and recommended to Badiul that a woman's only Animators Training be held. There was some resistance to this idea internally, as it hadn't been done before, and the logistics were not going to be easy. But Badiul was on board. He'd seen the value in the female only VCAWs that were pioneered earlier, and he was curious to see how this would work. So, in 2001, the first women's Animators Training was held with Deborah and a trainer she had worked with before, Felicity McRobb, leading, and Tazima, Jolly, and Elisabeth supporting.

It was agreed that this training for women would happen at the same time as a standard one led by Badiul, both occurring in different rooms of the same building. For the first two days of the training, they would keep the cohorts separate, except for lunch and tea breaks, but on the third day, the women would join the men's training to deliver the VCAW to them. The fourth day would again be separate sessions for men and women.

Thirty women came from all over Bangladesh to participate, saving up money to come, getting permission from their husbands, and ensuring their household duties would be managed in their absence. Badiul was sharply aware of what a big deal it was for them to attend. The substance of the Animators Training for women was the same as the standard training, in that the same manual was used, but it differed remarkably in other ways. What made the women's training so remarkable were the quality of sharing, and the stories women told, as many were heart-rending and would never have been shared in a mixed group. A lot of time early in the training was given to building relationships between Deborah and Felicity and the other women. There was no rushing of the timeline or elevation of the manual over what was happening in the room. Because what was happening was uniquely feminine, thick with women's stories, tears, and shared pain. Many women had had terrible things done to them: sexual violence, being married as a child, being born a girl into a family that wished they had been born a boy. Being together as women to have their experiences and feelings validated, and to know deep in their beings that their work as animators would help prevent this for other women, had many, many layers to it.

This training also highlighted the very different experiences women and men have in how they each moved and lived in the world. At a typical Animators Training, it was obvious that men were used to standing up and claiming space. They expected to belong and be heard. They believed that what they had to say was important and warranted attention. Their attitude to the training was more linear—*this is what I need to do, and I'll go through this step and that step and come out the other side an animator.* It was expected.

Women, on the other hand had layers of conditioning and lived experiences that told them they did not belong, and it was risky to speak up. The deep and honoring space of the women's only Animators Training gave them the taste of being heard and knowing that who they were and what they had to say mattered. All this came together on the third day when the women walked in to lead the VCAW for the men, and for Badiul, it was spectacular. The transformation of the women was remarkable. They led with a boldness, clarity, and vivacity that inspired deep engagement, respect, and applause. Badiul could tell that the men were blown away. Their preconceived ideas about women's leadership and their inability to make an impact dissipated. And for the women themselves, they owned their power and their leadership. There was no going back for anyone after that.

After that training, both Deborah and Badiul felt her job was done. A milestone had been reached and now it was up to the local team to work through what the new frontier could look like. At first, Badiul and the other trainers tried to integrate the lessons learned and adapt how Animators Trainings were conducted to be more inclusive, but even with these efforts, the special needs and issues women faced were not getting addressed. The reality of speaking in front of the men in the training was a big obstacle that even the cajoling and respectful support of Badiul and the other trainers could not overcome. The suffering women endured, and their specific challenges could not be covered in the necessary depth during a single Animators Training. It became clear that adaptation wasn't what was required. A new leadership approach was called for, one that was designed and based around the women themselves, and what they needed to succeed as animators and leaders. A retrofit would not do the job and indeed would miss the opportunity this new idea offered.

The female only VCAWs and the first Animators Training for women only proved that women only spaces were beneficial in attracting and mobilizing rural women who would otherwise miss out on this knowledge, and the spread of courtyard meetings demonstrated the demand was there. Badiul, Jolly, and the head of the training team, Jamirul Islam, sat down to think through how to leverage this. Using experiences gained from the female only VCAWs and Animators Training, and through holding in-depth consultations with women leaders in the field, they developed the plan of creating a training and mobilization structure for women.

To get it right, Badiul reached out to Shaheen Rahman, a supporter who was also a gender expert consultant, to help them design how this new program could work. Badiul's only stipulation was that the Animators Training be a prerequisite, as he believed it was important that women already understood the principles of mobilizing and how to run a VCAW. Rahman agreed and put together the outline for a three-day residential program—the Women's Foundation Course (WFC)—to activate and support women's leadership. The program's objective was to "mobilize, empower, and inspire the women of Bangladesh by building their capacity and developing their leadership skills to powerfully confront the issue of gender inequality and thereby create a hunger free, self-reliant Bangladesh."

The Women's Foundation Course had at its heart the recognition that the marginalization of women was structural to Bangladesh society. It didn't skip over the unique challenges and difficulties women faced, from harassment, to restricted movement, to dowry torture, and more. The program did not dilute the institutional and cultural barriers against women, and participants would spend time analyzing the situation of women in Bangladesh. It addressed topics such as what gender is; the role of women in families and society; patriarchy and women's rights; and development initiatives.

This was all groundbreaking stuff in the context of rural Bangladesh, and some of the team, including volunteer animators, wondered how it might be received there. Would the Women's Foundation Course upset the men too much? Would there be a backlash? Maybe it should be softened somewhat to prevent raising any ire. This questioning made sense: the many unlawful activities against women were often unimpeded and unprosecuted. Would this program make women an even bigger target?

In considering this, the team believed the program must be as potent as it could be, and they decided not to dilute its message and impact. Women lived and worked in an already unimaginably restrictive and punitive context, and anything less than a full accounting of this would have done everyone a disservice. Badiul was clear that radicalizing women with information, context, and tools for resistance was part of what was needed to confront and transform the situation they faced.

The first WFC was held in Dhaka in 2006, and Tuhin Afsari, Shashanka, and Shukomoy, under the leadership of Jamir and Jolly, were instrumental in its successful roll out. Women came from all over the country to participate, with every district in the nation represented. Mr. Rahman led the first training and the two subsequent ones, using these to train Badiul, Jamir, and other trainers in how to lead the training.

The participants' experience in the Women's Foundation Course had many similarities to the women only Animators Training, but they were further amplified as women stayed overnight together. An important part of the training's success were the profound and intimate opportunities for sharing. Woman after woman stood and divulged her life's story, telling of the trials and suffering they had endured, and each woman's story was received with a depth of listening and resonance that was deeply healing. There was a lot of crying and sobbing since it was the first time women had a space that was just for them. Their lived experience and the enormity of the task ahead to end the subjugation of women finally had room to be felt, seen, and heard. Every woman got the message that they were a powerhouse. The crying was cathartic and enriched their deep engagement with the course material.

Focusing on gender roles provided one of the earliest breakthroughs. When women met in small groups to describe the different tasks women and men did on a typical day in a rural family's life, the inequity was laid out and it was shocking.

WOMEN	MEN
Many tasks	Few tasks
No rest	Many naps
More working hours in a day	Less working hours in a day
Less important (valued) work	More important (valued) work
More household work	More income-generating work
Less time for recreation	More time for recreation

In analyzing the value placed on the different tasks men and women did, and the amount of time dedicated to each, women could view their lives in the context of a larger picture of structural imbalance. It became clear to them that although they worked longer and completed more tasks, their tasks were not seen as having value, and the women received little to no compensation for their work. In the discussions that followed, women shared their new realizations: "Women in Bangladesh are the first to rise and the last to bed…there is no rest in a day." "Women are treated like unpaid servants, while men who do the same work in restaurants or hotels are paid." "Women are responsible for caring for three generations—their parents, themselves, their husbands, and their children and yet this is considered nothing."

Throughout the training, women also confronted how they might also perpetuate these very structures of inequality, through choices they made in elevating their son's education over their daughter's, whether they accepted dowry, or how they might treat their own daughters-in-law.

One unplanned element that arose, which became part of every WFC and conference, thereafter, was dancing. The lack of freedom for women to express themselves included the freedom to dance and sing. At the end of the first day of the training, women started singing and clapping to popular songs, while other women began dancing and swirling around. Tears of joy and laughter intermingled with the voices. The freedom they felt to just dance and sing had long been denied them. Doing so together felt both radical and healing. One young woman came to the course wearing a burqa and was quite subdued, but through the days and evenings of the training, she became the dancing queen.

With the success of the first Women's Foundation Course, it became clear that it needed to be more than a three-day residential program; ongoing empowerment and leadership development was vital so that no woman was left isolated and alone. It was also important that the trainings take place where THP was already working, so engaged men could amplify the message of women and girls' inclusion and involvement in ending hunger.

To design what this longer program should entail, Badiul invited eleven village women leaders from the ten regions to meet in Dhaka. Together they created a four-year program of training and empowerment, starting with women getting unleashed as leaders through the Women's Leadership Course, and then ongoing support and training to consolidate their growth and impact. The program would include the role of women in their *union parishad*, how to hold courtyard meetings, how to address dowry and child marriages, and how to establish income generation for women. Women would also learn how to advocate at the policy level and develop the necessary skills to champion their rights and mobilize other women in their community. And so, the Bikoshito Nari Network (Unleashed Women Leaders Network) was born.

The Unleashed Women Leaders Network took off and Badiul was extraordinarily proud of what was being achieved by thousands of women around the country. In Rejbina Akter, a student nurse who was part of the network, he saw a common thread—women redefining leadership on their own terms. Rejbina was passionate about stopping child marriages and told Badiul how she had halted the marriage of a twelve-year-old girl in her area. "I took the initiative, talked to the parents, involved other Unleashed Women volunteers, and convinced the family," she told him. As part of her broader activism, Rejbina went to schools to speak about stopping child marriages, as well as advocating for reproductive hygiene and women's health. She shared that her own previous lack of confidence allowed her to connect with the girls at school. Before becoming an Unleashed Woman Leader, Rejbina did not see herself as a leader or someone who could have these discussions and influence positive outcomes, yet through her participation she imagined and then created a style of leadership that was most suited to her. Badiul observed this in countless other women: they weren't modeling old norms, but rather had the courage to lead in ways that were most authentic to them.

Besides tackling systemic and village level issues, members addressed challenges they had in their daily lives. As Romela from Pabna District shared: "After being trained as an Unleashed Woman Leader, I started my own family garden. The food I grow feeds my family, saves us money, and I can even sell what's left over to bring in more income. I want others to have what I've now got, so I've started a savings group for women in my village." For Akhi, a young woman from Jessore District, the reason was more poetic: she joined the Unleashed Women's Network because "the darkness that is in my village needs to be lifted."

Anju Anwara Moyna from Tangail took the Women's Leadership Course, and during the COVID-19 pandemic created a Facebook group called *Amra Gopalpurbashi* (We are the Gopalpur residents). She mobilized more than 15,000 people in her area to join The Hunger Project's very successful Coronavirus Resilient Villages (CRV) initiative to prevent and mitigate the spread of the virus. On one of the hundreds of Zoom calls Badiul held during that time to keep his activists connected, Anju told Badiul it was he who made her realize that her life becomes worthwhile when it makes a difference in the lives of others.

The seismic shift Unleashed Women Leaders created in women's lives could not be overestimated. Learning about their rights was a big factor in why it was so impactful. It was common for women not to speak up when their husbands hit them, because they thought it was his right, or to not know they were legally entitled to have their dowry returned to them in the case of divorce. Understanding how the government worked was also incredibly useful. One woman came to Badiul at a large public gathering to share that she now knew which local government member to approach regarding a certain matter, and what to expect from them. The synergy between empowering the woman and holding the local government accountable was very interesting to him.

With the Women's Leadership Course and Unleashed Women's Network empowering women all over the country, Badiul wanted to address the marginalization and deprivation of women that started from their very birth. From the moment a girl drew her first breath, she was viewed as a burden and an expense. In a culture that prayed for sons, having a daughter was not celebrated. She was a problem to be offloaded as soon as possible, often through marrying her off quickly.

Conversations with Badiul's own driver, Sikander Ali, brought this home. Sikander had four daughters and no son, which he bemoaned as he believed there would be no one to take care of him in his old age. As was the norm, he considered his girls a burden and just an expensive problem. Providing a dowry would cost a lot, so he wanted them married young and out of his house. Sikander was not a bad person—he was typical in feeling disadvantaged by his situation. Fortunately, because of his association with Badiul, he came to realize that his girls were not liabilities, but humans to be cherished and celebrated. They were worthy of love, education, and respect.

Not everyone had the opportunity to work so closely with Badiul, and Sikander's original world view was the societal norm that Badiul wanted to address. He wanted to change the national conversation around girls, shifting it from girls as a strain and unwanted encumbrance, to girls as having inherent worth and value for their own sake. He knew this would require a bold approach and came upon the idea to have a national day to honor and celebrate girls. There were national days for so many other things, most not as vital and important as this. Badiul was intrigued about what might happen were the country to have a day to elevate the national conversation for girls, so he set this in motion.

Through his contacts with government officials, he petitioned the minister to declare September 30th as the "National Girl Child Day," and the government readily complied. Badiul was thrilled, and with his team, took the initiative to bring together nearly 200 civil society organizations to form the National Girl Child Advocacy Forum (NGCAF). Right from the beginning, he knew this day was bigger than any one organization —it needed to become as broad and large as possible. The first National Girl Child Day was celebrated with much fanfare on September 30th, 2000. There were rallies held across the country, with animators organizing events, speeches, and games on that day. News articles were published about why girls were a contribution to the family and how their development and investment uplifted all of society. Other organizations and government departments held events, and in schools there were parades and even sporting events created, especially to celebrate girls.

Every year, the activities increased, and its impact did not stop with Bangladesh. Following in the footsteps of Bangladesh, the United Nations declared October 11th as the International Day of Girls to recognize girls as a distinct category of development policy with the message that investing in them gave hope for a better future for humankind. Badiul was humbled by this and saw it as an acknowledgement of the pioneering role he and his team had played toward that goal.

The Unleashed Women Leaders Network activities also positively impacted men. This sentiment from Saiful, who lived in the Cumilla District, was common: "The Quran never said to suppress women. I believe the principles of THP, and the Quran are the same." Recognition of the state of women and its untenability broke through the conditioning of many men. Machmud from Barisal exemplified this: "My wife was imprisoned until the Unleashed Women Leaders Training and now she is free and very active in uplifting other women. My neighbors were against her activities at first, but now they are with us."

Mindsets and beliefs were changing in homes and hearts across the country, and this kept Badiul and his team uplifted and committed to keep going. For every step backwards for women's rights, there were countless inspiring examples of the breakthroughs in leadership and social conditioning the Unleashed Women's movement was activating. One of these was in Khulna, where Badiul met Keya, who was married at twelve and had her first child at fourteen. In her village were a number of Unleashed Women Leaders who went from hut to hut talking to women, including Keya, about their situation and what could be done about it. Keya learned a lot from them and wanted to join them, so, at the age of eighteen, she attended the three-day residential training.

After the training, one of the first things she did was set up a women's self-help group. To start the process, she went door to door to invite women to join; most of whom were like her—nonliterate and married too young. Even though they lived in very poor circumstances, each woman committed to bringing ten to fifteen taka (about twenty cents) every week to pool as a kitty for entrepreneurial endeavors. Within eighteen months, the women had created their own microfinance group savings pool by investing the money they each saved back into the group. Members used this as seed capital to set up small businesses like making the cardboard boxes in which local stores sold their wares. This was something Badiul saw regularly across the country—women leveraging the resources they did have to lift themselves out of poverty.

Keya's next focus was to stamp out child marriage in her village within two years, so no other girl suffered what she did. Badiul knew she would succeed because of her own determination, and because of the support she had from the other Unleashed Women Leaders. Looking into her animated face, he felt immense pride in being her partner. Her leadership was so unexpected given her background, and all the more powerful because of it.

The creation of the Unleashed Women Leaders Network became one of the most powerful interventions that The Hunger Project had implemented to help communities end hunger and poverty. It empowered the leadership of so many women in ways that were beyond Badiul's imagination. It was not uncommon for these leaders to run for office in local government, and some became important activists and office bearers within their political parties. Badiul looked for opportunities to give these women visibility and attention on the national and even global stage; he once took dozens of these empowered women to a global gathering in Bangalore, India where they met Joan Holmes and other women leaders. Badiul called them the "future Prime Ministers of Bangladesh."

Badiul had hoped more than a thousand women would eventually be part of the Unleashed Women Leaders Network over time, but this ambitious goal had already been achieved in its second year with 1,108 women trained from fifteen trainings. By the end of 2023, there had been 259 trainings for women through the program, unleashing more than 10,000 women leaders across every district in the country.[12]

12 Their impact is astonishing and most of it undocumented; courtyard sessions, conversations with families that stopped a child marriage, and other outcomes were not systematically reported back to the Dhaka headquarters, especially in the first decade or so when phones and the internet were not common. In recent years it has been easier to collect data and this snapshot between July 2017 and June 2019 shows the impact: the Unleashed Network collectively stopped 3,521 child marriages, oversaw 3,666 safe maternal deliveries, and ran 17,676 separate campaigns on child marriage, sanitation, nutrition, and dowry. It's a remarkable example of what's possible when women are empowered, and their leadership potential is activated.

CHAPTER NINE

Mobilizing the Leaders of Tomorrow

When Badiul returned home in 1991, the country was bursting at the seams. By the mid-1990s, there were 120 million people living in Bangladesh, with the population growing 2.32 percent each year. There were 24 million people between the ages of fifteen and twenty-four, and another 15 million between the ages of ten and fourteen. For most economists and development workers, the huge numbers of young people were a big problem.

Not for Badiul. He believed this burgeoning demographic was a potential resource for building the nation—an asset, rather than a liability, and he wanted to develop and mobilize that asset to end hunger. Badiul believed this new generation could—and should—play a role in the future of Bangladesh. Excluding them from this opportunity made no sense to him. He believed young people, the future leaders of the nation, should play a role in creating a prosperous, democratic, and peaceful Bangladesh.

This conviction would lead to the creation of the largest volunteer movement of young people in the country, a sweeping national cohort of more than 200,000 taking action to end hunger. Yet when he began, Badiul could not have imagined the scale and impact it would have.

Badiul was always looking out for the next dial to turn to build momentum, and the nation's youth, which made up 20 percent of the country's population, proved to be that. He had always recognized the important role young people played in the country's history, providing critical leadership at every important juncture. Between 1950 and 1952, in response to West Pakistan seeking to impose Urdu as the national language (when most of the population spoke Bangla), it was young people who protested, with some giving their lives.[13] Youths were at the forefront of the six-point movement, which galvanized the people of Bangladesh to protest against the exploitation of the Bengalis by Pakistan. Students, including Badiul himself, again provided the leadership in the 1969 Popular Movement that united the entire nation against injustices of the Pakistani rule, ultimately leading to the war of liberation. And it was the youth of the country who first took up arms against the Pakistani army and hoisted the flag of an independent Bangladesh.

Badiul felt very strongly that the nation's youth were an untapped resource, and he was ready to explore how to ignite their participation to end hunger. Not having lived through war and its traumatic aftermath meant young people were not yet handicapped by the mindset of dependency. They had also not yet gotten used to receiving handouts and becoming dependent on

13 Their efforts are now celebrated globally as the International Mother's Language Day on February 21.

the charity of others. They had not yet become like the proverbial parrot that could not fly.

He knew that by nature, young people are restless, willing to take risks, and blaze new trails. They are idealistic and want their lives to matter and count for something worthwhile. Young people were not yet conditioned by their lived experiences. As people grow older, they become risk averse—with families to support and obligations to meet, these entrenched adult behaviors can be hard to disrupt. However, since youth are not normally burdened by the obligations and stark realities of adulthood, Badiul realized that they can be true volunteers, doing things selflessly for others. He was already seeing this in the many young people attending local VCAWs who really took to the concepts. So it had already been on his mind to focus on ways to unleash the energy and dynamism of young people.

Badiul's thinking complemented the idea of the "Demographic Dividend" which proposed that if most of the population is able to work based on their age, the additional productivity from this group can produce increased benefits of economic growth for the whole country, i.e. the more youth a nation had in its population, the larger the potential windfall. However, the potential to capitalize on the situation, meaning, turn it into a positive economic benefit rather than a drag on resources, was also dependent on the nation's ability to give its young people quality education, good health, proper nutrition, ample opportunities, and a conducive environment for them to succeed. Failing to do this would turn the demographic dividend into a demographic nightmare.

Badiul could see how Bangladesh could take advantage of

its huge number of young people, yet this could only happen if appropriate policies were formulated, and the leadership qualities of young people were developed. Given the vastness of the demographic, Badiul wanted to mobilize young people to prevent them from being infected with the "dependency virus," as their parents and elders had been. The time was right to devise a strategy to include and mobilize young people, and so Youth Ending Hunger (or YEH, as it was called) was launched.[14]

Drawing his team together to design the best approach, the decision was made to focus primarily on students who came from less privileged segments of society, who had exposure to rural village life, and who were primarily born and brought up outside of metropolitan areas. Students at the better off English medium schools and from well-to-do families were not Badiul's priority, even though their education standards and levels of literacy were much higher. Due to the plummeting quality of rural education, the ambitions of the most deprived students had been marginalized and overlooked; when they finished school, they were resigned to low paying jobs, if they could get them. Many of Badiul's generation who did well in jobs and other pursuits had come from villages, but this had changed, primarily because of the deterioration of rural schools. As a result, the only avenue of success for promising rural students was being sent to the city to stay with relatives while they continued their schooling, or for

---

14 This became a full circle moment for The Hunger Project Bangladesh, which had been originally established by a group of students who were members of the global initiative of Youth Ending Hunger. YEH had started in the United States in 1985 and ran for twelve years in more than twenty countries, with an education platform in countries like the U.S. and Japan. Badiul's focus on youth leadership would start the next iteration of YEH, with Bangladesh as its epicenter. Later, as the strategy gained momentum and took off, it would be picked up and spread across Africa.

parents to move the whole family to the city. With most young people living in villages, Badiul wanted to change this.

YEH started with four interrelated objectives, and the aim was to get something going to see what stuck. Badiul was curious about what would work. He had two children in this demographic, but he was the first to admit he didn't know what motivated and intrigued this generation. Badiul began meeting with young people after they had done the VCAW, and this helped him frame the objectives. He also got advice from educators, youth leaders, women leaders, and others.

The first objective was to hone the students' leadership skills. Badiul believed that leadership could not be taught as a theory, but rather it must be learned through practice and action. He envisioned a community of courageous champions whose leadership skills would flourish from taking actions sparked by their vision and commitment. This would require transforming their mindset from not believing they could do things to developing determination and confidence. To achieve this, students would undertake social action projects to learn by doing. They would also show leadership by initiating income-generating activities to create a better life.

With that in mind, Badiul developed a partnership with the Directorate of Youth Development (DYD), which through their nationwide training centers provided skills training to young people for self-employment. Badiul knew that creating employment for the growing population was critical and would require self-employment along with jobs in the private and public sectors. He didn't need to look far afield to find the first cohorts of young people to participate, by going immediately to youth who had done the VCAW and who wanted to expand what they had learned by taking skills training at DYD facilities. DYD trainers were so impressed with the motivated young people Badiul and his team were sending, they asked The Hunger Project to provide VCAWs to all participants in their other training programs.

The second objective was to encourage youth to stay clean, be positive, and do good work. YEH especially emphasized helping them to resist substance abuse and being manipulated and exploited by vested interest groups. In post-independent Bangladesh, many student organizations had devolved into becoming affiliated with political parties, and were often involved in nefarious activities, including hooliganism, toll collection, and violence. Unfortunately, they had become protectors of the interests of political parties instead of supporting the students' best interests, and they used muscle power rather than brains to preserve those interests. Guiding youths to stay away from corruption was key to fulfilling the demographic dividend.

The third objective was to develop students' creative potential to the highest level. Government schools required rote memorization to pass public examinations, which Badiul, ever the educator, believed stifled critical thinking and creative approaches. To redress this, The Hunger Project initiated book reading competitions and study circles, and promoted debates and quizzes to expand the knowledge and critical abilities of young people. There was a science and technology focus, with special Math Olympiads for young students from rural schools. This was recognized with an award from the Bangladesh Math Olympiad Team.

The fourth objective was to create a sense of social responsibility among the youth. This was important to Badiul because Youth Ending Hunger wasn't designed to be a "fast track to success" program. A singular, individual focus on getting ahead would not help uplift the country, and indeed, could set it back. To implement this objective, Badiul looked for a pressing problem that youth could be successfully involved with and found it through public health campaigns that promoted Oral Rehydration Therapy (ORT).

Diarrhea accounted for 20 percent of all deaths of children under five at that time, and it was dehydration, as a result of the diarrhea, which made it so deadly. ORT, a fluid replacement made by adding salt and sugar to water, allows the body to absorb liquid and replace minerals and salts depleted by diarrhea. It was pioneered in Bangladesh by BRAC and could easily and affordably be made at home.

Badiul planned a community campaign, spearheaded by Youth Ending Hunger leaders, to promote ORT usage in villages, and UNICEF wanted to be involved. Rolf Carriere, head of UNICEF in Bangladesh, was familiar with The Hunger Project and occasionally had dinner with Badiul and Tazima. This relationship led to a UNICEF supported partnership for a big initiative called the ORT Declaration. This highlighted Badiul's ability to bring together for a larger purpose people and organizations who often competed with one another. Important national and international leaders attended the launch event, including UNICEF Executive Director, the legendary James Grant, along with many members of parliament and government functionaries, who all signed a pledge to help this campaign. A key to its success was Youth Ending Hunger members, who spread the information in communities across the country that diarrheal death could be prevented by using ORT. They demonstrated how to make ORT by mixing molasses with salt in clean boiled water, and they helped families make the formula. The campaign was a huge success, with THP's ORT declaration recognized as a significant contribution to the development of the health sector of Bangladesh over its fifty years in a book called *50 Years of Independence: The Development of Health Sector of Bangladesh,* published by Health Watch, a coalition of health experts of Bangladesh, in 2022.[15]

Young people initially found their way to Youth Ending Hunger through the activities of animators in their villages, and through doing the VCAW. Word then spread in universities and colleges of a movement where young people were welcomed as vital and important contributors, instead of being looked down upon or ignored, and more youth flocked to this invitation to make a difference.

As the demand for Youth Ending Hunger increased, Badiul needed to figure out a more systematic way to empower them. He believed the Animators Training wasn't suitable for widespread youth mobilizing, as the younger cohort didn't have the same bleak mindsets to break through. A shorter, rural-based training was

15 A by-product of Badiul's relationship with Rolf was the creation of a specialized nutrition program in Bangladesh. For some time, UNICEF had been trying to convince the Bangladesh government to adopt this, but the Finance Minister, Saifur Rahman, was not interested in funding it. Rolf turned to Badiul for help, and so Badiul, with his friend Abdur Rab Chowdhury MP, convinced the finance minister to start the Bangladesh Integrated Nutrition Programme (BINP), which was the first large-scale government intervention in nutrition. Badiul was deeply gratified by this because he knew that the lack of micronutrients and correct nutrition—even if calorie intake was sufficient, represented a hidden hunger, and caused stunting, lack of brain development, and even death, especially of children. This success was followed a few years later by the National Nutrition Programme (NNP), with Badiul thus playing a behind-the-scenes role in the birth of a large and successful public nutrition program in Bangladesh.

needed where youth could discuss social issues impacting their communities and explore both individual and collective ways to address them. Badiul wanted to unleash their spirit and instill in them the confidence and willingness to reach their potential. He believed that each young person, with the right support and mindset, could deepen their sense of social responsibility.

After consultation with his team, education specialists, and young people themselves, the Youth Leaders Training (YLT) was created as the next step for youth after doing the VCAW. A key principle of the YLT was the idea of youth paying back in some small way what had been gifted to them by society—be it the health clinic where they were born, the schools and trained teachers that educated them, or the national autonomy they now lived in. Honoring this created a framework for them to invest their time and energy to improve their society and make it better. Within this context, even the poorest person could contribute in some way.

The first Youth Leaders Training course was held in 1995 in Dhaka, with sixty young people (both women and men aged sixteen to twenty-five) attending. Badiul loved the energy and enthusiasm YEH members brought to the concepts. They were on fire to contribute to their village and had less resistance to ideas, such as self-reliance and empowering women that many adults initially had when doing the Animators Training. When asked afterwards what the students had enjoyed most, the overwhelming response was spending time together with other young people, learning from one another, and being able to discuss social issues openly and think critically about solutions. Badiul was energized by the response, and by the curiosity and action the course unleashed in the "youngsters," as he affectionately called them.

He genuinely believed in the power of young people and was committed to supporting them however he could in their efforts to make their mark on the country.

Badiul really came alive surrounded by people a fraction of his age—their unbridled sense of possibility and their "can-do" attitude always lifted his spirits. As a professor, he had always enjoyed teaching young open minds. Yet what he found through leading the YLT course was how much he was learning from them.

After the first Youth Leaders Foundation Course was held, demand took off, and finding young people was not a problem. Youth leaders receiving the training earned a reputation for their efforts and were provided opportunities for individual growth and accomplishment that were immensely appealing. Most importantly, they gained the feeling of being part of something bigger and making a difference with their lives. Even before smart phones, they shared freely and enthusiastically with their friends and other students.

However, keeping up with the increasing demand for youth trainings was not something The Hunger Project could afford to do, and so again Badiul needed to think outside the box for ways to make it happen. Focusing on increasing social capital provided a path forward. He knew that strengthening multi-generational connections within a community would have deep and lasting benefits, so he decided to invite active members of Youth Ending Hunger to become trainers and lead the program themselves. In some ways, this was a risky move, especially in a culture that revered the wisdom of older people and diminished that of youths, but Badiul knew it was essential to directly train the leadership ability of future leaders. This became a very popular invitation, with hundreds of young people going through additional training to be able to lead the Youth Leaders Foundation Courses.

After the first few YLT courses were delivered, additional training was then offered on governance matters and active citizenry, which was developed jointly with the British Council. These programs were eagerly taken up by youth wanting to develop themselves further, for personal reasons as well as communal ones. Any opportunity to grow and develop skills outside the schooling or university structures was appealing.

From schools, to universities, across villages—all over, young people got activated. They were critical for running campaigns against many social ills. One of their earliest successes was mobilizing to dispose of plastic bags thoughtfully. Plastic was ubiquitous and often thrown away without regard. An unintended consequence was clogging the water drains, which led to horrific flash flooding in the monsoon period. People were drowning and huts were being washed away because the drains designed to disperse the water were not able to. Youth Ending Hunger leaders across the country created a campaign to collect the plastic from clogged drains and educate their community about how to safely dispose of it in the future.

Activities sprung up around the country, initiated by young people's own priorities, and these included informal literacy camps for those unable to attend school. One afternoon, when Badiul was meeting with some animators in Khulna, he saw a group of primary school students sitting together under a tin roof. Curious about this as it was after school hours when most children were playing or helping with chores, Badiul wandered over and met three high school students who were in Youth Ending Hunger. Chitra, Santi, and Julie studied at the local high school, and they ran a remedial class for students who had fallen behind in their studies and were in real danger of dropping out of school. Most afternoons after school, they taught in this makeshift classroom without pay, and without extra credit from their school. Their reasons were simple. As they told Badiul: "We are committed to having every young person educated in our village, and this is our contribution to making that happen."

Another of the thousands of youth leaders YEH unleashed was Baharuddin Raihan, a young man who was electrocuted when he was eleven, losing both his hands. As a student, he took the VCAW and the Youth Leadership Training and became the coordinator of the Cox's Bazar district group for Youth Ending Hunger. This was no mean feat, as Raihan completed high school then university level education by writing with his mouth. His social action project involved providing educational resources and support to disadvantaged children, bridging the gap between rich and poor. As an activist, he even went to jail to protect the rights of expression and Badiul admired him immensely, telling him that with his leadership, Bangladesh will prosper. This became part of Raihan's own belief system, and further inspired his growth and leadership.

Initiatives that Youth Ending Hunger members took on included stopping girls from dropping out of school due to early marriage pressures. YEH members would identify who was not attending school and visit them to encourage them to come back. In her work as a volunteer, Tazima had met Rumi, a fourteen-year-old girl from a struggling family in Jhalakhati, Barisal, and she shared with Badiul her remarkable tale. Rumi was pulled out of school when her family could not pay the school fees, and then her parents decided to get her married because if Rumi was not at school studying, she would become a target for male harassment; her parents believing marriage was the only option to keep her safe. Rumi felt like her life had stopped. "My dreams were shattered when I was taken out of school. I wasn't ready to become a wife or mother."

Two of Rumi's friends were part of Youth Ending Hunger, and they visited her to find out why she had stopped coming to classes. In hearing that a time and date had been set for her marriage, the girls swung into action, assembling other YEH members to discuss what to do. They agreed a two-part approach was needed. First, they must appeal to the parents, and then the school. They went to Rumi's house to talk with the parents, letting them know that Rumi had her whole life ahead of her, and it was not right—nor legal—to marry her as a child. They said that marriage would destroy her life.

Next, the YEH members spoke to the headmistress of Rumi's school and asked if the school would cover the cost of Rumi's tuition, to which she agreed. The teacher and students then visited Rumi's home and met with the parents, with the teacher assuring them that the school would cover the cost of Rumi's education. On this basis, the parents agreed to stop the marriage preparations and return Rumi to school. This victory was one of many Youth Ending Hunger students had as they implemented campaigns across the country. With the support of their training and the adult animators in their area, they were able to leverage their enthusiasm with strategies to achieve their goals. Even when their actions were not successful—for every one girl saved from early marriage there was another one for whom YEH couldn't budge her parents from their decision to go ahead—they continued to step out in their society to help improve things for other people.

Boys, too learned to take action to improve conditions for girls. Badiul heard Tuhin Reza at a regional Youth Ending Hunger conference share about the activities of his YEH group to stop the harassment of female students. Tuhin and his friends took a coordinated approach, speaking to the men on the street who were harassing girls, and to boys at school before such behavior began. He'd also gone to the police station with some female students to get support for them. Tuhin was seeing the results of this approach, noting that while harassment was prevalent when they started, it was less visible now. He told Badiul how great it felt to be a member of the group. As he said: "We don't have any political motivation, or affiliation—we are united irrespective of our differences in political opinion. We feel part of a larger movement for Bangladesh."

As Youth Ending Hunger and the Youth Leaders Training course took off, Badiul was keen to extend the initial YLT by adding workshops that developed them personally. This was something members themselves really wanted—they were hungry to improve and develop, as well as ambitious to grow in their own lives. Subjects included building leadership that inspired confidence and trust; developing networking where they could participate in opportunities to meet and learn from other youth, entrepreneurs, and influential people; skill development, including facilitation, public speaking, project management, and self-awareness; and livelihood and economic trainings to help them build up financial competency. These trainings for developing soft skills were very attractive to young people and were a key part of YEH's rapid growth.

Empowering leadership was the heart and soul of Youth

Ending Hunger, and Badiul and his team designed it so that YEH members gathered monthly in chapters spread across the nation, each driven by a philosophy of local leadership. He traveled across the country to consolidate this by inspiring and recruiting young leaders—his dedication and charisma drawing passionate volunteers to the cause.

As it grew, the National Coordination Committee, a democratically elected body made up of Youth Ending Hunger activists and leaders, representing every region, was formed. Badiul guided the implementation of a framework where each chapter was led by a committed team of volunteers, with a National Coordinator at the helm. This system was entirely voluntary and built upon the democratic principles that Badiul passionately championed.

Youth ownership of the movement was not theoretical. Empowered by the new coordination structure and wanting to increase connections among members, YEH volunteer leaders devised a series of regional conferences to provide a youth led space for them to set their priorities, which they organized and funded themselves. Attending the first conference, Badiul watched with pride as hundreds of young people entered in groups, chatting, and sharing as they took their seats. He was exuberantly informed by the youth coordinators that the conference had been organized and funded by themselves, through holding market stalls and fundraising. Each attendee had also paid their own way to be part of it.

With his enthusiastic support, to date youth have hosted seventeen National Youth Conferences and ten Regional Conferences, each one drawing at least one thousand enthusiastic young participants. Badiul is always the honored guest, witnessing, and amplifying the remarkable energy and commitment of these young leaders. The conferences serve as platforms for young people to exchange ideas, learn from each other, and build a cohesive community of empowered leaders. Driven by the youth themselves, they foster a sense of ownership and accountability—they had the vision for it, and they made it happen. This self-sufficiency was a cornerstone of Badiul's philosophy, emphasizing the importance of grassroots leadership and initiative.

A terrorist attack in the heart of Dhaka, which killed twenty-two people, including eighteen foreigners and two police officers, brought youth into devastating focus for Badiul. Bangladesh, while a religious country, was always secular and democratic, with Muslims, Christians, and Hindus living peacefully side by side for the most part. But this noticeably changed as radical fundamentalism—something that hit the youth the hardest—increased globally. The pursuit of religious-based solutions to many of the world's ills was becoming more common, with young people particularly vulnerable to being pulled onto a radical path.

The urgency of addressing this came home to Badiul in a shocking way when he discovered that two previously active YEH volunteers, Abedatul Fatema (Asa) and her husband Tanvir Kaderi, were among the people behind the terrorist bombing of the Holey Bakery in Dhaka on July 1, 2016.

Tanvir and Asa had met as YEH volunteers, both taking the Youth Leaders Training course around 2000. They were attracted to YEH because it created a sense of social responsibility and provided a way to do something for society. In those early days, Tanvir was a student at Dhaka College and was a very serious and committed volunteer for Youth Ending Hunger, and Asa was an exceptionally bright student of journalism at Dhaka University who had participated in several YEH programs with Badiul. Like many other YEH volunteers, they moved on after completing their education, and Badiul had no further direct association with them. He had heard that Asa secured a job in an international NGO, where she was leading, among other things, gender training, and he was very happy for her.

According to their son's testimony, Tanvir and Asa were typical middle-class professionals, with a happy family, and looking back after the bombing, Badiul's impressions of them were that they were both clean, committed, and liberal minded individuals. He never saw any sign of radical thinking in them—in fact, in those days, radicalization was not even an issue.

When Badiul read their names in the newspaper in relation to the bombing, he could not believe it. How could two intelligent people with a bright future and two teenage children do such a thing? How could they mastermind the cold-blooded killing of innocent people? It made no sense to him. He needed to understand what happened and so he dug into the literature on radicalization. He learned that broadly speaking, there are two ways people get radicalized. One is what is called the "push factor" and the other is the "pull factor." When angry and alienated people, upset with the state of things, join a radical cause to seek a religious based solution, the push factor is said to have played its role. On the other hand, when a radical brainwashes others to join their cause, the pull factor is said to be at work. Often spouses radicalize each other and their families. Apparently, Tanvir was radicalized first by outsiders, then he radicalized Asa, and both of them radicalized their sons.

Badiul was most concerned that what had happened with

Tanvir and Asa could also happen to others. There were occasional signs of communal tension and violence between different religious communities, and more visible religious observances were also notable through an uptick in women wearing burqas and hijabs. All of this was underpinned by cynical political rhetoric in Bangladesh, but also India and elsewhere, that emphasized religion over secularism. Badiul realized how highly vulnerable Bangladeshi youth were and was determined to do something about it to prevent further radicalization. He consulted with experts across the country and as far away as the Middle East, the United Kingdom, and the United States. Bangladesh was still at a point where fringe ideas were not yet mainstream, and Badiul wanted to place his thumb on the scale to tip it toward pluralism and secularism.

In response, he and his colleagues developed the BRAVE (Building Resilience Against Violent Extremism) program to prevent young people from drifting onto the radical path, and THP received funding from the German Embassy to run it for three years. The purpose was to foment a social movement against violent extremism and intolerance, and it involved thousands of youths from all segments of society. The BRAVE initiative mobilized youth and community elders to prevent radicalization and promote tolerance and social cohesion by addressing three main drivers of radicalism: identity-based prejudices, especially those between Hindu and Muslim communities; settling opposing views, be they political or confrontations between neighbors; and providing new ways for young people to be involved in the community that engaged and fulfilled their self-worth. "Peace Ambassadors" were also created, who advocated for religious freedom and peacebuilding efforts in many subdistricts. Badiul also developed the Social Harmony Workshop to promote tolerance, religious harmony, and social cohesion. From this, activities for preventing political, religious, and ethnic violence arose with young people playing a key role.

Youth Ending Hunger volunteers made a courageous and acutely important contribution to the country during the COVID-19 pandemic, when Bangladesh, like the rest of the world, was in a state of crisis, faced with death and the collapse of economies and supply chains. Badiul stepped forward at the very beginning of the pandemic to design a highly innovative approach based on the World Health Organization's (WHO) risk communication and community engagement guidelines. Using YEH volunteers as his key partners, 2.5 million people from 1,200 villages across Bangladesh were mobilized by YEH under the banner of Coronavirus Resilient Villages (CRV). The purpose was not only to help support community members during the pandemic but also to help prevent the spread of infection. The essential idea was that every person—including the most marginalized—must be protected for everyone to be protected. YEH volunteers and Unleashed Women Leaders spearheaded this campaign, which involved creating awareness through house-to-house visits, distribution of food and other essentials, management of COVID-19 patients, and dealing with the gender-based violence and child marriage escalation which were rampant during the pandemic. Defying the risks, these young volunteers went to each household, held courtyard meetings, distributed food and information, got the infected patients professional help, buried the dead, enrolled the ultra-poor into the government's social protection scheme, and many other essential services to keep their communities safe. This was all carefully monitored, allowing Badiul to show that both infection and death rate from Coronavirus were substantially reduced in these areas.

THP's CRV initiative was highly acclaimed across Bangladesh. Dr. Mushtuq Husain, an Adviser to the government's IEDCR (Institute of Epidemiology, Disease Control, and Research), wrote to Badiul: "CRV is a model not only for our villages, it may be replicated in our cities and towns." This grassroots campaign was also recognized for how it helped communities become more resilient against other challenges they face, including climate vulnerabilities.

After attending an online meeting, where YEH volunteers shared their activities with experts, Dr. Taufique Joarder, a WHO consultant and professor at Singapore National University, declared: "I am elated, inspired and energized by today's discussion. This is an extraordinary, wonderful, and unique initiative undertaken during a pandemic. You must document it. I have only one request: you must not deprive the world of its knowledge." Badiul shared all this with the YEH network, making sure they knew how their actions and courage were recognized globally. He was deeply moved by what had been achieved. Again, it was the nation's youth who had stepped forward and led the way during a time of crisis, death, and despair.

Badiul's belief about the power of youth has been soundly validated. Youth Ending Hunger has contributed substantially towards ending hunger, through their local campaigns and activism, and in spreading the messages of self-reliance—their use of social media means they continue to find new ways to engage people for transformative change. But the impact is much more lasting than this. Young people are on the forefront again in Bangladesh, this time in rising up against the autocratic and corrupt stranglehold the ruling party has had on the nation. As was true when Badiul was young, students are leading the charge and have taken to the streets, calling for the government to be accountable and abide by the rule of law. Now, as this chapter is being written, hundreds of student protesters have been murdered, with thousands more rounded up and detained. They have faced intense state violence and intimidation, but still they gathered to demand change. Through their dogged and fearless activism, the autocratic dictator Sheikh Hasina has been deposed, and the students' demands for an Interim Government have been agreed to. Badiul was not surprised to learn that some of the leaders and many of the youth involved in this "Monsoon Revolution" were or had been members of the Youth Ending Hunger.

Youth Ending Hunger continues to grow as each new generation finds the context of empowerment and leadership incredibly rewarding.[16] As members get older and age out of Youth Ending Hunger, many stay in close contact, becoming mentors for new Youth Ending Hunger volunteers. Often, as adults, they become animators, continuing to lead their communities in innovative ways. Through Badiul's efforts and those of his colleagues, the nation's *demographic dividend* has, at least in part, been achieved.

16 By the end of 2023, the YEH network had 30,755 active members across 1,371 units nationwide, with countless others embodying the movement's principles informally. Cumulatively, more than 200,000 young people have been formally trained as leaders since 1995.

CHAPTER TEN

Taking on the Big Guns

After the deadly Bhola cyclone of 1970 and the war of liberation in 1971, reliance on overseas aid had been necessary for Bangladesh, yet it had become an addictive source of capital and investment long after the acute crises had ended. As money came in from abroad, Badiul observed that policy decisions were made through cronyism, kickbacks, and corruption. Money was mismanaged and misused, and policies that were good for the country went out of favor. Successive governments did little to strengthen accountability within the institutions responsible for managing the funds. A devastating consequence was that the kind of investments governments should have made in health, education, and infrastructure, were not made, and the funds were siphoned off instead.

Since independence, corruption had become endemic, emboldened by people entering politics purely for personal gain. Badiul despaired at how government had turned into a business, with Bangladesh becoming the "best democracy money could buy." The politicization of business, and the "businessization" of politics caused a serious deterioration in the quality of politics and governance. As a result, both major parties— Awami League and Bangladesh Nationalist Party (BNP)—had become dens of corruption, and almost all these corruptive deeds, big and small, were carried out under the patronage of political parties in power. Consequently, from 2001 to 2005, Bangladesh won the dubious distinction of being named the number one corrupt country in the world, as determined by Transparency International's Corruption Perception Index (and has hovered in the top 25 percent of corrupt countries since then).

It was, of course, the poor who paid the price for this deterioration. As hunger and poverty were societal issues, Badiul knew they must be addressed at the institutional and policy level, as well as at the community level by people in their villages and neighborhoods. Badiul found it infuriating and unjust that the share of national resources and the services people needed and deserved to have from the government were not flowing to them. The disabling environment fostered by the government was present in every aspect of life. Medical centers were not adequately staffed or funded. Across the country, sick people, ground down by poverty and malnutrition, went to health centers that had no doctors, or the medicines were out of stock. Parents would send their children to school only to find overcrowded classrooms, and no teacher present. Sometimes "teachers" were relatives and cronies of politicians, who were not trained to teach at all, but were given paid postings at schools. With the central government responsible for teacher performance, there was no local entity to hold them to account.

It was like this across the whole country. Roads were made without the right amount of road base—the money allocated for that stolen. Building projects either stopped or were built with low-quality materials. Necessary public works programs were not undertaken. Money allocated from the central government didn't make it to the villages— it was transferred to private bank accounts before it could be used for the purposes it was given. Kleptocracy was everywhere.

In addition, since 1971, Bangladesh had experienced immense political insecurity, including two periods of one-party rule; two military coups; and the assassinations of two heads of state. Believing it was vital that government be called upon to lead the country in a transparent and stable way, Badiul pondered the best way to meaningfully contribute to this. He decided that the lower tiers of government would be a good place to start, as it was the government closest to the people which had the most day-to-day interactions with them at the village level.

He began by inviting local government leaders to participate in the Animators Training, as they had access to some resources and, should they choose, an ability to mobilize more resources for their constituents in the villages. The training did activate their commitment, and there was a noticeable improvement in the progress villagers made in partnership with these local government animators. Badiul was pleased, but as this was happening in an *ad hoc* way, he reached out to the Ministry of Local Government to create a partnership with them to train the faculty and staff of three government run, rural development and training institutions. Shorter versions of the Animators Training (called "Catalyzing Self-Reliance") were also included in the training of government officials and through these efforts, lots of young, new recruits were trained. In total, nearly two dozen batches of government officials and local government leaders were trained in THP's methodology, where they too had the opportunity to imagine a country that worked for everyone. They wanted to play a role in making this a reality.

One of the outcomes was more transparency with how money was spent at the local level. With Badiul's encouragement, these local government animators arranged open budget meetings to demonstrate fiscal candidness and clarity, and many distinguished citizens participated in these events. Abul Hossain, a Union Parishad (UP) chairman, held one of the first of these open budget meetings, and nearly two hundred voters crammed into a small hall to listen. As he read out every line item from the local government budget, people paid close attention to what was spent on salaries, road works, etc. Hossain then invited people to ask questions and discuss priorities for spending for the next fiscal year.

Even though the politics of corruption seemed entrenched, it was sessions like this that gave Badiul hope. He always knew that ending hunger couldn't happen by the people's efforts alone—it would take the strengthening and resourcing of local government institutions. Activities like the open budget meetings gave him a taste of what was possible when civil society worked with the people. It was inspiring but still very uncommon and he was astute enough to acknowledge that the inroads he had made were merely a drop of water in a bucket. Transformation of the patronage paradigm, a concept he had introduced in the Animators Training, where people differentiated between being subjects or citizens; an "aid beneficiary" or a change agent, could not happen without addressing the corrosion at the heart of the body politic. Citizens could face their challenges courageously, yet the dysfunctionality of basic governmental functions and systems, and widespread corruption, only reinforced mindsets of feudalism and fatalism that worked against people's own interests.

The weakening of Bangladesh's democratic fabric was deeply troubling to Badiul. As a former student activist for a liberated Bangladesh, it was unacceptable to him that the country had deviated so much from its founding values of democracy and justice—political, economic, and social—which were enshrined in its constitution. He observed with dismay how the erosion of rights and authoritarianism were increasingly taking root, threatening to strangle the aspirations of millions. But rather than resign himself to despair, he resolved to fight for change. Yet he knew this would not be easy, as doing so would involve going against the power structure—the big guns! There was also a risk for him personally, and The Hunger Project, however he knew it must be addressed. He broached tackling these democratic deficits with his THP colleagues, and while they agreed something needed to be done to address the dysfunctions, there was serious hesitation on their parts. Most thought that like other civil society organizations, THP should take the safe course and not rock the boat—THP was already doing good work—why put that in jeopardy? They were also concerned about their own safety and livelihoods—it was no small thing to speak out against the powerful elites.

As Badiul canvassed this new direction more broadly, his many friends and well-wishers cautioned him—they wanted him and his family to be safe and they were not convinced that would be the case. They urged him not to "poke the bear." Badiul's children were also not initially on board. They were worried for their father as they knew from their friends that getting embroiled in Bangladesh's politics of annihilation could be dangerous. However, Tazima was solidly behind him from the beginning, and she smoothed the way for the children and the family's close circle to support him.

Badiul himself, even knowing the danger, ultimately decided to take it on. If he was successful, the rights of others, including his children, would be safeguarded into the future. However, given the risks, Badiul wanted to be strategic and include important public figures to be part of his initiative.

From early on, influential people of Bangladesh had become great supporters of The Hunger Project and of Badiul personally, and through informal discussions, he learned that others were also deeply worried about the effects of political degeneration and corruption on the country. Badiul decided to bring together the people he believed could collectively wield enough influence to steer the government back towards a more transparent democracy. To begin, he called upon the former Cabinet Secretary, Mujibul Huq, and told him that esteemed and irrefutable leaders like him should come together to bring their moral weight to bear and speak up, as the state of the nation was degenerating. Huq agreed to convene *Nagorik Sanghati* (Civic Solidarity), an *ad hoc* group of distinguished citizens Badiul brought together, who issued statements on major issues, and published pieces in the newspapers. However, there was no sustained advocacy or activism, and after a while Badiul felt not enough headway had been made. He wanted to move beyond good people saying nice things. He wanted to do something that would really make a difference.

He shared these thoughts with Professor Muzaffar Ahmad, a

member of the group. Ahmad was a very distinguished economist, intellectual, and activist with a reputation for being the most outspoken and courageous of all civil society leaders. Both he and Badiul wanted to take more concrete action against governance by the "goons," and they were intrigued by a methodology developed by the Public Affairs Center in Bangalore, India, which had collected information about candidates running for office. These candidates filled in a questionnaire about their background that was then collated and made public to help voters make informed decisions at the ballot box. Badiul and Ahmad thought it would be a useful experiment to try something similar in Bangladesh to help clean up the tainted political sphere. As a result, they formed Citizens for Fair Elections (CFE) in November 2002 to promote clean candidates in elections and improve the quality of elected leaders to help the poor succeed. Professor Ahmad was made Chair and Badiul became the Secretary of CFE. As he saw it, Ahmad was the irrefutable national figure, and he was the activist.

With local elections coming up, CFE decided to implement the Bangalore strategy and initiate a clean candidate campaign in Bangladesh. As a preparatory step, Badiul and Ahmad, along with a senior journalist from a major newspaper, visited villages in the Sonargaon sub-district of Dhaka, where they asked people how important the upcoming *Union Parishad* (local government) election was, and what type of person they wanted elected. People uniformly expressed that they didn't want "land grabbers," people who were corrupt, or those known to mistreat women to win. The sentiment was clear—people did not want "bad dudes." They wanted "good guys" in those positions.

While the journalist had privately agreed with Badiul on what

CFE was aiming to achieve, when none of these villagers' opinions were reported in the newspaper, Badiul was disappointed. This was a good story, and it was worth covering! However, the reasons became clear when a prominent journalist Badiul knew well, called to warn him to stop the clean candidate campaign. He asked if Badiul was mad: "What are you doing? If you take information about candidates to the voters, you and your people will be beaten up." Badiul took this in stride. For him, it was an indication that what they were trying to do was right. He knew a shakeup of the system would entail personal and professional risks, and he was prepared for that.[17]

Based on the inputs from the villagers, Badiul and Ahmad developed a questionnaire to distribute to candidates for chairmanship of Union Parishad, the lowest tier of local government in Bangladesh. The questionnaire was very simple. The questions for candidates were:

> Are there any allegations of corruption against you? Yes, or no?
>
> Are there allegations of land grabbing against you? Yes, or no?
>
> Are there allegations against you of violence against women? Yes, or no?
>
> What do you plan to do if elected?
>
> If you don't get elected, will you support and work with the one who got elected?

17 Fortunately, the threats of violence against Badiul at this time did not materialize.

How much money you are going to spend in the election? Where will this money come from?

When the information was collected, CFE put together a comparative statement that made the answers explicit. For example:

Candidate Name:

Corruption? No.

Land grabbing? No answer. And so on.

These comparative statements were printed on big pieces of paper and posted on the walls of tea stalls, shops, and other public places. The statements didn't accuse anybody. The questions and answers were quite mundane. But people could see the candidates' responses, including who had not filled in everything, and who had not provided the correct information. What made this so radical was that the voters knew these candidates either personally or by reputation as they were from that area. So, when wrong answers or no answers were given, people knew. They knew who the land grabbers were. They knew which candidates were accused of violence and mistreating women—who the "bad dudes" were. Being transparent about it broke the mindset of malaise and cynicism. It gave voters agency to question the "business as usual" roll out of patronage politics. They realized there might be other options. Publicly displaying what people knew created a commotion. It created discussions in tea stalls, marketplaces, and wherever people congregated. The information spread like wildfire, gaining the interest of the national media.

"Meet-the-candidate" forums were then arranged so that

voters could directly ask candidates questions. Badiul loved these sessions, as for him they were an example of democracy in action. To create some accountability, candidates signed a written statement agreeing they would abide by all laws and refrain from violence and vote buying, and voters also publicly took an oath to exercise their voting rights judiciously and refrain from casting votes for criminals and corrupt candidates. These were revolutionary initiatives which had never been done before in Bangladesh and it completely changed the dynamics of the election.

The campaign was run across fifty-five Unions, each made up of about twenty thousand people. Running an operation this large required a lot of organizational support, which CFE did not have. The logistics were massive as the population involved was over one million people. Badiul was able to involve animators in this process, as The Hunger Project had thousands of dedicated people who could mobilize others. After the election, the team surveyed voters and found a significant percentage of them had changed their minds about who they voted for. Even if their candidate choice remained unchanged, they said they now knew it was their right to be represented by honest people.

Citizens for Fair Election's focus on clean candidates seemed at first a way to redress the disabling environment that disenfranchised the people, especially the poor, but Badiul soon realized that getting good people elected at the local level was not enough, although it is critically important. He had seen how the system itself didn't allow good candidates to fully express their leadership and do things differently. They were too often rendered impotent, caught up in a morass of failed promises, squandered money, and the venality of the functionaries that held the system in place. They were unable to do what they came to do. Badiul realized it was time to move beyond CFE and make way for an even more robust and courageous group at all levels to agitate for the systemic change that was required.

As a result, SHUJAN: Citizens for Good Governance—or "the Good Guys" as it was called—was created by Badiul and Ahmad on December 21st, 2003, with a mandate to establish democracy and good governance in Bangladesh. Ahmad was again the Chair and Badiul played the (unpaid) Chief Executive role. Many distinguished citizens joined SHUJAN, and to insulate THP from any political risk and fallout, SHUJAN became a separate organization and was not part of THP, though THP became its secretariat. Badiul kept his work in THP and SHUJAN separate, though he viewed both organizations as having intersecting purposes to improve the conditions of the common people.

Encouraged by the voters' positive response to the clean candidate experiment, one of SHUJAN's first victories was in 2005, when it filed a writ before the High Court asking for candidates running for national office to disclose their antecedents (such as educational, professional, and criminal backgrounds), and financial information (such as income and the assets and liabilities of themselves and their dependents). These were to be disclosed in the form of affidavits, which would empower voters with information to make informed decisions at the ballot box. The Court agreed and directed the Election Commission to distribute the disclosed candidate information. It was a big victory for Badiul and SHUJAN, and was not easy to achieve as vested interest groups tried to overturn the High Court judgment by filing a fraudulent appeal.[18] Thankfully, this was unsuccessful, and the Supreme Court directive stood.

This set the stage for one of SHUJAN's biggest legacies. Following the judgment, affidavits on all candidates' backgrounds were collected, and comparative statements were prepared which were made available to voters through printed forms and press conferences. This was a mammoth undertaking, and again, the thousands of volunteers Badiul had mobilized through The Hunger Project provided the arms and legs to implement the initiative. To his immense satisfaction, the use of disclosure became institutionalized, with journalists and citizens routinely using the information that was stored on SHUJAN's robust website to verify candidate's claims.

SHUJAN then cemented its national and international reputation with a victory against voter fraud. Ahead of the scheduled 2006 election, the Election Commission (EC) had prepared a fresh electoral roll with more than 90 million voters' names on it. The authenticity of the electoral roll generated considerable controversy, as there were credible accusations that it was not accurate. Badiul believed this struck at the heart of Bangladesh's democracy: if the voter roll was not legitimate, or was not perceived to be legitimate, then how could any election result be trusted?

SHUJAN took on checking its accuracy, and with the support of the Dutch Embassy and some other organizations, it surveyed a number of *Upazilas* which showed the electoral roll was indeed not correct. SHUJAN then prepared a database of the entire electoral roll, which was a monumental undertaking.

---

18 Justice M A Matin who authored the High Court judgment is now the Vice President of SHUJAN.

The Election Commission refused to give them the information they needed, so SHUJAN went directly to the political parties, which gave them the electoral roll for each constituency on a disk.

With the correct records in hand, Badiul enlisted John Coonrod's help in New York to make a secure database of voter names, using the crosschecked information. John did this and uploaded it onto the SHUJAN website (www.votebd.org), where voters were encouraged to search for their names on the uploaded electoral roll. It was a database of about 80 million names and proved that the formal roll was padded with over 12 million fake voters. This all became an international sensation. Badiul and Ahmad were interviewed by news sources around the world and *Time Magazine* hailed SHUJAN as "democracy activists."

Bringing to light the electoral roll's many inaccuracies caused widespread voter outrage. The opposition parties, led by Awami League, organized street agitations, hartals, and rallies, blaming the ruling BNP for tinkering with the electoral roll. There were also newspaper headlines accusing BNP and its allies of doing this to influence election results. In reality, SHUJAN found the discrepancies had happened largely because of multiple registrations of the same voter in different locations, e.g. a voter could be registered in Dhaka as well as in their village home, which meant they could technically vote more than once, and this was leveraged politically by both parties. SHUJAN's initiative paved the way for voter roll reform that required identification, which led to the Bangladesh Supreme Court directing the Election Commission to prepare a new electoral roll with photographs, something SHUJAN had advocated for many years and had proved its technical feasibility. The new electoral roll was audited by an independent international organization and was found to be very accurate.[19]

Badiul and SHUJAN achieved an additional significant breakthrough when governance reforms they had articulated and championed were written into law. To promote decentralized governance, the Caretaker Government, responding to intense advocacy by SHUJAN, formed a panel of experts with the aim to "Strengthen and Revitalize the Local Government." Badiul was appointed to it, and with his fellow experts, rewrote the local government law, enshrining key requirements for citizen engagement and transparency. These laws contained far-reaching reform ideas, including the preparation of five-year plans, open budget meetings, and bottom-up planning that The Hunger Project had pioneered.

While this was immensely exciting, momentum soon stalled. The Awami League won the December 2008 election in a convincing landslide and, since they promised to institute the sweeping voter and political reforms espoused by SHUJAN, Badiul was initially pleased with their victory. He hoped this would be the moment where Bangladesh could begin to restore impartiality to institutions, adhere to the rule of law, and address

19 The Election Commission was required by law to send enumerators to each household annually to update the electoral roll. Unfortunately, due to the gutting of the funding for public services and the lack of accountability in public institutions, the enumerators do not go to every household, and as a result inaccuracies have crept up again in the electoral roll. For example, the electoral roll with photographs initially had over 1.2 million more women voters than men, but now men outnumber women in the electoral roll—despite that millions of men are working abroad. SHUJAN has flagged this "gender gap" issue in the electoral roll that cannot be accounted for in population analysis.

the dysfunctional governance system. However, this was not to be. Even though the Awami League came to power with an election manifesto titled "A Charter for Change," the change that took place was in the wrong direction. Over time, experienced leaders and government functionaries were moved on and replaced with inept, partisan, and corrupt people to lead major institutions. Local government elections were rigged, and even professional bodies had party leaders and cronies running them. Political repression and human rights violations proliferated, and cronyism, corruption, and the flight of capital accelerated. It was the start of the state capture of all institutions. Things had become so bad that Justice Habibur Rahman, the former Chief Justice and later Chief Advisor of the Caretaker Government, stated in 2011 that "the whole country is in the hands of the goons."

Badiul's dismay deepened further when the Awami League—enabled by its capture of the court system and its large parliamentary majority—abolished the Caretaker Government system in 2011. The Caretaker system was a mechanism to ensure free and fair elections and consisted of eleven distinguished non-partisan citizens headed by a former chief justice, which formed a government for three months in between two elected government cycles. The system was popular in the country as it afforded a better chance for unimpeded, just, and equitable elections to occur. The Bangladesh Nationalist Party (BNP) first tinkered with the Caretaker system for partisan advantages when it was in power in the early 2000s, but the Awami League abolished it altogether to cement its hold on power. Not long after this happened, Badiul lost his good friend, mentor, and SHUJAN co-founder, Professor Muzaffar Ahmad, who passed away after struggling with serious health problems. His loss at this time of political turmoil was hugely felt, and it increased the pressure and responsibility Badiul felt to honor what they had started and steer the country back to democracy.

This was not to be. With the removal of the Caretaker system, the BNP and its allies were adamant they would not participate in the 2014 election unless the system was reinstated. When the government led by Awami League refused this demand, the path was set for BNP to boycott the election. Across the nation people went to the polls with only Awami League candidates or their allies on the ballot paper, and as a result the Awami League was returned to power with 153 of 300 MPs elected unopposed. This one-sided election invited Court challenge, and Badiul readily accepted his appointment as *Amicus Curiae*—friend of the Court—by the High Court of Bangladesh in a seminal case that challenged the 2014 election. Badiul made both oral and written submissions to the Court, which according to Dr. Kamal Hossain, the framer of the Bangladesh's constitution, made a significant contribution to the jurisprudence of elections. The Court itself, in its judgment[20] observed that Badiul had:

> "Rendered real and valuable assistance to the Court with his versatile wisdom and experience in the field of election matters. His use of current laws and citations from different judicial decisions in support of his submissions reflect enormous industry and vast erudition; his attitude in seeking substantial and real justice by a Court are a lesson to all."

This stolen election was an incredibly low point for the country, and for Badiul, who knew the cost the poorest would

20 Khandker Abdus Salam vs Bangladesh

pay with such rampant illegality and corruption entrenched at the very top. While his work at The Hunger Project was going well, Badiul understood better than most that without a change in the way the country was governed, all that the people had built for themselves could be lost. He knew he had to continue to find ways to shake up the system through SHUJAN.-

With this in mind, Badiul seized upon the Right to Information (RTI) Act as a tool to equip voters and activists with the information they needed to keep the government transparent and answerable to the people. SHUJAN played an important role in the passing of the RTI law, and Badiul saw it as a potent lever for democracy activists to use—RTI is the only law whose implementation depends on the initiative of citizens; as people submit more and more RTI requests, the law's ability to hold those in power accountable increases. Once the law was passed, Badiul and his colleagues trained volunteers and journalists as RTI activists and facilitated the filing of their RTI requests.

Badiul himself used the RTI tool to highlight corruption, and he became a thorn in the side of government interests. In 2015, he filed an RTI application to the Election Commission to get the audited statements of the political parties, which the EC refused to provide. Aggrieved, he went to the High Court and received a seminal judgment which confirmed that information held by government offices was public information and subject to disclosure. This was the first major case for the RTI, and it opened the doors for wider use of RTI for safeguarding people's voting rights.[21]

Badiul's biggest success from filing RTI applications came during the 11th Parliamentary election held in 2018. Ruling party

21 See *Badiul Alam Majumdar and others v. Bangladesh* [69 DLR (2017)].

activists and highly partisan law enforcement agencies, in collusion with the Election Commission, had stuffed the ballot boxes the night before the election. Such blatant rigging of the election took place despite Hasina's public pronouncement—presumably made to overcome the legitimacy crisis her government faced due to the one-sided election of 2014—that free, fair, and competitive elections would be held.

This would not be the case, and Hasina and her cronies again seized an unfair victory in the 2018 election. Badiul responded by filing an RTI application, and the information he received provided irrefutable evidence that the 2018 election had been rigged. Under increasing pressure and with much prevarication, the Election Commission was forced to disclose the center-wide election results, with the EC's own data confirming the election outcome was manipulated. With the Awami League retaining their grip on power, Badiul then facilitated a petition by forty-two distinguished citizens to request that the President of Bangladesh form the Supreme Judicial Council to investigate and take appropriate punitive action against the Election Commission for committing gross misconduct.

Badiul kept up the pressure in multiple ways: SHUJAN surveyed voters to assess their perception of the 2018 election, with more than two-thirds of the respondents believing the election was not fair or acceptable; and fifty-one experts, asked to rate the 2008, 2014, and 2018 Parliament elections using a set criteria for election integrity, gave the lowest score to the 2018 election. Badiul was also the lead applicant in filing another writ before the High Court against the Government of Bangladesh to gain evidence to prove the appointment of members to the Election Commission was manipulated. Failing to get the necessary information from the Cabinet Division and the Information Commission after filing an RTI application, Badiul and his SHUJAN colleagues filed the writ, which is still pending.

Through all these activities, Badiul sought to create accountability, pressure, and public awareness on the stolen elections and governance failures, which blatantly undermined Bangladesh's declaration of independence. He was determined to restore people's right to self-determination.

It is hard to overstate just how persistent and dogged Badiul has been against powerful elites. In 2022, he again bested an attempt to subvert the democratic process when SHUJAN unearthed voter machine irregularities. The partisan Election Commission had purchased low-quality voting machines—machines which did not have any paper trail backup—that could be used to produce manipulated voter results. SHUJAN thwarted this by organizing a seminar to highlight the pitfall of the machine and mobilizing distinguished citizens who signed statements and successfully prevented the machines' implementation.

Having failed in their attempt to use the low-quality voting machines to steal the January 2024 election, the ruling Awami League, led by Sheikh Hasina, set out to manipulate the electoral process by co-opting the highly partisan police force. Using tear gas and rubber bullets, the police attacked a mass political protest rally on October 28, 2023, and this was followed by filing fake cases, which led to the arrests of 25,000 opposition leaders and activists over the following months. As a result, opposition political parties, led by BNP, boycotted the 2024 election. At great personal risk, Badiul and his SHUJAN colleagues raised hue and cry about these efforts to yet again steal the election and perpetuate Sheikh Hasina's autocratic rule. Badiul was regularly interviewed by national and global media to highlight the seizure of state power. The eventual election result which showed Hasina's inevitable victory was the death knell to Bangladesh's claim of being a democratic nation.

With the electoral system compromised, Hasina did not need to pay attention to the views and aspirations of the voters, and this allowed her to control Bangladesh with an iron fist for over fifteen years. Her autocratic rule proved that modern-day dictators do not come to power wearing olive green uniforms and riding on tanks—they initially come to power through a fair election, as Hasina did in 2008.

The last ten years have been very difficult for Bangladesh and for Badiul. He had given decades of his life to helping democracy flourish, only to see it become more volatile and unstable. Draconian laws, repressive measures, and the capture of institutions with partisan appointments took away people's rights, including voting rights. The encroachment on media freedom meant the country was devolving into an autocratic state, with far too few people willing or able to speak about what was happening. *The New York Times* reported that millions of opposition activists faced politically motivated charges, extra-judicial killings, and enforced disappearances. Given Hasina's absolute and autocratic control over all apparatuses of the state, criticizing the government was therefore extremely risky.

Although he was deeply concerned for his own and his family's safety, Badiul did not stop—he would not let these entrenched forces win. Despite blatant lawlessness, his determination for SHUJAN's aims only strengthened, and in return, SHUJAN's principled position and persistent campaigning gained traction and admiration. While many of his friends went quiet, Badiul stood up to Hasina's autocratic rule, relentlessly informing citizens through his writings and speaking of all the harm she and her cohorts had been doing to them and future generations.

Badiul was the face of SHUJAN, and through his hundreds of uncompromising op-ed pieces in major newspapers, inclusion in a dozen books by major publishers in Bangladesh, and increased television and radio presence, he became a mouthpiece for the nation's frustrations. He did not mince his words or change his stance, even with increasing pressure to do so. He had become not only one of the most prominent activists but also the recognized expert on elections and local governance in Bangladesh. At a time of disappearances, executions, and political arrests, his fearless willingness to call out government corruption for what it was endeared him to people everywhere, including overseas. On a few occasions in New York City, a taxi driving past him would suddenly swerve to the side and park, with the Bangladeshi driver coming out to pay his respects to Badiul. Even on the other side of the world, Badiul was recognized for his bravery and outspokenness.

Badiul's reputation did not protect him from violence. His home was attacked on August 4, 2018, before the 11th Parliament election. As the US Ambassador Marcia Bernicat was leaving his home after a farewell dinner, ruling party goons attacked her motorcade outside his house. After the Ambassador's vehicle sped away, they then attacked Badiul's home and tried to break the security gate to enter the premises. Thankfully, their attempt was unsuccessful. Police were called, but they failed to provide any protection for Badiul's family. These acts of violence against their home worried Badiul and Tazima immensely, but both were united that Badiul should not stop.

There were even efforts to buy him off. His son, with degrees from MIT, Stanford, and Cambridge Universities, and a post-doctoral stint at Imperial College, was denied a faculty position at Dhaka University, and Badiul's own appointment as a Member of the Board of Governors of Bangladesh Academy of Rural Development was rescinded after he wrote too many articles that were critical of the government.

The mounting pressure that SHUJAN applied on the government also affected his work at The Hunger Project. In 2023, The Hunger Project, among other organizations, was targeted when the government used the NGO Affairs Bureau to refuse to approve donor funded projects and did not release approved funds. There were also repeated investigations into The Hunger Project by the security forces. Badiul understood this was clearly payback for SHUJAN, which had been vocal against human rights violations, corruption, and the lack of free and fair elections. As SHUJAN itself was not registered as an NGO, the regulatory authority could not put it out of business, therefore THP was targeted. THP serving as the Secretariat for SHUJAN linked the two even closer. Badiul's continued activism would require separating SHUJAN from THP even further.

Badiul and SHUJAN's work was not enough to stem the country's slide into autocracy, yet without a group of people standing up for the rule of law, human rights, and the democratic process, things would have been much worse. SHUJAN made significant strides in promoting reforms, requiring disclosures, and empowering voters with information, and it has been crucial in galvanizing public opinion in favor of change. SHUJAN has been a light in the darkness, and this light has kept many people hopeful. Badiul and SHUJAN's relentless social agitation and education helped make Hasina's autocratic rule unsupportable.

How did autocracy take hold in a nation of freedom fighters? As Badiul sees it, with the country doing better economically, people were initially willing to let things be. However, by using law enforcement agencies and state institutions as instruments of repression to keep people subdued, overlooking the illegalities was never going to be sustainable. As the student uprisings occurring as this book is being written prove, the Bangladeshi people will not submit to authoritarian rule forever. They will rise up and demand their voices be heard, and Badiul will continue to be their partner to see that vision of a just and free Bangladesh fulfilled.

PART THREE

QUESTIONS OF LEGACY

CHAPTER ELEVEN

A New Paradigm of Development

Badiul's leadership in ending hunger was deeply influenced by two things: his own lived experience of hunger and starvation as a child; and spending the first twenty-five years of his life under two separate colonial rules—being born at the end of British rule in India and raised under a second foreign rule by Pakistan. His deeply negative firsthand experiences of colonization and his radical awakening as a young student to the price his nation had paid would fuel his critical views on foreign aid in later years. With a permanent move back to Bangladesh in 1991, Badiul spent time both listening to villagers and examining the patterns of exploitation he saw across the country. This led him to question the very nature of aid and its impact. He came to see that traditional aid not only failed to address the root causes of poverty, but it was also a modern-day extension of colonialism, where donor countries perpetuated a cycle of dependency and control under the guise of generosity and support.

Having lived through two separate colonial periods, where decisions were made by outside forces that diminished the nation and took from the people, Badiul saw similarities with what was now one of the biggest industries in the nation—aid. For him the aid paradigm was rooted in colonial thinking and ripe for disruption.

At its core, colonialism is an extractive process that leaves the colonized nation poorer. Be it minerals, textiles, or location, the ruling power takes what it wants and convinces the colony's people they are better off for it, and over time, people can forget what was lost. They are given trinkets in exchange for their land and its natural resources, and a legacy of hopelessness becomes entrenched unless it is actively thrown off. In comparing the traditional aid paradigm to colonization, Badiul observed that, in the former, what was extracted was power and money by organizations claiming to 'help' communities, which drained or redirected resources that could have otherwise been used to genuinely empower people in need. Equally insidious, a sense of purpose and meaning was also extracted by external actors and do-gooders, which overshadowed local leadership and left people poorer in spirit and dignity. The best outcome in this paradigm was to place the "beneficiaries" in a slightly better-off state, but even then, Badiul rarely saw this happen. Instead, the dignity of resilient and hardworking people was undermined.

For Badiul, using the word "beneficiary" encapsulated this ruler/subject mentality that he found so abhorrent. In the paternal context rife within the aid paradigm, human beings living in poverty were seen as "beneficiaries"—passive recipients of services and donor largesse, with little say, if any, about what they get. In recent years, using the term beneficiaries has become unpopular, with donors preferring to call the people receiving the benefits "partners." However, despite the change in the term, Badiul believed the underlying attitude remained largely unchanged—"partners" may be involved in superficial consultation and participation, but they enjoy little role, responsibility, or influence regarding the design and delivery of the benefit or services provided to them. In other words, the responsibility for decision making still rested with the donors and external agents and experts and not the people themselves.

Traditional anti-poverty projects were maintained in a benevolence paradigm which made critiquing them sound like ingratitude. Usually designed and implemented by external experts, these programs treated the women and men who made up the "target population" as passive recipients of aid, rather than active participants in their own development. This was the hallmark of the donor/recipient relationship that was at the center of the aid paradigm: local people barely contributed to, let alone led, any aspect of the service delivery system designed to help them. It was done to them and for them—not with them or by them. Badiul hated how the more powerful outsider was the center of activity, ownership, and decision making: for him, it was essential that local people were at the center of decisions that impacted them. Any external agents' place should be in the back seat, providing services and assistance as needed—and not in the driver's seat, setting the course and direction.

Badiul believed the ubiquity of traditional development thinking was a major source of his country's inability to gain traction after liberation. His criticism was rooted in his observation that this model failed to address the multifaceted nature of poverty and overlooked the structural barriers that undermined justice and prevented equitable distribution of resources. He knew this had to change and that people's ownership was an essential prerequisite for the decolonization of aid.

As a result of his observations, reflections, and analysis, Badiul championed a community-led development approach that was ahead of its time. Here, as has been seen throughout this book, local actors set their own agendas, developed solutions, and took voluntary actions to implement those solutions. This model was grounded in the unshakeable belief that people are inherently capable and creative, and that empowering them to lead their own development is both more effective and more sustainable. More than that, it was life affirming—people are not passive bystanders in the matter of their own life and treating them as such was demeaning. Badiul saw beyond the conditioning people had been burdened with and recognized the potential for powerful leadership that was within each person. He recalled his interaction with the parrot all those decades ago, where the bird's seeming inability to fly reminded him of his country's learned helplessness. That parrot informed his seminal understanding: people had only forgotten their birthright to be fully human and respond rigorously to life, and they could be awakened to remember.

As this work began to take shape on the ground and the results showed the approach was working, Badiul began to distinguish between what he called "top-down development" or the "service delivery" paradigm that was the norm, and "locally led development" or the "empowerment" paradigm that he advocated, and the contrast between the two became a hallmark of how he approached the huge issue of ending hunger.

In the top-down paradigm, service delivery organizations hold preconceived notions about who "poor" people are and design their interventions based on this. Typically viewing people as uneducated and unable to help themselves, the governing mindset is there are "millions of mouths to feed," a Sisyphean task with no possible resolution. This treats the people as a passive bloc of helplessness and neediness, with no ability to engage robustly in their own future. In this framework, only a few can be helped to solve their specific problems—the issues are too large and complex for anything other than a tinkering on the sidelines of the problem. In contrast, the empowerment paradigm favored by Badiul and The Hunger Project held that people can help themselves, they have the agency and inherent ability to do so and are the most invested in improving their lives. They are the solution—not the problem, and so the question becomes not "How do we feed and help all these people?" but rather, "How do we unleash their inherent power?" and "How do we unlock their leadership and capability so they can feed themselves and their families?" Answering these last two questions offered a completely different set of strategies and approaches.

TOP-DOWN DEVELOPMENT	LOCALLY LED DEVELOPMENT
Preconceived ideas that poor people are "uneducated and cannot help themselves"	Recognizes that people can help themselves and they want to improve their lives
Non-participatory design approach creates disconnect	Mobilize - Provide training and facilitation, identify community issues together
Small fraction of money and support reaches people	Leverage existing institutions and focus on local needs
Project focus creates short-term and siloed efforts	Longer-term view addresses the nexus of interlinked issues. People learn together to scale up

TOP-DOWN DEVELOPMENT	LOCALLY LED DEVELOPMENT
Non-sustainable (dependent on others)	Sustainable because personal and community leadership increases social capital
People removed from the outcome	Pride in and ownership of achievements
Creates "beneficiaries"	People become change agents

Badiul noticed how often short-term thinking got in the way of the strategic interventions that would make a sustainable difference. Aid and development projects were typically timebound with specific end dates, and were delivered with help hired from outside the community, who would leave at the end of the period. As a result, there was little scope, if any, for a continued engagement with the people that the project served, and this brought the sustainability of the project into question. Interventions with short life-spans were not conducive to creating locally led initiatives which required considerable energy and sustained efforts over a longer time. Too often Badiul witnessed how such short-term thinking and donor driven management deadlines led to shortcuts to achieve the project's stated outcomes on time: in a clean water project for example, where one of the objectives was to train people to maintain the equipment, that outcome would be jettisoned if the project ran out of time or money. While traveling across the country, it was common for him to see the heads of tube wells missing, farming irrigation infrastructure broken and idle, and health care campaigns abandoned. As they were created by external parties and not by the people themselves, most gains collapsed once the funding was withdrawn, and the experts left.

Badiul was constantly dismayed at how little of the money and support for projects actually reached the people—the rest was sequestered for expert remunerations, staff salaries, and the needs of bureaucracy. As a counterpoint, the empowerment paradigm was highly leveraged, as the investment of time, energy, and creativity by community members magnified the impact of external support. Here, a little money went a long way: as well as leveraging people's own abilities, partnerships were created, and pressure applied for government functionaries to provide the services the people were entitled to. Instead of using donor money to pay for teachers and doctors, his approach called functionaries to be held to account to provide these for the people. He had seen too many schools close when donor priorities shifted from education to something else, leaving teachers unpaid and classrooms empty.

Yet another drawback to the top-down approach was the siloed nature of traditional aid. Projects usually focused on only one aspect of what was needed, like providing water, or microfinance, and ignored the nexus of interlinked issues that gave rise to poverty in the first place. In contrast, with the empowerment approach, local projects were multidimensional and could be scaled through people's own action. Badiul demonstrated this repeatedly—one animator would start an initiative that was then taken up by others in the village, and then a whole Hunger Free Zone would be formed that encompassed many thousands of people.

When people were mobilized and awakened through tools like the VCAW, supporting and growing their leadership becomes the priority. However, in the traditional paradigm, this does not happen because, while a service might have been delivered, the people stay the same. Ownership and responsibility were not catalyzed as the accomplishment remained that of the organization and not of themselves. In contrast, Badiul's approach created enormous pride and a heartfelt celebration of achievements. Rather than feeling grateful, people became change agents. They authentically knew they had done it themselves, and that they could achieve even more through working together.

Badiul was not blind to the deep structural and racial inequities that lay at the heart of the top-down approach to development. Much of the funding for traditional aid came from the Global North via international NGOs and bilateral organizations, where people were conditioned to feel sorry for the "starving millions." Unconsciously or not, there is an "of course" mindset to the challenges people from the Global South, including Bangladesh, face that overlooks the structural nature of why this is happening. As a nation, Bangladesh only recently achieved Independence, after being ruled by foreign powers for more than 200 years, and it is inordinately impacted by climate related disasters that are exacerbated by climate change it had little hand in causing. Bangladesh's problems were not solely of their own making, and traditional donor's failure to recognize this grated on Badiul. Treating his people like hapless children was deeply offensive and unjust. Badiul was not beholden to these sorts of funding constraints and was able to have the freedom to develop a new approach because the money he had for his work came from The Hunger Project "untied," meaning he could use it how he saw fit, in line with the strategy he created. This was only possible because the global leaders at the organization were also deeply committed to working in this empowerment paradigm, and Joan Holmes, John Coonrod, and others were his complete partners, standing with him to transform the way development was done. Hence, while in comparison with other NGOs, THP Bangladesh was not well funded, there was enough to give him flexibility to pioneer and run a true community-led paradigm of development. He did not have to defer or seek permission from outsiders from a foreign land.

In response to the top-down approach, The Hunger Project Bangladesh's strategy was based on the local leadership and a community-led paradigm. This blossomed into a pioneering array of activities and solutions that were not even fathomable at their inception. Central to this approach was the Vision, Commitment, and Action Workshop (VCAW), which aimed to inspire and empower individuals to take proactive steps toward self-reliance. This workshop became a cornerstone of THP's methodology, fostering a sense of ownership and agency among participants. It was the springboard into further training and inquiry about one's own conditioning as well as what could be possible when a person is unshackled from old mindsets and steps into their agency.

The VCAW and Animators Training began in 1993 and was followed two years later by mobilizing youth through the new Youth Ending Hunger strategy. Unleashing the power of women soon followed. Inspired by the trainings, over the years hundreds of thousands of volunteers have initiated countless activities to create self-employment and cause improvements in their communities in the areas of health, education, income, sanitation, and more. In the 2000s, the strategy for grassroots mobilization really came together, which Badiul consolidated into four pillars:

mobilizing and empowering communities; alliances and network building; strengthening local government; and empowering women and girls as key change agents.

Through his empowerment approach, local people in rural villages became leaders, unleashed through various trainings, including Youth Leaders Training (YLT), Women Leaders Foundation Training, and People Against Violence Everywhere (PAVE) Training. THP-Bangladesh also developed important tools for increasing awareness around civil rights such as the Citizenship Workshop and Democracy/Election Olympiad, and around inclusion and dispute mediation, such as the Social Harmony Workshop. In addition, THP accessed various types of skills training provided by government and non-government organizations and made them available to rural people who would not normally be invited.

This enabling of leadership at the grassroots level was unprecedented, and it led to the formation of several key networks which included: Girl Child Advocacy Forum (NGCAF); and Participatory Action Research (PAR) for creating self-help groups, which brought together thousands of mostly ultra-poor women. These networks encompassed volunteers from different walks of life and contributed to fomenting a broader campaign for ending hunger and poverty. Badiul's belief in awakening and mobilizing this leadership was the key that turned development projects into a movement.

The network of grassroots volunteers and local government leaders that Badiul formed was tied together through the formulation of the MDG (Millennium Development Goal's) Union Strategy in 2010. With a grant from BRAC, THP-Bangladesh sought to localize the MDGs by forging a partnership between the people; their elected *Union Parishad* representatives; civil society; THP-Bangladesh's trained grassroots level volunteers; and the government functionaries. This was a powerful manifestation of community or locally led development. The building and enhancing of community trust that the initiative created was studied by four professors from Columbia, Princeton, and Cambridge Universities, and written up in the American Academy of Sciences Proceeding, thus representing the best academic recognition one can get. And with the declaration of the Sustainable Development Goals (SDGs) by the world leaders in 2015, THP-Bangladesh's MDG Union Strategy turned into SDG Union Strategy, and Badiul and his team continued to use the empowerment approach for localizing SDG activity.

Through the decades of applying a community-led approach, Badiul has come to expect something remarkable. When people within a particular geographic area come together, working shoulder to shoulder to reach shared goals, a kind of miracle occurs—a form of capital is created that allows for greater outcomes than previously imagined. This capital is called "social capital" and is solidified through goodwill between people and a readiness to work together for the common good. Unlike financial capital, you can't count or measure social capital, so it is often overlooked and undervalued. However, its presence can make up for the absence of financial capital in very tangible ways. Exponential outcomes become possible when people shift their worldview from "me" to "we." Social capital is foundational to the success of the empowerment paradigm because hunger and poverty are community-wide issues. And as Tagore aptly said, poverty is like the fear of ghosts—when you are alone, it engulfs you, but it goes away when you are together with others sharing a common purpose. Building up the bank of social capital means communities can weather hardships and disagreements much more cohesively and robustly than when it is absent. It is the secret sauce to collective action.

Badiul's focus on building a civil society to advocate for policy changes was also his expression of the community-led development paradigm. In creating a political citizens' movement, he challenged the top-down paradigm. Decades of charity had muted or misdirected valid political anger, and Badiul's activism via SHUJAN gave focus to the legitimate political outspokenness and critique that must accompany the shift toward engaged citizenry. This is what he set out to do—to speak truth to power, without fear or favor, to ensure systemic change took hold. This truth telling has created awareness amongst the people, who, as the recent uprisings show, are increasingly no longer willing to put up with the deprivation and criminalization perpetrated by the Hasina regime. Amongst the chicanery and corruptions at the highest level, it is this broad, people-powered network of citizen action that gives Badiul immense hope.

In the last thirty years, Badiul has made scrupulous efforts to practice development of the people from the community or locally led paradigm. This work has been a long and arduous path for him, with much trial and error. He did not have a manual to guide him, or many examples to follow. Instead, he went through a constant process of action, reflection, and then action again, trying to find the best approach to solve the next piece of the never-ending hunger puzzle. His has been an adaptive exercise based on learning by doing: solutions did not fall like manna from heaven or come from textbooks, but were carved out and discovered in the process of figuring out what was next needed to end hunger in his country.

Thankfully, this approach is not unique anymore. Around the world, others have also discovered that empowerment must be led by the people, for the people, and more donors are prepared to invest in this iterative, complicated, and long-term process. Badiul's rejection of how aid was done traditionally, and his forging of a new path more than thirty years ago, contributes to this body of experience, and offers substantial evidence that empowering people is the best approach to solving complex challenges.

CHAPTER TWELVE

Reflections on a Revolutionary

A sunny morning finds Badiul sitting on some wooden steps, sipping water. He is in Australia at Cathy's home and the mood is contemplative. From the idealistic boy who left his small village with dreams of an education, to the seasoned leader now sitting in quiet reflection, Badiul's journey has been marked by transformation at every turn. Born into poverty, he became a professor, and then the leader of a people-powered movement. None of this was expected or anticipated because he was born without any advantage other than his parent's love, and his own curiosity.

Badiul was born in an undivided India, and raised in the backdrop of World War II, the tragic Bengal famine, and partition. Extreme poverty and hunger were not theoretical concepts used to propel an ambitious trailblazer. Rather, they were an intimate and challenging lived experience that shaped his very nature and gave him the authority and immense compassion which fueled the largest movement to end poverty his country had ever known. From a young age, Badiul had been involved in student activism, protesting the exploitation of the people of East Pakistan by successive Pakistani regimes, and this questing, justice seeking nature of his continued and grew through the course of his life. After finishing university and teaching for a few years, Badiul went to the United States as a student on a scholarship. Staying there, he completed a PhD in Economics and taught at several universities where he rose to the rank of full professor, before returning permanently to Bangladesh in 1991. During his twenty-one years in America, he also raised a family, lost a wife, remarried, and worked for NASA and the Saudi Royal family. Yet thoughts of his homeland were never far from his mind.

Badiul's return to Bangladesh was a chance to reignite his sense of purpose, and a meeting with Joan Holmes, The Hunger Project's founding president, transformed his inner need for meaning into a powerful outer expression that would change millions of lives. Badiul joined the organization in April 1993 as the Global Office Representative, with his title later changing to Country Director. At that time, The Hunger Project in Bangladesh was little more than a bold idea; Badiul's undertaking offered no guarantee of success—only a conviction that the status quo could not stand, and that the suffering of millions could not be ignored. Badiul could not have foreseen the full extent of the grassroots revolution he would foment. What began as a mission to empower the hungry to take control of their own futures caught fire: it was truly an idea whose time had come.

That said, when Badiul began this journey, the odds were stacked against him. No one believed hunger could end, and the poor were written off as helpless and pitiable. The top-down development paradigm was entrenched, and corruption was rife. Along the way, he faced obstacles that would have caused many to falter—political repression, personal threats, and the constant challenge of working in a system stacked against justice and progress. Bangladesh, with its complex history of poverty, political instability, and social inequity, presented challenges that seemed insurmountable. But Badiul didn't see these challenges as barriers that could not be overcome; rather, in each, he saw an opportunity to reshape the future by empowering those who had been marginalized and silenced for too long.

Although Badiul had studied under the brightest minds, including famed management thinker Peter Drucker, it was rural countryfolk who sparked his greatest growth. Sitting with people in villages and listening deeply, changed him profoundly. He says of this time, "I did not just see with my eyes and hear with my ears—I listened and observed with my heart." Thus began a lifelong process of unlearning what he had been conditioned to believe about himself, his people, and his country, and it was this ability to analyze his own thinking that made him so brilliant at facilitating spaces for others to also examine the beliefs that held them back. Accompanying Badiul on some of his visits to the villages, I saw firsthand the deep connections he forged with people—a connection rooted in mutual respect and a shared vision for change. Over the years, it became clear to me that his greatest source of inspiration was the leadership emerging from those ground down by generational poverty who were now discovering their rights as citizens and taking action. It was in their eyes, in their voices, and in their actions that he first sowed the seeds of a revolution—a people-led awakening of activism and agency that would help unshackle the nation from its legacy of despair, dependency, and poverty. For Badiul, while educated at some of the best universities in America, it was these grassroots people who were his greatest teachers.

Developing leadership was not theoretical to Badiul—he was deeply committed to his own growth, and this included confronting the deep-seated biases ingrained since birth. It was in his conversations with Joan Holmes, for example, that he first confronted his own blindness regarding his limiting, conditioned beliefs about women. Coming face to face with his privilege as a man in a deeply patriarchal society was challenging, but Badiul faced this fight with himself head-on. His willingness to address these and other uncomfortable truths was something I deeply admired, and this relentless self-scrutiny set him apart as a leader. Badiul's leading-by-doing was his hallmark; all who met him knew he would never ask them to take on anything he wouldn't do himself. This approach lent him undeniable credibility and as a result, his philosophy resonated deeply with those he sought to empower.

This commitment to his ongoing growth meant Badiul developed immense self-awareness about his own mindsets, and he was vigilant to not let hopelessness, cynicism, or resignation get any purchase. He was careful not to let feelings of frustration get in the way of showing up powerfully in his mission. Even when witnessing very bleak things like meeting Rahima, who was pregnant and married at thirteen, he would not let his anguish win—there was too much at stake and he would not add to the country's despair. So while he often felt enormous grief at the many things he saw, Badiul managed his internal state very cautiously, and was careful about this when communicating with others.

In a country of 170 million people, stories of struggle and endurance were universal, and Badiul, having been raised in deprivation himself, understood them viscerally. Be it in a small hut, a rice field, or a training, Badiul listened to each person sharing their story with the empathy of someone who had walked that path and understood the weight of it. This earned him the permission to help people think differently about themselves and their situation, and he was never complicit in another person's small version of themselves.

His country's people, who had risen up to secure their freedom, had become moribund, and Badiul was committed to reawakening the spirit he knew was there. This desire was the genesis of the Vision, Commitment, and Action Workshops (VCAW), which would become the cornerstone of everything that followed. The workshop was simple in design but revolutionary in purpose: it gave people an experience of imagining a different future, one where they saw themselves not as victims of circumstance but as agents of change. More than five million people in Bangladesh have participated to date, and Badiul's influence didn't stop at the border—across Africa and Latin America, the VCAW was adopted as a tool to mobilize the leadership to end hunger in rural areas.

From the success and expansion of the VCAW emerged a strategy that would unleash a movement: the creation of animators—local people who supported their community through leading the VCAW and assisting the activities that were initiated. These weren't leaders in the traditional sense; they were farmers, mothers, laborers—ordinary people who had, until that point, never imagined themselves capable of anything beyond survival. But Badiul saw in them what they hadn't seen in themselves: leadership potential. Animators mobilized their communities, and organized efforts from local sanitation issues to larger economic projects. Their achievements were proof that Badiul's belief in grassroots leadership—which had initially been met with skepticism—worked.

The animator movement also spread to Africa, where I have seen the local version of Badiul's pioneering approach save lives in communities deeply affected by HIV and AIDS, poverty, and hunger. Meeting animators in Malawi or Ethiopia, I recognized that same fire and deep commitment that was present in Bangladesh—people who were active agents of their own development.

The animator cohort in Bangladesh, which has grown to more than 250,000 people, laid the groundwork for an even broader transformation. Badiul understood that to truly end hunger, women must be empowered, and by unleashing the untapped potential of women in rural areas, he catalyzed a fundamental shift in the social fabric of these communities. Women who once saw themselves as powerless and without rights now stood at the forefront of change.

For me, having seen in too many villages the suffering that the subjugation and marginalization of women inflicts, this part of his work was the most transformative. When 1,200 women came together in the Unleashed Women Leaders conference in 2019, and declared their progress with comments like "I played a role in eradicating illiteracy, early marriage, and improving sanitation in my village," and "I have stopped more than twenty child marriages," Badiul's legacy could not be denied. The 10,000 rural, village women he trained as leaders to end hunger are at the forefront of change where it matters—in the homes, hearths, and bellies of the rural poor.

Youth, too, found their voice, activated by Badiul's deep belief that they had an important part to play in the development of the nation, and his leadership role in politically engaging young people would deliver in time. As this chapter is being written, young people have thrown off the chains of an autocratic government and put their bodies on the line. Hundreds have been killed but their sacrifices were not in vain—Prime Minister Hasina was ousted and subsequently fled the country, and the students' demands were granted for Nobel Peace Prize winner Dr. Muhammad Yunus to lead an interim government. Badiul is not surprised by any of this—he always knew young people would lead the change when the time came.

Empowering individuals was not enough to end hunger—the system had to change too. SHUJAN, the advocacy group that Badiul founded with Professor Muzaffar Ahmed, pushed for the transparency, accountability, and democracy essential for good governance. It became a force for change at the highest levels and helped set the stage for the autocratic reign that had strangled the country to be overthrown.

Badiul's legacy goes beyond these specific initiatives. His work laid the foundation for Bangladesh's progress on the Millennium Development Goals (MDGs) and later the Sustainable Development Goals (SDGs). What started as a series of workshops in villages grew into a national movement, influencing policies, changing lives, and demonstrating that change, when driven by the people, is not only possible—it is unstoppable.

Though Badiul's achievements are remarkable, he has never viewed his life as "heroic." For him, the real heroes are common folk who, often at great personal risk, stand up to be counted, and it is their combined strength that has driven this revolution. Badiul's story is an example of what is possible when ordinary people come together with a shared purpose. Whatever he has achieved is a testament to this power of individual and collective action, and the potential within each person to contribute to meaningful change. His approach to leadership is not about commanding from the front, but rather, walking beside people, encouraging them, and calling them forth. He creates spaces where people feel seen, heard, and capable of shaping their own futures.

I have seen Badiul demonstrate this in so many ways. Even though he is a public figure, he does not seek the spotlight for himself, but instead focuses it on the community—the volunteers, the local leaders, the countless individuals who have taken up the mantle alongside him. One fond image I have is of a woman standing on the stage in a small village hall, to share about what she had accomplished since becoming an animator. She was feeling hesitant and shy in front of the crowd, but Badiul stood below her, his face and eyes beaming at her with encouragement and joy. As she looked down at Badiul and began to speak, I could see her draw courage from him. When the audience applauded, no one was more pleased than Badiul.

Badiul's life has been one of continuous learning, adaptation, and persistence, and as he looks toward the future, he has wisdom to share with those who seek to make a difference.

Curiosity has been a guiding force throughout Badiul's life, and he encourages the next generation of activists to keep questioning the status quo and challenging entrenched beliefs. He was able to break free of the limitations of his upbringing and culture and forge a completely new path for himself and his country, by being open to new ideas and perspectives. So for him, embracing curiosity and a willingness to learn is essential—as is not being afraid to be *unreasonable*. In a world that values conformity over innovation, looking good over doing what's right, and appeasement over saying what needs to be said, his call for unreasonableness is a radical and necessary one.

Badiul advises those who are unsure where to start that they should not wait for the perfect moment or ideal conditions. Too often, leadership potential is stifled because people feel they either need to have it all figured out before they begin, or they must get themselves ready in some way. This is tempting, but it's based on a false premise—that somehow you are not enough as you are now to take action in something meaningful to you. Change, as he has demonstrated, is not the result of a single grand gesture but the accumulation of small, consistent actions which build muscle, capability, and confidence over time. The most important step, he advises, is to start where you are—whether that means addressing an immediate need in your community or taking the first step toward a larger goal; and then start with what you have—your own resources and abilities are enough to begin. This idea of starting where you're at and using what you already have—is a fantastic way to help us shake off hesitation and begin. Everyone, regardless of their background, has something valuable to contribute.

Fostering solidarity as both a mindset and a pathway for

action, was central to Badiul's success. The challenges of creating lasting change are too great to be faced alone, and Badiul always worked with others who shared his vision and values—he could not have achieved what he did without trusted advisors, dedicated colleagues, and a nation of courageous people. He shows that effective leadership is not singular or solitary; it does not occur in a vacuum. Solidarity is an antidote to the despair that can be felt when problems seem overwhelming; with collective action, people who come together with a common purpose can achieve far more than they could individually.

Integrity is something Badiul considers necessary to cultivate and practice. For him, integrity is more than being honest and truthful—it encompasses remaining true to the purpose, and includes being present, listening to others with respect, and following through with your promises, both big and small. He calls this "keeping my word" and it is not performative to him—it shapes every aspect of his life, including his personal life, where he is careful to live in a clean, frugal, and disciplined manner. Badiul's authentic connection with people living in hunger is because of his integrity—when he says he is their partner to end hunger, they know this to be true, even if they don't know the details of his life. Badiul believes that ensuring you can be counted on, and not someone who is frivolous, is fundamental to crafting the type of leadership that lives beyond you. Integrity extends to making sure the work you do is not about you and is instead grounded in a deep alignment of both values and mission. Ego driven leadership is antithetical to Badiul's meaning of integrity.

The idea that we can't often choose what happens to us, but we do have a choice in how we respond, is one Badiul encourages. It is true that there are many things that cannot be individually determined—the enabling environment for success is rigged toward those who already have easy access to it. But Badiul maintains that it is most important to attend to one's mindset—those beliefs and attitudes that frame how you respond to the world. This includes getting clear on who you want to be—and why. Rigorously question what you are saying and believing about yourself and your situation. Are you letting your circumstances define who you are, therefore limiting what is possible for you? As Badiul has shown, jettisoning unhelpful beliefs, even when they seem true ("I am poor!") and developing the muscle to choose your response, is an essential practice.

Most profoundly, Badiul's vast experience shows that progress takes time, and tends to take longer and be more frustrating than you expect. This is something I personally take comfort from—it's allowed me to settle into the longer term, gnarly work that goes with creating change. It's helped me stay the course, especially when things don't go well or seem to be taking too much time. There's a maturity to this hard-won perspective of Badiul's, and one I believe is minimized in the discourse around what it will take to create a more just and equitable world for all. Badiul suffered many setbacks and moments when progress seemed elusive, but these were the times when perseverance was most crucial. Making headway in something big and meaningful is often a marathon, filled with obstacles and opposition, but while forward movement is often slow and incremental, there is still progress, nonetheless. It is naïve to expect instant success, but with steady, determined effort over time, transformation does become possible. For those engaged in activism already, his advice is clear: remember the reasons you started, involve others, and be prepared for a long, possibly difficult road ahead. Don't be put off by that—expect it and you will not give up or lose faith when it gets hard and unpleasant. The fight against hunger, against inequality, and against injustice are struggles that may never be fully resolved in our lifetimes, yet this does not make them any less worth fighting for.

At nearly eighty years old, it's natural that Badiul's thoughts turn to the future. The progress he has made is real and meaningful, yet the complexity of these issues underscores that no single individual, no matter how visionary, will ever live long enough to see everything resolved. The truth of this sits heavily on Badiul. In the winter of his life, he's thinking more and more about the future of what he has built, its sustainability, and his own legacy.

For the Hunger Project Bangladesh, Badiul's imminent retirement poses a looming challenge. With the huge loss of Nasima (Jolly) Akhter's recent passing, and a number of his earliest colleagues also now retiring, institutional memory and organizational leadership is stretched thin. The Hunger Project Bangladesh is facing an uncertain future, made more so by the absence of a person to assume the mantle of Country Director. There are several reasons for this, but the simplest one is that Badiul has not been ready until now to step aside, and yet, as with all things, his official leadership of The Hunger Project cannot last forever. Eventually, he would need to retire.

Managing this transition is also an existential concern—who is Badiul if not The Hunger Project Bangladesh—and what is The Hunger Project Bangladesh without Badiul in it? Sorting through his thoughts and feelings on this has been complex. Visiting Cathy in Australia, away from the demands of his Dhaka office, affords him some space to reflect and begin the process of separating his public and political identity from the vision that fuels him. In a quiet moment, he is moved to realize that his vision remains even as he prepares to release the role. This is a time of profound letting go for Badiul—he knows the future of The Hunger Project Bangladesh will be for others to decide, and perhaps that is best for him. Badiul is not done with his activism, but he is almost done with running an organization and everything that entails.

That said, there are some key areas of unfinished work which occupy his mind. One is the continued struggle for women's rights in rural Bangladesh. Though the Unleashed Women's Network has empowered thousands, issues like early marriage and violence persist. Badiul knows these challenges will require sustained efforts to ensure progress isn't lost.

The youth movement that Badiul inspired also faces its own set of challenges. While young people have been at the forefront of demanding change, from environmental protection to educational reform, they are often met with violence, repression, or apathy from those in power. The recent youth-led protests calling for political accountability and equity highlight the dangers these young people face. Badiul knows that nurturing and supporting this next generation of changemakers is critical.

The ongoing challenge of political corruption and democratic deficits is the most pressing unfinished work for Badiul, and this is the area he is drawn to focus his leadership on once he retires from The Hunger Project. While SHUJAN has made remarkable strides in advocating for transparency and accountability in government, the political landscape in Bangladesh remains volatile. Badiul's efforts to promote good governance have laid the groundwork for change, but he is acutely aware that the road ahead is long, and the forces of resistance are powerful. The recent uprising in Bangladesh was possible, in part, because of the years of campaigning and outspokenness of Badiul and SHUJAN, and he knows the work to restore democracy is just beginning. This is a fight he wants to be in, and his voice and deep experience is desperately needed. The next chapter of his life will most certainly involve his continued leadership in this area.

In writing this book and reflecting on Badiul's journey, I am struck by the sheer persistence required to build and sustain a movement over decades, and the joy and energy he brought to it. The challenges Badiul faced, both personal and professional, would have overwhelmed most people, but his commitment and equanimity never wavered. He demonstrates that perseverance doesn't have to be a grim, white-knuckle slog through adversity. Instead, by staying true to your values, even when compromising on them would offer a quick win; holding onto hope even when others have given up; and continuing to work for change even when it seems impossible, a profound inner contentment arises, which is all the more satisfying because it is not linked to a specific outcome. As Badiul and other wise people have found, the path itself becomes the reward.

"Today I Saw a Revolution" isn't just about Badiul; it's a story for anyone who has ever dared to believe they can make a difference. As I complete this book, I'm filled with a deep sense of gratitude—for the chance to share Badiul's journey, for the lessons I've learned, and for the privilege of contributing to a movement much larger than any one person. Badiul's legacy is a reminder, as Martin Luther King Jr. once said, that the arc of the moral universe bends toward justice—but it's never a straight path, and it is never finished. We all have a part to play in shaping that arc.

The revolution Badiul helped ignite continues to grow, and it needs each of us to carry it forward. His legacy is not limited to Bangladesh—it is a clarion call to shake off the shackles of despair and dive into the waters of change and possibility. This book is a call to action—the torch will soon be passed, and Badiul's example urges us to take it up. The future we create can be determined by us all.

Postscript

As this book was on its way to the printers, dramatic developments took place in Bangladesh.

Widespread discontent with the autocratic rule of Sheikh Hasina had been brewing for some time. The frustration people increasingly felt from being locked out of free elections and being denied human rights and equal opportunities in all spheres, led to an explosive situation which sparked a student-led revolt against the regime.

The "Monsoon Revolution" began in the summer of 2024 when students demanded reform of the quota system in government employment. This reform pressure was the tip of iceberg, as their protests were underpinned by the deprivations and lack of justice and recourse that Badiul had been writing and speaking about for decades.

Students rallied throughout the country, and as the protests grew and more people joined, Hasina, instead of paying attention to the students' demands, used force to deal with them. Hundreds died and over 18,000 were injured, with some losing eyes and limbs due to violence inflicted by state forces. This transformed the student protest into a mass movement, with people from all walks of life taking to the streets in defiance of the government's extreme measures.

As a result, on August 5, 2024, Hasina was forced to flee the country—her iron, autocratic grip finally broken. In the political vacuum that followed, student leaders called for the most distinguished Bangladeshi to take the helm, leading to Nobel Peace Laureate Dr. Muhammad Yunus becoming head of the Interim Government on August 8, 2024.

As Yunus took office, he sent a message to Badiul saying he needed Badiul's help, and so these two esteemed leaders met to discuss the situation and what was required.

Soon after, in a televised address to the nation on the evening of September 11, 2024, Yunus announced that Badiul Alam Majumdar would head the Electoral System Reform Commission to overhaul the electoral framework of the country. Badiul's work would pave the way for free, fair, and competitive elections.

Badiul has called this appointment the "ultimate recognition," and it combines the many threads of his life's work. It validates the understanding he gained so many years ago that empowering the poor, and accountable governance and rule of law, were interlinked necessities, each vital for ending hunger and poverty. In the twilight of his life, Badiul will again be bringing his leadership to bear in the service of his nation, as he helps set the path for an inclusive, just, prosperous, and democratic Bangladesh.

September 12, 2024

Acknowledgments

This book would not have been possible without the incredible support, guidance, and dedication of many remarkable individuals. With immense gratitude, I acknowledge the people and communities who contributed to bringing this project to life.

I start by paying my respects to the traditional owners upon whose land I have written most of this book—the Widjabul Wiabal people of the Bundjalung Nation. I recognize their 50,000-year connection and commitment to Country, which was never ceded, and I pay my respects to Elders past and present.

To the extraordinary staff of The Hunger Project Bangladesh—your innovation, compassion, and dedication have been instrumental in shaping the path toward a self-reliant Bangladesh, and your work in empowering communities is the cornerstone of this project. Thank you for your ongoing vision, commitment, and action despite numerous challenges (and a revolutionary uprising!), and for your invaluable assistance in helping me piece this story together. I am honored to be your partner.

To the countless volunteer leaders of Bangladesh, who lead in the face of adversity—your courage and determination inspire me every day. You've shown that we, the people, are enough to create lasting change, and this book is a testament to your incredible efforts. Whether you are an animator, a woman leader, or a student activist, *Today I Saw a Revolution* is for you.

To my beloved family—Steve, Bronwen, Patrick, Roshni, and Leo—thank you for being my unwavering pillars of support. Your love, patience, and unending belief in this book, plus the tea and snacks, gave me the fortitude to complete this journey. I love you all.

And to Badiul—my fearless friend and steadfast partner on this wild ride. Your irreverence and humor found their match in me, and it has been a privilege, in every sense of the word, to witness and document your remarkable journey. You continue to inspire me, and I can't wait to see what you will contribute next. And Tazima—your wisdom and generosity have been integral to all that Badiul has achieved; it would not have been possible without your support and leadership. Thank you for our friendship and for helping me tell this story.

To Badiul and Tazima's children—Mahboub, Mahfuz, Shahirah, Rozana, and Samira—thank you for allowing this global eye on your father's life. I hope you approve, and any mistakes are mine alone.

I am deeply grateful to the incredible leaders of The Hunger Project, past and present—Joan Holmes, John Coonrod, fellow staffers, volunteers, village leaders, and activists. Thank you for your vision and service—and for shaping me into the leader I've become.

To my clients, who have been incredibly understanding as I put work on hold to see this book finished, and who still hired me anyway—thank you! I'll carry everything I've learned from this book into helping you all.

And finally, to every reader, supporter, and believer in the power of collective action—whether your mission is to end hunger, fight for justice, or create positive change in any part of the world—may this be your inspiration to continue the work. Together, let's carry this revolution forward and create the future we long for.

One last thing: I'm committed to ensuring *Today I Saw a Revolution* makes the greatest impact possible. That's why all profits after costs will be donated to The Hunger Project to further its incredible work. This entire project has been a matter of soul for me, and it feels right that any monies made through sales be used to help others.

Cathy Burke
Repentance Creek, Australia
2024

About the Author

Cathy Burke is a renowned global advocate, writer, and speaker on leadership, transformation, and social impact. As CEO of The Hunger Project Australia and Global Vice President, Cathy spent two decades helping build one of the world's most successful organizations focused on empowering communities to end hunger and poverty.

Now an author, leadership coach, and trainer, she helps organizations and individuals worldwide develop the mindsets, leadership skills, and heart needed to address 21st-century challenges. At the core of Cathy's work is a commitment to people—engaging deeply, inspiring leadership, and sparking collective action.

A recipient of the Australian Davos Leadership Award and the Financial Review Women of Influence Award, Cathy is the author of *Today I Saw a Revolution: From Grassroots to Global Change* (2024), *Lead In: Mindsets to Lead, Live and Work Differently* (2022), and *Unlikely Leaders: Lessons in Leadership from the Village Classroom* (2015).

Cathy lives on 85 acres in the subtropical rainforest of northern New South Wales, on the unceded lands of the Widjabul Wia-bal people of the Bundjalung Nation.

Cathy can be contacted at www.cathyburke.com.

About The Hunger Project

The Hunger Project is a global, non-profit organization committed to ending hunger and poverty by pioneering sustainable, community-led development initiatives. With programs in Africa, South Asia, and Latin America, The Hunger Project empowers people—especially women—to take charge of their futures through economic empowerment, and social mobilization. The Hunger Project helps communities break the cycle of hunger and build long-term resilience, ensuring a future free from hunger for generations to come.

More information about The Hunger Project can be found at www.thp.org.

Printed in the USA
CPSIA information can be obtained
at www.ICGtesting.com
CBHW030219270924
14982CB00003B/5